A *Celebration* of

HER*story*
QUILTS

Strong Women

Susanne Miller Jones

Carol,
Celebrate strong
women!
Susanie M. Jones

Schiffer
Publishing Ltd

4880 Lower Valley Road • Atglen, PA 19310

Other Schiffer Books by the Author:

Fly Me to the Moon: An Art Quilt Journey, ISBN 978-0-7643-5400-7

Other Schiffer Books on Related Subjects:

Art Quilts International: Abstract & Geometric, Martha Sielman, ISBN 978-0-7643-5220-1

Artistry in Fiber Series, Anne Lee and E. Ashley Rooney. Vol. 1: *Wall Art*, ISBN 978-0-7643-5304-8; Vol. 2: *Sculpture*, ISBN 978-0-7643-5342-0; Vol. 3: *Wearable Art*, ISBN 978-0-7643-5399-4

And Still We Rise: Race, Culture and Visual Conversations, Carolyn L. Mazloomi, ISBN 978-0-7643-4928-7

Designed by Molly Shields
Cover design by Danielle Farmer
Type set in Weidemann Bk BT/Times New Roman

ISBN: 978-0-7643-5460-1
Printed in China

Published by Schiffer Publishing, Ltd.
4880 Lower Valley Road
Atglen, PA 19310
Phone: (610) 593-1777; Fax: (610) 593-2002
E-mail: Info@schifferbooks.com
Web: www.schifferbooks.com

For our complete selection of fine books on this and related subjects, please visit our website at www.schifferbooks.com. You may also write for a free catalog.

Schiffer Publishing's titles are available at special discounts for bulk purchases for sales promotions or premiums. Special editions, including personalized covers, corporate imprints, and excerpts, can be created in large quantities for special needs. For more information, contact the publisher.

We are always looking for people to write books on new and related subjects. If you have an idea for a book, please contact us at proposals@schifferbooks.com.

All *HERstory* fiber art photographs were taken by Todd Jones.
Portraits of the author and the jurors were taken by Bonnie McCaffery.
Thanks to:
The *Milwaukee Journal Sentinel* for the photo of Dorothy Day (*Dorothy Day* by Diane Cadrain)
Allan Warren for his photo of Phyllis Diller (*Humor Has It* by Denise Currier)
Anna Zollicoffer for her drawing of Lucille Ball (*Lucille Ball: A Multimedia Megastar* by Meena Schaldenbrand)
Antonio Olmos for his photo of Malala Yousafzai (*Malala* by Gabriele DiTota)
Annette Polan for her painting of Wilma Vaught (*The Women in Military Service for America and General Wilma L. Vaught, Retired* by Starla Phelps)
Michael Solovey for his artwork *Athena's Watch* (*The Women in Military Service for America and General Wilma L. Vaught, Retired* by Starla Phelps)
Miami News Collection, History Miami Museum for their photo of Gloria Steinem (*Gloria* by Bonnie Askowitz)
The Green Belt Movement for their photo of Wangari Maathai (*I Will Be a Hummingbird* by Lisa Arthaud)
Tony Cunha for his photo of Beatrice Wood (*Beatrice Wood: A Life Colored by Art* by Mary McLaughlin)
Dan Oppenheimer for Jack Robinson's photo of Nina Simone (*Nina: A Theme with Variations* by Sherri Culver)
Tennille Granson for her photo of ballet dancers (*Misty in the Making* by Nneka Gamble)
Alan Light for the photo of Oprah Winfrey (*Oprah Winfrey: Overcoming and Conquering* by Leo Ransom). It is used under the conditions outlined in Creative Commons Attribution 2.0 Generic.
J. Nguyen for the photo of Harpo Studios (*Oprah Winfrey: Overcoming and Conquering* by Leo Ransom). It is used under the conditions outlined in Creative Commons Attribution 2.0 Generic. It is used under the conditions outlined in Creative Commons Attribution Share Alike 3.0 Unported.

QR Code is a registered trademark of DENSO WAVE

This book is dedicated with great love to six women who are my heart. It is dedicated with love and in fond memory of the three most important women in my early life: my mother, Sue Mullins Miller; and my grandmothers Annie Gragg Mullins and Anna Bruce Miller. They loved me unconditionally and raised me to be a strong woman. It is dedicated with love to my mother-in-law, Marna Bromberg Williams, who has loved, accepted, and encouraged me. It is also dedicated with love and hope for the future to my daughter Sarah Susan Jones and my future daughter-in-law Amber Lynn Paulson. Sarah and Amber, I hope that the inspiration that I found in my mother, my grandmothers, and Marna, will be evident in the pages of this book. The future is in your hands and those of your generation.

Contents

Foreword

Karey P. Bresenhan
Founder, International Quilt Market and Quilt Festival
Cofounder, International Quilt Association

Man's influence on history is well recorded, but to paraphrase Virginia Woolf, "Anonymous was a woman." But after this groundbreaking book and exhibit, anonymity will be far less prevalent, at least in the quilt world.

Homemaker. Mother. Wife. Chef. Nanny. Housekeeper. Chauffeur. Cheerleader. Teacher. General. Pilot. Museum director. College professor. Doctor. Lawyer. Governor. Women are famed for their ability to multi-task and take on many different roles. Over the last century, these "traditional" roles have been expanded thanks to the modern-day pioneer women who have shattered glass ceilings in fields that were previously dominated by men. This book and the exhibit that inspired it are a welcome and long-overdue tribute to just a selection of women who have shaped history through *HERstory*. From politicians to scientists. Environmentalists to entertainers. Activists to artists. Athletes to authors. There are even some fictional heroines as well as personal heroes in this mix.

The use of quilting as the medium by which to honor these women mirrors the advances they have made in their own fields. Traditionally, quilting was a skill learned from necessity. Born from the need to keep loved ones warm and protected using whatever materials were available, from finest fabrics to cheap feed sacks, quilting has progressed into an art form all its own. The art quilt movement has allowed women to express their creativity in a new way and it has allowed the artists in this book to demonstrate their respect and even affection for those remarkable women by visually presenting their roles in *HERstory*.

In the quilt world, many of us were privileged to know such enormous talents as Yvonne Porcella, one of the first major names in the world of art quilts, whose quilts have even been seen through the famed Smithsonian Institution and in many museum exhibits.

In the real world, we can vote because of women like Elizabeth Cady Stanton and Susan B. Anthony, early suffragists. But today it is the work and accomplishments of activist women in government that have enriched our lives and opened opportunities for women everywhere. Thanks are due to women such as Barbara Jordan, widely acknowledged as one of our earliest and most effective black politicians . . . Margaret Thatcher, the first woman prime minister of the United Kingdom . . . Angela Merkel, the chancellor of Germany . . . Golda Meir of Israel. Even in the face of terrible violence, some women stood tall. Rosa Parks faced down racist oppression with stoic determination. Bullets could not silence Gabrielle Giffords and Malala Yousafzai, who continue to advocate for their causes with grace and dignity.

Also acknowledged are authors like Pearl S. Buck and Agatha Christie, Simone de Beauvoir and Gloria Steinem, J.K. Rowling of *Harry Potter* fame, even Ann Landers, all of whom have influenced the world with their writing. Artists like Dorothea Lange, the photojournalist who documented the

Great Depression of the 1930s, or Frida Kahlo, the extraordinary painter, used visual means to change the world.

So many everyday things in our lives today, things we take completely for granted, are due to the efforts captured in *HERstory*. Marie Curie and the actress Hedy Lamarr make an unusual pairing, but Madame Curie helped to discover x-rays and the actress was a gifted inventor who is credited with developing the principles of Wi-Fi, Bluetooth, and radar.

Then there are those whose achievements showed the world that, for women, even the sky had no limit. Jacqueline Cochran, Amelia Earhart, and Amy Johnson all showed immense bravery flying solo across continents, as did Sally Ride when she became the first American woman to go into space.

I could go on, but instead, I will leave you to enjoy celebrating and discovering all the women honored in this marvelous book through the medium of quilting. The love, care, and talent each artist has shown in the creation of these quilts is a testimony not just to the influence the subjects themselves have had on *HERstory*, but a testimony to the influence the art quilt movement has had on the world of quilting. No longer confined to making quilts for necessity, these artists have the freedom to express their skills and creativity in an exciting and powerful medium.

My wish is that you enjoy the quilts as much as you enjoy finding out more about the women who have had such an impact on *HERstory*.

Coline Jenkins
Greenwich, Connecticut
2017 | Centennial of New York State women's suffrage

*W*hat is a quilt?

It is our most intimate cloth. It covers us during the night. A quilt's warmth settles our minds and souls while we sleep. It witnesses conception and is passed from generation to generation. It is a mosaic of stitches and patterns made by a woman's hand. It is a work of life.

Who is Elizabeth Cady Stanton?

Elizabeth is my great-great-grandmother. She is my mother's mother's mother's mother. We all share the same genetic material—mitochondria, known as the powerhouses of our cells. Elizabeth Cady Stanton is also our nation's fore-mother, celebrated for connecting women to law. Her life's work was the exploration of the rights and wrongs of women. Her powerful claim is based on the underpinning of our country, "We hold these truths to be self-evident: that all men and women are created equal; that they are endowed by their Creator with certain inalienable rights; that among these are life, liberty, and the pursuit of happiness."[*]

In 1815, during wintery November in upstate New York, Elizabeth was born—perhaps warmed by a quilt. She was born into a family steeped in law. She was the daughter of a lawyer, who counseled clients in his office, attached to their home, within earshot of Elizabeth. As well, Elizabeth visited her father while he presided in the courthouse down the street. As a girl, Elizabeth soaked up the discussions of law and was especially stirred by the complaints of the women who had turned to her father for

help. Alas, in the eyes and ears of Elizabeth, the law was unfair to women. So stirred was she that at the age of ten, she envisioned cutting out those nasty paragraphs from her father's law books that made women so distraught. In essence, the law decreed that a married woman was "civilly dead" before the law.

Forward to 1848: Elizabeth, age thirty-two, and a handful of women convened the first women's rights convention to address the rights of women. They wrote and presented a women's declaration of independence in Seneca Falls, New York. Their "Declaration of Sentiments" demanded woman's access to higher education and professions, the right to own her wages, and the fundamental right to vote. The rest is history as this cast stone created ripples for generations to follow.

Dear Artists,
Thank you for telling powerful women's history—American history—by using the iconic American art form, the quilt.

Dear Readers,
Now the quilt book—full of lives and creation—is in your hands. Be enriched and inspired by the quilters and the women they honor.
Please leave your mark on the world.

[*] From the "Declaration of Sentiments," as written by Elizabeth Cady Stanton and the women who attended the first Women's Convention.

Preface

I registered to vote on August 18, 1971, the fifty-first anniversary of the ratification of the 19th Amendment giving women the right to vote. I voted for the first time in the presidential election in 1972, the first time that my paternal grandmother was eligible as well. Her name was Anna Bruce Miller, and her story was one of the inspirations behind this collection.

Anna was born to Norwegian immigrants in South Dakota Territory in 1888. South Dakota was admitted to the Union the next year. Being a citizen with a vote must have been a very exciting thing to her father and brothers, but it didn't make a difference to her mother and the three girls. Women got the right to vote on August 18, 1920, when the 19th Amendment was ratified. Anna married my British grandfather a few months later. Unbeknownst to her, the Expatriation Act of 1907 stated that if you married a citizen of another country, your citizenship morphed into his. So she lost her citizenship and with it, her right to vote. In 1921, my grandfather, grandmother, and father, three days old, were all naturalized. They moved to Washington, DC, whose citizens did not have the right to vote for president until the DC voting rights amendment was ratified in 1961. The first election that DC citizens could vote in was 1964, but by then my grandmother had moved to Maryland. However, she could not vote there because she moved after the voter registration deadline for the 1964 election had passed. There must have been another Maryland move later, into a different voting district, as she wasn't eligible in 1968 either.

So my grandmother, Anna Bruce Miller, at the age of eighty-four and I, age nineteen, voted for the same candidate and for the first time each in the 1972 election. She was very proud of the one and only vote she ever cast.

My mother, Sue Mullins Miller, was born after women had the right to vote. She worked on Capitol Hill for Senator Lister Hill from Alabama, Representative Armistead Selden from Alabama, Senator John Carroll from Colorado, and Senator Abraham Ribicoff from Connecticut. She was a dedicated public servant, and she never missed an election. My mom believed in our electoral process and the responsibility of voting. Because of her, I've never missed a vote either. The suffragists and those who came before us fought too hard to gain this right. We stand on their shoulders.

My mother-in-law, Marna Bromberg Williams, never had to fight to get the right to vote either. I admire the fact that even though she was born in privilege, she worked tirelessly to help those denied their rights. Following the bombing of the Sixteenth Street Baptist Church in 1963, which killed four little girls in Birmingham, Alabama, Marna decided that she must help. Her work is the subject of a personal hero piece that I made in her honor. Putting her relationships with family and friends at risk, she did what she knew was right. That is the story of each woman in this collection.

So this collection was inspired by all three of these women: Anna who wanted to do what she couldn't do; Sue who always did what she could; and Marna who did what she could for those who could not.

Meet the Jurors

Lisa Ellis

Church Windows for YP

Fairfax, Virginia

isa Ellis is President of the Board of Directors of Studio Art Quilt Associates (SAQA). She is dedicated to helping SAQA members get to the next level of their personal artistic journey. Lisa has degrees in Math and Computer Science. She worked for twenty-three years in the aerospace industry. She retired in 2003 to focus her energies on volunteer work and her passion for quilting.

In addition to her art, Lisa seeks to make the world a better place through the Healing Quilts in Medicine initiative, which commissions art quilts for installation in hospitals to improve the healing environment for patients and their families. Lisa is the chairwoman of Sacred Threads, a bi-annual quilt show and moving exposition that focuses on inspirational, religious, and personal growth themes. She also serves on the board of directors of the Quilt Alliance, a non-profit organization dedicated to preserving the stories of quilts and their makers.

In 2010 she formed her company, Giving Back Technology, to provide information technology services to non-profit museums, galleries, and other art organizations. She frequently teaches quilting techniques and lectures on Healing Quilts in Medicine and Sacred Threads.

Lisa made *Church Windows for YP* in memory of Yvonne Porcella (1936–2016), who founded Studio Art Quilt Associates. Lisa explains her piece:

I engineered a pieced cathedral window block that can be constructed on a domestic machine and becomes a true quilt with batting. As I thought about Yvonne, the cathedral window was appropriate as a connection to her faith and the inspiration she found during her travels and viewing of stained glass windows. In tribute to Yvonne, I used bright silks and checks of black and white to capture her sense of whimsy and colorful design.

As I think about Yvonne, I naturally ponder her legacy. We spent some treasured times together these last three years. We shared our mutual faith, she filled in some gaps about the history of SAQA, and we talked about supporting the benefit auctions with donation quilts for causes we love. We bought these silly rubber bead bracelets. We would meet up at various quilt events:

Houston, Quilter's Take Manhattan, SAQA Conferences, and Sacred Threads. She would always give me the precious gift of her time. Often we would go to museums. Wow. She was smart and knew her stuff. I was lucky to hear her views on the art and soak up her knowledge.

What is her legacy to me? Make the most of your iPhone. Text your friends and loved ones frequently. It makes your friends feel close and special. Send goofy pictures occasionally, everyone needs and loves a laugh. Ask for prayer when you need it. Be kind, be courageous, keep your faith, light candles, and pray for those in need. Be generous with your time, give people your undivided attention, dress like your voice as an artist, donate to your causes, live life to the fullest, don't give up, and don't stop creating. I miss her every day.

Cyndi Souder
Memories
Annandale, Virginia

Cyndi Souder is an award-winning quilt artist whose work has been shown nationally. Cyndi teaches locally and nationally, as well as online for Craftsy. Her classes include surface design, machine-quilting, design, and an ongoing series of art quilt classes. Much of her work involves creating celebration quilts for clients.

Cyndi is a Juried Artist Member of Studio Art Quilt Associates and is a BERNINA brand ambassador. She co-founded two art quilt challenges: *Power Suits* and *Arts & Old Lace*, both of which traveled nationally. In addition to her book, *Creating Celebration Quilts*, she has written for a variety of national magazines and has appeared on *Quilting Arts TV* and *The Quilt Show*.

Cyndi's quilt *Memories* is a memorial piece to her sister. She explains:

I created this celebration quilt in tribute to my sister, Victoria Zacheis Greve. Vicki made a difference in so many lives through her unwavering encouragement and support. She taught me to help others and to look for the best in people. I would be a vastly different person if Vicki had not mothered me, mentored me, loved me, and utterly convinced me that I could do anything I set out to do. She lost her battle with ovarian cancer in 2004 at age fifty-eight. I still miss her so much it is sometimes hard to breathe.

Introduction

*D*ear Reader,

History books are filled with stories of the accomplishments of men. There have always been women achieving amazing things, but they have largely gone unreported in the annals of history. It's time that we added *HERstory* to history. This collection celebrates the amazing things that women everywhere have accomplished since 1920 when women were given the right to vote in the United States. Stories of courageous, intelligent, and ground-breaking women are told here in fabric, thread, paint, and embellishments. This exhibit, by eighty-five artists from seven countries, includes tributes to women well known to us, as well as those who worked behind the scenes. These quilts celebrate strong women who cracked glass ceilings and those who made discoveries. Women who shook the world by breaking into fields previously reserved for men are commemorated, as are those who were the first to do something before any man. Art quilts honor athletes, authors, artists, aviators and astronauts . . . business leaders, educators, entertainers . . . mathematicians, scientists, writers, and world leaders.

The first section is about the suffragists who fought to give women the most important voice that women have, the vote. There are still many countries where women have no voice. Our work is not finished.

The second section consists of women who did something that was a first for humankind or for a woman. Some are household names, and some are unknown to most of us. Each of them inspired the artist who created the tribute, hoping to inspire you to want to know more.

The third section is dedicated to groups of women. Sometimes when we work together, we are capable of doing things that are impossible for us as individuals. Las Sinsombrero was a group in Spain working to win rights for women. In the case of the ENIAC Computers and the Bletchley Girls, they were called upon when men were not available due to war. The first female Rangers were out to prove that they were just as capable as any male.

The last section is about personal heroes. These women are relatives of the artists or people that are greatly admired by the artists. The final three women are treasures in the quilt world.

This collection is by no means an exhaustive list. Many outstanding women are missing. Who would be on your list? Why not make your own?

If you are a quilter, perhaps your guild would like to have a Mini-*HERstory* gallery at your local show. There will be an online gallery where we will honor other strong women who inspire us all. The URL is www.herstoryonline.gallery. Write to me at susanne@susannemjones.com, and I will tell you how to participate.

The technology elements of *HERstory* don't stop with the online gallery. One of the quilts just cried out to share a story with you in the form of a video, so a **QR code** on that page offers it to you. Watch for it. Use your QR code reader on your phone and you can experience a multimedia event right in the comfort of your chair.

Also included is a chance for you to get directly acquainted with the artists. To listen to them speak to you as you go through the book, download the **audio files** at www.schifferbooks.com/HERstory.html.

Sojourner Truth (1797–1883)

. . . first black woman to succeed in challenging a white man in a US court; credited with delivering the "Ain't I a Woman?" speech.

Sojourner Truth
Carol Vinick
West Hartford, Connecticut

"Life is a hard battle anyway. If we laugh and sing a little as we fight the good fight of freedom, it makes it all go easier. I will not allow my life's light to be determined by the darkness around me." — Sojourner Truth

Sojourner Truth, a freed Northern slave and lifelong activist for human rights, was a key figure in both the Abolitionist Movement and the fight for Universal Suffrage for Women. Ninety years before Rosa Parks sat at the front of a bus in Montgomery, Alabama, Sojourner Truth sat in the white-only section of a Washington, DC, streetcar to protest segregated transportation.

Born into northern slavery in 1797 in Swartekill, New York, she was one of twelve children. She was named Isabella Baumfree. She fought to free herself from slavery. Although New York State began negotiating abolition in 1799, the emancipation of New York slaves didn't occur until 1827. In 1826, after her owner went back on an emancipation promise, she escaped with her infant daughter, Sophia, leaving two other children. When she found out that her son, Peter, age five, was illegally sold to a plantation owner in Alabama, she went to court and got him back. This was the first case where a black woman was successful in challenging a white man in a US court. In 1843 she changed her name to Sojourner Truth. She worked with the National Freedmen's Relief Association to improve living conditions of former slaves. In 1864 she met with President Abraham Lincoln. She tried, unsuccessfully, to secure land grants for former slaves, but helped freed slaves find homes. She also recruited black troops into the Union Army.

Although she could not read or write, she was not afraid to speak up and tell her story. In 1850 Sojourner published her memoir, *The Narrative of Sojourner Truth: A Northern Slave*, which she dictated to Olive Gilbert. That same year, Truth spoke at the National Women's Rights Convention in Worcester, Massachusetts, and toured with abolitionist George Thompson, speaking about slavery and human rights.

Truth was most well-known for the speech she gave at the Ohio Women's Rights Convention in Akron, Ohio, dubbed "Ain't I a Woman?" It is unlikely that she ever uttered the words "Ain't I a Woman," but it is clear that she made strong a case for equality for women. Women's suffrage advocates Lucretia Mott and Susan B. Anthony were among her friends and comrades.

Until Sojourner was too old to do so, she gave speeches about women's rights, the injustice of slavery, race relations, prison reform, property rights of former slaves, and her opposition to capital punishment. Sojourner lived to see the abolition of slavery, but women's suffrage was not achieved until 1920, thirty-seven years after her death.

Artist Carol Vinick's method is fabric collage. Carol arranges tiny pieces of fabric to create the picture and glues them down to the muslin. She used raw-edge appliqué for the four peripheral figures. The baby's chains were painted on with Inktense Blocks and then stitched over with free-motion quilting. The text was added with free-motion quilting. Carol used commercial cottons, batiks, hand-dyed cotton, vintage lace, hand-painted cotton and silk, which she designed, and hand-painted string. The paints used included Jacquard's Dye-Na-Flow, Lumiere, and Opaque, as well as Liquitex Basic Acrylic Color and Inktense Blocks.

Elizabeth Cady Stanton (1815–1902)

. . . suffragist who organized the first women's rights convention; was the first woman to run for Congress.

Elizabeth Cady Stanton
Tammi Daubenspeck
Sherman, Texas

"We hold these truths to be self-evident: that all men and women are created equal; that they are endowed by their Creator with certain inalienable rights; that among these are life, liberty, and the pursuit of happiness; that to secure these rights governments are instituted, deriving their just powers from the consent of the governed." —Elizabeth Cady Stanton

Elizabeth Cady Stanton was born in 1815. Since her father was a lawyer, she had access to an education about the unequal laws that restricted women. As a young girl, she worked hard to excel in fields that were male dominated.

Elizabeth was active in the abolitionist movement, during which she met Henry B. Stanton. When they married, she insisted on removing the word "obey" from their wedding vows. When they attended an anti-slavery convention, she learned something about women's inequality: she would not be able to speak because she was a woman.

The Stantons had seven children. As Henry traveled extensively, she was left to raise the children and keep house in addition to her women's rights work. She and Susan B. Anthony were a great team. Stanton wrote many of Anthony's speeches and Anthony helped care for Stanton's children when she was busy working for equal rights.

Elizabeth held the first women's rights convention, the Seneca Falls Convention in 1848. At this convention, the women rewrote part of the Declaration of Independence to include men and women. It became known as their "Declaration of Sentiments." Elizabeth was the first woman to run for Congress. With her daughter, Elizabeth wrote *The Woman's Bible* in two volumes.

She inspired many women's rights activists, and her descendants are active in today's fight for equality.

Coline Jenkins, Elizabeth's great-great-granddaughter wrote a foreword for this book (see page 7). She interviewed artist Tammi Daubenspeck, who explained she was saddened that Elizabeth was not as well-known as Susan B. Anthony, although Stanton wrote many of Anthony's speeches. Tammi wanted to recognize Elizabeth, believing that without her efforts, the right to vote would have been delayed.

Elizabeth's ability to raise a family of seven children while fighting for truth, freedom of speech, and equal rights for all, was inspiring to Tammi. She found Elizabeth's refusal to include the word "obey" in her wedding vows an act of bravery, and something that she and Elizabeth have in common.

The sunflower figures prominently on Tammi's piece as it was Stanton's pen name and the symbol of the National Woman Suffrage Association. The American suffrage movement used purple, yellow, and gold on banners and ribbons, so it became her palette. *The Woman's Bible* was included as it was very controversial, but was important to Elizabeth Cady Stanton that it be written. The quotes on the quilt show Elizabeth's writing style and humorous personality. Elizabeth's quote from her letter to President Theodore Roosevelt was written at the age of eighty-six. Having spent her lifetime fighting for women's rights, she mustered the strength of mind and conviction to remind the President: "Surely there is no greater monopoly than that of all men denying to all women a voice in the laws they are compelled to obey."

This piece was machine appliquéd. Tammi used fabric pens to add handwritten quotes attributed to Stanton on parchment-like pieces of fabric. It was painted using acrylic paint, ink dye, and Inktense Blocks. Lace trim and a vintage button add to the authentically old look of this piece.

Kate Sheppard (1847–1934)

. . . the most prominent member of New Zealand's Women's Suffrage movement, which gained the vote for women in 1893.

Kate Sheppard
Claire Passmore
Trowbridge, United Kingdom

"All that separates whether of race, class, creed, or sex, is inhuman, and must be overcome."
—Kate Sheppard

Catherine Wilson Malcolm was born in Liverpool, England on March 10, 1847. Named after her grandmother, she preferred to go by "Kate." Following the death of her father, Kate's mother moved her four children and immigrated to New Zealand in search of a better life. Three years after arriving Kate married Walter Allen Sheppard, a merchant, and gave birth to their only child, Douglas in 1880.

In 1885, Kate became involved in establishing the New Zealand Women's Christian Temperance Union. She was a powerful speaker, a skilled organizer, and quickly built support for her cause. She began advocating for the cause of true equality for all, particularly women's suffrage. In 1887 on the introduction of the First Suffrage Bill to Parliament, she published a pamphlet entitled "Ten Reasons Why the Women of New Zealand Should Vote." Nothing became of this bill. Kate and other members of the Temperance Union began touring the country, wearing a white camellia as the symbol of their movement, holding meetings in towns and cities across the nation. About 30,000 signatures were gathered from all over the country and sent back to Kate, who glued them together, end to end, and wound the joined list around a piece of broom handle. (Two of these are preserved at Archives New Zealand.) In 1893 Kate Sheppard dramatically presented her "monster petition" to both Houses of Parliament. The document was carried into Parliament in a wheelbarrow and John Hall, Member

of Parliament and suffrage supporter, unrolled it down the central aisle of the chamber until it hit the wall with a thud. The women's suffrage bill was successfully passed, granting the women of New Zealand full voting rights. It was the first self-governing nation in the world where women had the right to vote.

With the election only ten weeks away, Kate worked tirelessly to register women voters. Despite the short notice, nearly two-thirds of women cast a vote in that historic election. Opposition had been strong from Parliamentarians, powerful men, and the liquor industry, fearing for its continued business. Bribes were paid and threats issued to try to stop the movement. The wearing of red camellias (opposite in color to the suffragists' white) became the symbol of solidarity against equal voting rights for women. Despite the opposition, Kate Sheppard and her fellow suffragists won the day.

British artist Claire Passmore depicted Kate Sheppard in classic Victorian dress and pose. Although she looks rather severe, Kate was known for her broad knowledge, good judgment, tolerance, and charm. Claire chose to cascade the iconic camellias down the side of the quilt. In the center are the signatures taken from the first page of the famous petitions. Kate Shepherd's signature is at the center.

Claire created this whole cloth quilt with hand and machine-appliqué, hand and free-motion machine embroidery. It was made with commercial prints, hand-dyed fabrics, tea-stained fabrics, discharged fabrics, recycled vintage kimono silk, velvet, brocade, and broderie anglaise from old clothing. It was quilted on a domestic sewing machine. Derwent Inktense pencils were used to add details.

Susan B. Anthony (1820–1906)

. . . suffragist who worked for over fifty years to get women the right to vote.

Susan B. Anthony
Suzanne Evenson
Inverness, Florida

"We shall someday be heeded, and . . . everybody will think it was always so, just exactly as many young people think that all the privileges, all the freedom, all the enjoyments which woman now possesses always were hers. They have no idea of how every single inch of ground that she stands upon today has been gained by the hard work of some little handful of women of the past." —Susan B. Anthony

Susan Brownell Anthony was born to a Quaker family in Adams, Massachusetts. Her father, who was active in the anti-slavery movement, encouraged Susan to be included in meetings and discussions for the cause of emancipation.

At that time, women were quite restricted. They belonged to their husbands and had no legal rights to own property, earn money, or even maintain custody of their children. And women were not permitted to vote! Susan and other women of her generation made a conscious decision to not marry for these reasons.

Susan became active in the emancipation and temperance movements. Women and children often suffered poverty and abuse at the hands of a drunken spouse or father. Involvement in these two causes provided Susan with experiences that were eventually put to good use.

Susan attended a women's rights convention in 1852 in Syracuse, New York. She and Elizabeth Cady Stanton were friends and revolutionary partners for more than fifty years in the cause of women's suffrage. Stanton was a mother with a large family. Skilled at writing and unmarried, Susan was free to travel, deliver the message, and encourage action toward the cause for suffrage which the pair saw as a necessary precursor to other rights for women.

On November 5, 1872, Susan B. Anthony voted, having been given permission to register several days earlier. She was arrested and put on trial for violating the law. In the end, she had to pay a fine of one hundred dollars and went home. Fortunately for the cause, the incident was newsworthy!

Susan did not live to see the 19th Amendment passed in 1919 but the work she and Elizabeth put forth was critical in contributing to its passage and its ratification in 1920. Here are Susan B. Anthony's wise words spoken toward the end of her life, in 1905:

When we all saw with clear eyes the future spread out before us with all its grand possibilities for women . . . We were not seers, but we did see that something must be done for women, and Quaker though I was, I had to do my part. That is all.

She said in 1906:

I have met and known most of the progressive women, who came after [Mary Wollstonecraft] — Lucretia Mott, the Grimke sisters, Elizabeth Cady Stanton, Lucy Stone—a long galaxy of great women . . . There have been others also just as true and devoted to the cause . . . but with such women consecrating their lives . . . Failure is impossible!

Throughout her life Susan B. Anthony dared to travel the country speaking on behalf of women's rights at a time when most men and many women believed that women should not speak out at all.

As artist Suzanne Evenson researched Susan, it became clear to Suzanne that Susan's profuse words mattered. In this quilt, Susan is surrounded by a selection of her spoken, printed and written words, some of which Suzanne chose because she saw parallels with women's lives in America and across the globe today. Suzanne selected the colors of the USA as her palette. White was used for the background and words were printed on fabric then stitched to the surface. Suzanne added the red and blue stars to symbolize her stellar place in the early years of the suffrage movement and American history. Suzanne digitally printed an image of Susan B. Anthony and the quotes.

"Well I have been & gone & done it!!—positively voted…& swore my vote in, at that…"
Rochester, Nov. 5, 1872

"…I never dreamed of the…officers prosecuting me for voting…" *1873*

"The women of this nation must be awakened to a sense of their degradation — political —or at least *we who are awake* —must make an effort to awaken those who are dead asleep." *1875*

"We shall some day be heeded, and …everybody will think it was always so just exactly as many young people think that all the privileges, all the freedom, all the enjoyments which woman now possesses always were hers. They have no idea of how every single inch of ground that she stands upon today has been gained by the hard work of some little handful of women of the past." *1894*

"God never made a man who is good enough to govern any woman without her consent." *1895*

"It was we, the people, not we, the white male citizens, nor yet we, the male citizens, but we, the whole people, who formed this Union." *1873*

"I have met and known most of the progressive women who came after /Mary Wollstonecraft/—Lucretia Mott, the Grimke sisters, Elizabeth Cady Stanton, Lucy Stone--a long galaxy of great women …There have been others also just as true and devoted to the cause …but with such women consecrating their lives …
Failure is impossible!"
1906

Susan B. Anthony
1820-1906
Women's Suffrage
Leader

"Why cannot these earnest, patriotic women be judged by the facts of their lives, and the dignity and justice of their demands and arguments, rather than by the clothes they wear, their age or personal appearance?" *1884*

"…Woman will never have equality of rights anywhere, she never will hold those she has now has by an absolute tenure, until she possess the fundamental right of self-representation. This fact is so obvious as to need no argument." *1902*

"…when we all saw with clear eyes the future spread out before us with all its grand possibilities for women…We were not seers, but we did see that something must be done for women, and Quaker though I was, I had to do my part. That is all." *1904*

19

Lucy Burns (1879–1966)

. . . founded the National Woman's Party.

Night of Terror
Lesly-Claire Greenberg
Fairfax, Virginia

"I think, with never-ending gratitude, that the young women of today do not and can never know at what price their right to free speech and to speak at all in public has been earned." —Lucy Burns

Lucy Burns was raised in Brooklyn believing that all children should be educated, even the girls. She graduated from Vassar College, taught for several years, and then went on to do post-graduate work at prestigious schools in both the United States and Europe. While she was at Oxford, she joined the Women's Social and Political Union to work with the suffrage movement in Britain. Arrested for picketing Parliament, she met Alice Paul at the police station in London. They became good friends and worked together to forward the cause of women.

Back in the US, they staged parades and pickets in Washington, DC. Shifts were rotated in front of the White House. Signs and banners were hung on the gates; placards were carried. They continually asked Woodrow Wilson, "How long must women wait for liberty?"

Lucy and Alice were more militant than many of their followers. They wanted to make sure the women that were demonstrating knew that there could be consequences to their actions. They were forcibly arrested for "blocking traffic" on the sidewalks surrounding the White House. The police along with more than forty guards from DC corrections moved in on the women. They were pushed, dragged, lifted, and thrown in jail. Lucy was imprisoned at the Occoquan Workhouse.

Conditions were deplorable. The only water was from an open pail, and they were fed slop full of worms. Because she was identified as "The Ring Leader," Lucy's attack was extremely brutal. She was stripped bare, and her hands were manacled to the bars above her head where she remained in the cold all night. This night was referred to as "The Night of Terror." When the prisoners staged a hunger strike, they were force-fed via tubes in their noses. They endured much to gain our liberty.

Soon after these events, in June of 1919, Congress passed the 19th Amendment to the Constitution. It was ratified in August 1920 granting women the right to vote. After winning this victory, Lucy Burns retreated into private life in Brooklyn where she and her sisters raised their orphaned niece.

Artist Lesly-Claire Greenberg has been making art quilts for over forty years. Lesly-Claire likes to make small test pieces or studies to determine what will work best. While she was working on this quilt, she was physically challenged. She tore a ligament in her dominant hand, and it was a trial to do handwork. Due to this, she tested machine and hand-quilting, deciding that the quilt and bars could be machine appliquéd and quilted. However, the handcuffs cried out for hand-quilting. The handcuffs were made using the Apliquick method of turned appliqué, turned under using an interfacing and fabric glue. Further construction was done using machine piecing, hand, and machine appliqué. Lesly-Claire often uses thorns in her work to represent pain and suffering. There is desolation in a garden gone to briars and weeds. Lesly-Claire created this tribute to Lucy Burns using Cherrywood hand-dyed suede-look cotton fabric.

Alice Paul (1885–1977)

. . . initiated and organized the 1913 Woman Suffrage Procession in Washington.

It's About Justice
Janice Paine-Dawes
Lakeview, Arizona

"There will never be a new world order until women are a part of it." —Alice Paul

Alice Paul was born into a Quaker family, where she was taught that men and women are equal. But there was little equality in America in the early 1900s. Women could not vote and had little say over their own lives. Women who attempted to vote were either turned away or jailed.

Alice's mother was active in the National American Woman Suffrage Association, and Alice would often accompany her to meetings. Alice continued to be politically active in college, and during graduate studies in England, she was exposed to the Pankhurst women, some of the UK's most militant suffragists. She joined their ranks and returned to the states ready to battle for the cause.

In 1912 she joined the National American Woman Suffrage Association (NAWSA) which had been led by Susan B. Anthony, Lucy Stone, and Elizabeth Cady Stanton.

Alice Paul assumed the leadership of the Congressional Committee of NAWSA in Washington, DC. She assembled a mass march of suffragists around the White House, the United States Capitol Building, and the Treasury Building on March 3, 1913, the day before President Wilson's inauguration. It is still viewed as one of the biggest protests in American history and brought more attention to the struggle for the vote. The NAWSA was not pleased with the militant tactics, and as a result, Alice started the National Woman's Party in 1916.

Alice Paul was a woman of strength and conviction. In 1917 she was jailed. The suffragists were subjected to inhuman treatment in prison that included being force-fed during hunger strikes and living in rat-infested squalor. When the public and politicians learned of these conditions, the movement began to garner support.

At the end of World War I, President Wilson encouraged Congress to pass the 19th Amendment. On June 4, 1919, the 19th Amendment giving women the right to vote passed both houses of Congress. On August 18, 1920, it was ratified by the states, and on August 26, 1920, the 19th Amendment was officially added to the Constitution.

Artist Janice Paine-Dawes' portrait of Alice is a freehand wash of textile paints that was then fused and applied to the base. The design inspiration came from a white muslin child's pinafore, with appliquéd stars, that was worn for Lincoln's inauguration, which Janice saw at the Lincoln Museum in Springfield, Illinois. Janice could envision a child wearing that pinafore with lavender or gold stars, the colors of the American suffragist movement. The design morphed into this tattered, aged campaign poster. The bottom stripe is pieced in the colors Alice used for the suffragists' flag. The arch of nineteen fused appliquéd lavender stars represents the 19th Amendment. Janice painted some edges to appear as a torn poster and other areas were dry brushed to look like aged paper.

Edith Abbott (1876–1957)

. . . first female to chair a graduate school in the US, the University of Chicago School of Social Service.

Grace Abbott (1878–1939)

. . . top female in the federal government during the Depression; director of Children's Bureau.

Sisters and Comrades through All the Years
Linda Syverson Guild
Bethesda, Maryland

"Grace used to say that a small Midwestern town was the most honestly democratic place in the world. There were no people who were rich, and the poor we knew as individuals. They were people to whom we were expected to be especially polite and kind— people who had had one misfortune or another, people whom we should try to help." —Edith Abbott

The Abbott sisters, Edith and Grace, grew up in Grand Island, Nebraska, daughters of a pioneer lawyer and a Quaker suffragist. They were raised believing in the power of the written word and were advocates for people who did not have a voice: immigrants, women, and children. Both sisters were invited to join Jane Addams at the Hull House in Chicago, working with newly arrived immigrants. The sisters were concerned with women's right to vote, the inequity of women, and children in wage-earning positions. Grace and Edith believed that children should enjoy childhood and attend school rather than support their families. Due to Edith's intense interest in mothers, children, and their welfare and the knowledge that it took figures to change the minds of the government, she was frequently referred to as the "passionate statistician." Edith worked to negotiate the transfer of the School of Civics and Philanthropy to the University of Chicago. This new department became the graduate school of Social Service at the University.

Grace worked with the Immigrants' Protective League until 1917 when immigration into the US was restricted during World War I. She was named President Wilson's representative to the League of Nations and spent time in Europe attempting to improve immigrants' rights there. Feeling defeated and frustrated in her inability to bring about change, she moved to Washington, DC and began her work with Julia Lathrop and the Children's Bureau, where Grace was named "chief" in

1921. Her dedication prompted the press to call Grace the "the mother of America's 43 million children."

President Hoover nominated Grace for a cabinet position in his administration, the first woman to receive that honor. However, her nomination ran into a great deal of opposition, finally from Hoover himself.

Edith became the first female chair of a US graduate school at the School of Social Service, University of Chicago. Grace became the Director of the Children's Bureau; she was the highest ranking female in the federal government at that time. As head of the United States Children's Bureau, she was in charge of the first federal grants-in-aid welfare program in US history: the influential Maternity and Infancy Act. They worked together to improve the function of their administrations. Edith educated the people that Grace employed at the Children's Bureau and Grace made certain that Edith's programs continued to find funding. Grace suffered from ill health for many years and passed away in 1939. Edith never recovered from her loss but continued to oversee the School of Social Service. Eventually, she returned to Grand Island where she died in 1957.

In 1954, a naval destroyer was launched with the name USS Grace Abbott. In 1974, Grand Island, Nebraska dedicated a new library: Edith Abbott Memorial Library.

Artist Linda Syverson Guild grew up in the Abbotts' hometown. Linda hand painted the background and the silhouettes. The column was rendered in crayon. The "Votes for Women" image was free-motion stitched. The sisters' faces were pieced using a pattern made from filtered photographs of Grace and Edith and machine quilted to reinforce the structure of each face. Quotes on silhouettes were hand embroidered. The filmstrip, containing pictures and quotes, was pieced. It was machine quilted except for quotes. It was created with Cherrywood, Kona cotton, and commercially printed cotton fabrics.

THE CHILDREN'S AMENDMENT—VICTORY, 1939

...S OF UNSKILLED LABOR • AFTER SUFFRAGE—CITIZENS

...WOMEN A FORCE FOR GOOD GOVERNMENT?

...LABOR LEGISLAT... • WOMEN IN MANUFACTURIN...

...IME AND ...N TO FOREIGN BORN

...UNEMPL... ...ERAL RESPONSIBILITY

...LIC PROT... ...DDRE... ...HICAG...

• PUBLIC ...

...CIAL SECUR... ...HE IM... ...EM

...OR D... ...OVEM...

...ILD WELF...

Grace used to say that a small Midwestern town was the most honestly democratic place in the world. There were no people who were rich, and the poor we knew as individuals. They were people to whom we were expected to be especially polite and kind – people who had had one misfortune or another, people whom we should try to help.

Edith Abbott, A Sister's Memories

Breaker boys working in Ewen Breaker of Pennsylvania Coal Co. Location: South Pittston, Pennsylvania. Photographer: Lewis Hine August 1911

The statute that created the Children's Bureau had said that the bureau was to investigate all subjects relating to "the welfare of children and child life among all of the classes of our people."....

Grace saw this mandate for "social research" as one of the key functions of the bureau. It is difficult for us to realize today, but at the time that the Children's Bureau was set up [1912], there had never yet been a comprehensive statistical survey of the mortality rate of mothers and infants in childbirth.

John Sorensen, A Sister's Memories 2015

Newberry Mills (S.C.) Noon hour. All are working here. Witness, Sara R. Hine. Location: Newberry, South Carolina. Photographer, Lewis Hine December 1908

There is no easy explanation for the vast success of Miss [Grace] Abbott's career. She was not a reformer in the ordinary meaning of the word. Rather she was a builder... She constructed new social values in people. To hear her speak was to catch a vision; to labor with her was to share in a dream being made real. She quickened hundreds, perhaps thousands, by the fire of her own spirit... Her fame then was not temporary. She created immortality for herself... Her inspiration is a living force now and forever.

Washington (DC) Evening Star 1939

History will include her (Edith Abbott) name among the handful of leaders who have made enduring contributions to the field of education. Social work has now taken its place as an established profession. She, more than any other one person, gave direction to the education required to that profession. Posterity will not forget achievements such as these.

Wayne McMillen, Social Service Review 1957

I am looking for an Abbott to give a Suffragist speech.

Jane Addams, Hull House in Chicago

Local government local taxes, local poor relief had some significance in the pioneer days— and so did slavery, squatter sovereignty, free soil and the controversy over the 'subjugation of women' – but they have no relation to the facts of modern life.

Edith Abbott

VOTES for WOMEN

In general, however, the difficulties encountered by the immigrant will be the same and we can, therefore, on the basis of our past experience make intelligent plans for the future.

Grace Abbott

Maggie Aderin-Pocock (1968–)

. . . broke stereotypes about careers in science regarding gender, class, and color, and communicated to others that they are only myths.

Watching the Sky at Night
Alicia Merrett
Wells, Somerset, United Kingdom

"As a child growing up, I wanted to reach the stars, but by making this instrument, I was doing the next best thing. I could look into the hearts of stars."
—*Maggie Aderin-Pocock*

Dr. Maggie Aderin-Pocock, MBE was born Margaret Ebunoluwa to Nigerian parents in Islington, North London, United Kingdom, in 1968. While in school Margaret looked up to the sky, liked what she saw, and being short of money, built her own telescope. She finished secondary school with the highest possible marks in math and science. When she told a career teacher that she loved science and wanted to be an astronaut, it was suggested that she try nursing— "because that is scientific too." She was not considered university material due to the color of her skin.

Margaret went to Imperial College London, where she earned a Bachelor of Science in Physics and a Doctorate in Mechanical Engineering. After working in private industry, she went into university research, developing a high-resolution spectrograph for the Gemini Observatory in Chile, which is now widely used by other space scientists. Maggie has made instrumentation in both industrial and academic environments. As manager of a multidisciplinary team, she has been instrumental in the development of optical subsystems for the James Webb Space Telescope, due to replace the Hubble Space Telescope in 2018. Maggie manages instruments in a satellite, Aeolus that measures climate change.

Her main passion is bringing science and astronomy to the public and school children, encouraging them to choose scientific careers. She is a veritable pioneer in this field and has set up her own company, Science Innovation, Ltd. Its aim is to engage people in the wonders of space science and encourage a new generation of astronauts, astronomers, scientists, and engineers.

Maggie is one of two presenters on the long-running, popular BBC program *The Sky at Night*. She has made and presented the fascinating, oft-repeated program *Do We Really Need the Moon?* She has been instrumental in a number of other televised events and programs about science and cosmology, including *Dr. Who Confidential* and *How Satellites Rule Our World*.

Maggie Aderin-Pocock has been made an MBE (Member of the British Empire) for services to science and education. She was named one of six UK "Women of Outstanding Achievement" in 2006. Her most important accomplishment is to have broken stereotypes about careers, gender, class, and color and to have communicated that those stereotypes are only myths.

Growing up in Argentina, artist Alicia Merrett wanted to be an astronomer, but her weakness in math and the lack of encouraging teachers made it difficult. However, she retained a strong interest in science and cosmology, which Alicia has been able to indulge in England, her adopted country. This interest prompted her choice of Maggie as the subject of her piece. It is inspired by views of the sky at night, Alicia's knowledge of the solar system and the universe, and by photographs from the Hubble Telescope. Alicia loves the shapes and lines offered by representations of our earth, which she interprets with her own color palette, and adds texture with dense quilting. Alicia also likes incorporating text in her work. Alicia's pieced, stitched, fused, and collaged textile works aim to convey symbols and meanings. It was made with hand-dyed fabrics and was created using fusible appliqué. It features hand-cut fused fabric lettering and was machine quilted.

Space Scientist

Inspirational Communicator

Maggie Aderin-Pocock

27

Marian Anderson (1897–1993)

. . . first African American to perform as a member of the New York Metropolitan Opera and to perform at the White House.

Marian Anderson
Margaret Williams
Tucker, Georgia

"When I sing, I don't want them to see that my face is black; I don't want them to see that my face is white—I want them to see my soul. And that is colorless." —Marian Anderson

Marian Anderson, a gifted contralto, inspired a nation and broke down barriers for African American performers. Born in Philadelphia in 1897, she first sang in the choir at the Union Baptist Church. She began training with a vocal coach in her teens and was soon performing in concert halls. In the 1930s she toured extensively in Europe, Scandinavia, Russia, and Latin America.

Back in the US, Marian suffered many personal indignities as a result of racism. She never became bitter, instead making it her mission to "leave behind the kind of impression that will make it easier for those who follow." With grace and dignity, she began to open doors for other black performers during a time of institutional segregation.

The most famous example of discrimination against her occurred in 1939 when the Daughters of the American Revolution (DAR) refused to let her perform in Washington, DC's DAR Constitution Hall. First Lady Eleanor Roosevelt resigned her membership in the DAR and encouraged Secretary of the Interior Harold Ickes to arrange a free concert on the steps of the Lincoln Memorial. The concert took place on Easter Sunday with 75,000 people of all races attending and an audience of millions listening to the live radio broadcast. In her autobiography, Anderson wrote, "There seemed to be people as far as the eye could see. The crowd stretched in a great semicircle from the Lincoln Memorial around the reflecting pool onto the shaft of the Washington Monument. I had a feeling that a great wave of good will poured out from the people, almost engulfing me." The Easter concert is recognized as a milestone of the early Civil Rights movement in the US. In 1943, the DAR apologized, changed its rules, and invited Marian to perform at Constitution Hall in a series of benefit concerts for war relief.

Marian Anderson's career was marked by many firsts and awards including NAACP's Spingarn Medal, for the highest achievement of an American of African descent. She was the first African American to be invited to perform at the White House in 1939 when King George VI visited from Great Britain. In 1955, she became the first African American to perform as a member of the New York Metropolitan Opera. President Eisenhower appointed her to be a delegate to the Thirteenth General Assembly of the United Nations in 1958. Marian sang at the inaugurations of Dwight Eisenhower and John F. Kennedy. She was awarded the Presidential Medal of Freedom by President Kennedy in 1963 and the United Nations Peace Prize in 1977. In April 2016, the US Department of the Treasury announced that her Lincoln Memorial concert will be depicted on the reverse of the newly redesigned five dollar bill.

Artist Margaret Williams works with what she terms fused mosaic enhanced with thread painting and free-motion quilting. She uses commercial fabrics often hiding little surprises in the mosaic design. There are many music-related fabrics; if you look closely, you can see a woman's face in the corner of one of Marian's eyes. Margaret thinks of her as Eleanor Roosevelt. There are images of the Lincoln Memorial and the Paris Opera House hidden in there. The background is orange, the color of the jacket she wore for the Lincoln Memorial concert. Margaret used a permanent marker and textile paint to highlight her work.

Lucille Ball (1911–1989)

. . . first woman in television to head a
production company, Desilu.

Lucille Ball: A Multimedia Megastar

Meena Schaldenbrand

Plymouth, Michigan

*"Enrich the world through the healing powers of love
and laughter." —Lucille Ball*

Comedy is often the outgrowth of a life marked by tragedy
during childhood. Such was the case with Lucille Ball, whose
father died when she was three years old. When her mother
remarried, she and her new husband left the children behind
to be raised by grandparents. After her parents had returned to
Jamestown, New York, Lucy begged her mother to send her
to drama school. She was dumbstruck by fellow student Bette
Davis and was said to be too shy to do well at the school. She
quit school, but found work as a model first for a fashion
designer, then for Chesterfield cigarettes.

In the 1930s, she began her work in films, appearing in
more than eighty films during her career, earning her the
unofficial title, "The Queen of B Movies." It was on the set of
one of these B movies, *Dance, Girl, Dance,* that she met and
fell madly in love with Desi Arnaz. The couple stayed together
twenty years, during which they did a radio show together, *My
Favorite Husband*; starred in I *Love Lucy* and *The Lucy–Desi
Comedy Hour*, had two children, and started Desilu Productions.
She was the first woman in television to be head of a production
company. After their divorce, Ball bought out Arnaz's share
of the studio and was a very active studio head. Desilu was a
highly successful productive studio responsible for such shows
as *Our Miss Brooks, Make Room for Daddy, The Untouchables,
Star Trek, The Dick Van Dyke Show, Mission Impossible, The
Andy Griffith Show*, and *My Favorite Martian.*

Although Lucille Ball was also a producer, director, and
author, she was best known as the star of sitcoms: *I Love Lucy,
The Lucy–Desi Comedy Hour, The Lucy Show, Here's Lucy*,
and *Life with Lucy*. Her costars were her husband, Desi Arnaz,
and her children, Lucie Arnaz and Desi Jr. Her TV shows
earned her four Emmy awards. For many years she was *the*
star of the small screen. She was on thirty-nine *TV Guide*
covers, more than any other person.

Lucille Ball has two Hollywood Walk of Fame stars. One
is for her television work and the other for motion pictures.
Her hometown of Jamestown, New York, proudly named a
museum in her honor and renamed their community theater
Lucille Ball Little Theatre. Ball was one of *Time* magazine's
"100 Most Important People of the Century." On August 6,
2001, which would have been her ninetieth birthday, the US
Postal Service created a commemorative stamp in her honor.

Lucy was honored at the Kennedy Center for the Performing
Arts receiving the Lifetime Achievement Citation in 1986.
President George H. W. Bush presented Lucy with the Presidential
Medal of Freedom posthumously in 1989. Her autobiography
Love, Lucy was published after her death.

Artist Meena Schaldenbrand surrounded a portrait of Lucy
with eight hearts forming a star design to showcase her and
her many multimedia roles. Meena used aqua tulle and net for
the background behind Lucy. She used lace for her dress. It is
hand embroidered and free-motion quilted. Meena embellished
it with tubes, couched yarns, beads, sequins, pearls, rick rack,
and trim.

Mary McLeod Bethune (1875–1955)

. . . served under four presidents; president of the National Association of Colored Women; founded the National Council of Negro Women.

Mary McLeod Bethune, Educator and Activist

Betty Hahn

Sun City, Arizona

"I leave you a thirst for education. Knowledge is the prime need of the hour." —Mary McLeod Bethune

Mary McLeod Bethune was one of seventeen children born in 1875 to former slaves and the first of their children to be born free. A benefactor approached the family and said she would pay for one of their children to attend the new school opened by a missionary two miles from their home. Mary was considered the smartest of the children, so she was given the opportunity. She had always wanted to read. She shared her newfound knowledge with her family.

She later received a scholarship to the Scotia Seminary, a school for girls. After graduating in 1893, she attended Dwight Moody's Institute for Home and Foreign Missions in Chicago. After completing her studies, she went home and began her career as a teacher. In 1904, believing education was the best way for racial advancement, she opened the Daytona Normal and Industrial Institute for Negro Girls in Florida. The school grew to more than 250 students after starting with five. She served as the school's president and remained so even after it was combined with the Cookman Institute for Men in 1923. The merged institution became known as the Bethune-Cookman College.

She became the president of the Florida chapter of the National Association of Colored Women, serving as its national president from 1924 to 1928.

Mary assisted four presidents and became friends with Eleanor Roosevelt. President Calvin Coolidge invited her to participate in a conference on child welfare. President Herbert Hoover asked her to serve on the Commission on Home Building and Home Ownership and appointed Mary to a committee on child health. Bethune became a special advisor to President Franklin Roosevelt on minority affairs in 1935. That same year, she started the National Council of Negro Women to represent groups working on important issues for African American women. Also in '35, she received the Spingarn Medal from the NAACP, for outstanding achievement by an African American. In 1936, Roosevelt appointed Bethune to be the director of the Division of Negro Affairs of the National Youth Administration, becoming the first black woman to head a federal agency. Helping young people find job opportunities was one of her main concerns in this position. President Harry Truman appointed Bethune to a committee on national defense in the early 1950s and asked her to serve as an official delegate to a presidential inauguration in Liberia.

Artist Betty Hahn loves to paint stories. In researching Mary, Betty found beautiful photos to use to show the stages of her life, from early youth to advanced age. Betty fell in love with her as she painted her. In describing her process, Betty says that it feels like she is watching the painting grow. It is not something that she does, the painting just becomes. Betty used sepia tones, black, brown, and gray and left areas clear in which to quilt phrases and statements relating to the pictures. This whole cloth quilt was painted with Tsukineko ink on paper-backed silk crepe de chine. It was quilted on a movable machine.

33

Mary Blair (1911–1978)

. . . one of the first women to work in a creative capacity at Disney Studios, producing concept art for *Peter Pan* and *Cinderella*.

Mary Blair
Tanya Brown
Sunnyvale, California

"You get an education in school and in college. And then you start to work. And that's when you learn!"
—Mary Blair

Mary Blair was an American artist best known for producing concept art for the Walt Disney Company. Her film assignments included *Peter Pan, Alice in Wonderland*, and *Cinderella*. She also designed murals for *Tomorrowland* and *It's a Small World*. Post-Disney, she created illustrations for advertising and children's books, such as the Little Golden Book *I Can Fly*.

Mary's interest in art became apparent at an early age. She had a great deal of drive, taking lessons, entering competitions, and even politicking for a share of the family budget to purchase art supplies. "I have heard from my mother," one of her nieces later recalled, "that they sometimes did with less food, so that Mary could buy her paints."

As a young adult, she attended San Jose State and then won a scholarship to Chouinard Art Institute in Los Angeles. While at Chouinard, she met a fellow student and artist, Lee Everett Blair. A year after graduation, they married. Lee's later employment at Disney Studios perhaps opened doors there for Mary. She initially worked for a competitor, Ub Iwerks, as a cel painter, but she left that studio after a couple of years and was hired by Disney.

She began working in Disney's Character Model department in 1940, garnering Walt Disney's attention in 1941 during a three-month trip to South America. The trip was intended for Disney studio artists, including Mary's husband Lee, but Mary approached Walt and asked if she might come as well.

Her work transformed during this trip, evolving from a realistic, painterly style into a vibrant style with more simplified shapes and bright colors. Disney was enchanted. "Walt said that I knew about colors he had never heard of," she later proudly recalled. She became one of the first women to function in a creative capacity at the studio, rather than as an inker or painter of cels. Some said that she was Walt Disney's favorite artist.

In 1953, she left the studio and performed freelance design and illustration work for children's books and companies such as Nabisco. However, she and Walt remained close; and he included her in projects such as the mural art for *Tomorrowland*.

When popular styles changed, her career experienced a downturn. In 1978 she succumbed to a cerebral hemorrhage, not surviving to see a resurgence in admiration for her work.

Artist Tanya Brown's goal was to create a piece which would not only be an homage to Mary Blair's life and works, but would stylistically reflect the media for which she was most famous, animations and children's books. The quilt depicts a birth to death sequence, with the stork symbolizing her birth and the lilies symbolizing her passing away. Vignettes represent her marriage, her two sons, and some of the movies and books on which she worked. To create the surface design for the fabric, Tanya sketched on paper and refined them with ink. Then they were scanned and colorized in Procreate on an iPad. The resulting images were composited into a final layout using Photoshop on a Mac, printed on cotton fabric, batted, and densely stitched.

Ruby Bridges (1954–)

. . . first black child to integrate a white school in New Orleans, Louisiana.

Ruby Bridges, Age 6, 1960
Willa Downes
Fairfax, Virginia

"Don't follow the path. Go where there is no path and begin the trail. When you start a new trail equipped with courage, strength, and conviction, the only thing that can stop you is you!" —Ruby Bridges

Ruby Bridges helped change the educational future of thousands of children in the United States. In November of 1960 six-year-old Ruby was escorted by US Marshals into the William Frantz Elementary School in New Orleans, Louisiana. The Federal Marshals had been sent by President Eisenhower to protect Ruby from crowds of angry, jeering people after city and state police had refused to protect her.

Until then the school had only admitted white children, but the Supreme Court had decreed that school segregation must end and Ruby was African American. She was the only one of the six African American children who had chosen to attend the all-white school who had passed the school's admission test. The parents of all the white children immediately withdrew their children from the school, and all the teachers refused to continue teaching. Ruby became the only child in the school. Her teacher, Barbara Henry, a white woman who had been raised in Massachusetts, taught her alone in that school for over a year. Even though they had been a classroom family of two, Ruby and Mrs. Henry hadn't seen each other for many years. They were reunited on *The Oprah Winfrey Show* in 1996. It is a relationship that they both treasure.

Ruby serves as a role model for both children and adults today. So often our young children are in situations where they encounter bullies, acts of prejudice, hate, and other forms of degrading behavior by others. It is important for these children to understand they can have the courage to stand up to unethical, unfair, discriminatory, and intimidating behaviors, as Ruby did every day as she walked bravely past angry mobs to an otherwise empty school.

Often we recognize adults who exhibit courageous behavior as role models for ourselves and our children. We must also recognize, honor, and encourage the courageous behavior of children as they stand up against bullying, meanness, cheating, and discrimination, just like six-year-old Ruby Bridges did.

An empty school is always strange to former teacher and artist Willa Downes. Schools are meant to be bustling interactive worlds. Willa wanted to show the stark emptiness of the school by featuring row upon row of empty desks and the absence of anything else on the quilt. She wanted the simplicity of the quilt to reflect the vacant building.

Schools are usually filled with the incredible uniqueness of many children. Willa screen-printed the desks, using a thermofax screen that she designed herself. Each desk is distinctive in its printing and represents an individual child who is not there.

The quilting lines are linear to reinforce the barrenness and lack of movement within the school. By presenting Ruby as a felt appliqué silhouette, Willa hopes the viewer will focus on Ruby's solitary experience.

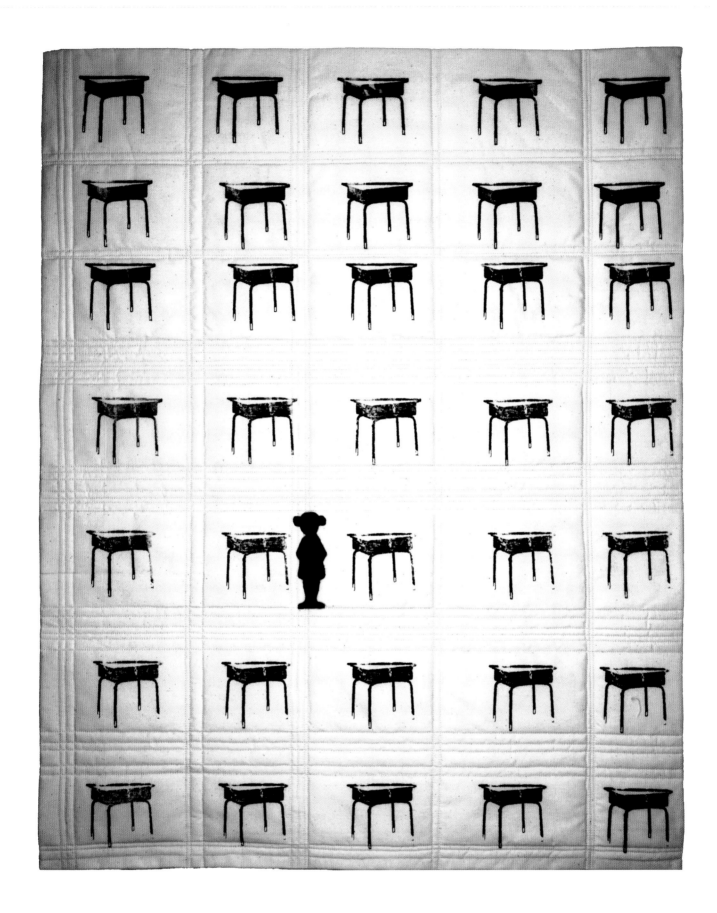

Pearl S. Buck (1892–1973)

. . . wrote brilliantly about China, winning
both a Pulitzer and a Nobel Prize.

A Pearl of Great Value
Rose Legge
Castle Rock, Colorado

---

*"You cannot make yourself feel something you do not
feel, but you can make yourself do right in spite of
your feelings."* —Pearl S. Buck

As a young girl growing up in Edmonds, Washington, in the 1960s, artist Rose Legge checked out a library book called *The Good Earth*. Written by Pearl S. Buck in 1932, it brought to life a whole world Rose had never imagined. The ancient, exotic culture of China was peopled with peasant field workers who endured much hardship and with rich, self-indulgent landowners. These characters were unforgettable, painted in fine detail and vivid color by Pearl, who knew them so well growing up as the child of missionaries. Over fifty years later, quotes from these characters in Pearl's authentic phrasing still come to Rose's mind.

Born Pearl Sydenstricker in 1892, she spent virtually all of her first forty years of life in China. She witnessed the age-old customs of a culture that no longer exists. Pearl had a gift for understanding and describing human nature as portrayed individually in her characters, as well as on an epic scale in an entire society undergoing rapid change. Her wise, moving style of writing was popular on bestseller lists, and *The Good Earth* won the Pulitzer Prize in 1932. It's still a familiar work and was selected for Oprah's Book Club in 2004.

Pearl S. Buck won the Nobel Prize for Literature in 1938, the first American female ever to do so. Writing was the vehicle Pearl used to express her views on women's rights, immigration, war, and violence long before average Americans were concerned about these issues. A caring activist for human rights, her efforts were not limited to her written words. In her later years, she devoted much of her time and effort establishing Welcome House, an adoption service for Asian children previously considered unadoptable. She founded Pearl S. Buck International which provides opportunities to explore and appreciate other cultures, builds better lives for all children around the world, and promotes her legacy.

Pearl remains an important woman of the twentieth century, and in 1983 a US postage stamp was issued in her honor. In 1999, she was designated a Women's History Month Honoree because of her achievements as a groundbreaking novelist.

Pearl died in 1973 of lung cancer. She had designed her own tombstone, inscribed with Chinese characters that mean "Pearl Sydenstricker."

Artist Rose Legge tried to create a quilt as rich in layers and contrasts as Pearl S. Buck herself. Rose hand-dyed and discharged fabric to evoke an Asian feel. She decided to create a balance between the opulent, colorful fabrics worn by the wealthy landowners Pearl wrote about, and the humbler homespun material worn by the fieldworkers she loved. Hand stitching was used for added textural interest and to give a worn, hand sewn look.

Rose included a deconstructed screen print to give an ancient, timeless element because the culture portrayed in Pearl's books had endured since antiquity. In stark contrast is her portrait, an independent, accomplished, educated woman of the twentieth century in a 1930s coat and hat. Rose created the portrait and the peony in pencil and watercolor in her sketchbook, printed it on fabric, then appliquéd it in the center of the quilt. She added hand painted and screen printed transparent silk and polyester organza overlays. Details were added with embroidery floss. The piece was embellished with beads.

Emily Carr (1871–1945)

. . . Canadian author and artist honored as the "Mother of Modern Arts."

Woman of the Deep Woods
Maggie Vanderweit
Fergus, Ontario, Canada

"I think that one's art is a growth inside one. I do not think one can explain growth. It is silent and subtle. One does not keep digging up a plant to see how it grows." —Emily Carr

Emily Carr, the first lady of Canadian art, studied painting in the US, England, and France before making British Columbia her home. She was taken with the art of the Post-Impressionists. In the 1920s she met the Group of Seven: Lawren Harris, J.E.H. MacDonald, Arthur Lismer, Frederick Varley, Frank Johnston, Franklin Carmichael, and A.Y. Jackson, who collectively dubbed her the "Mother of Modern Arts." After that, she was often included in their exhibitions.

Her works were heavily inspired by the Pacific Northwest Coast indigenous people, particularly the First Nations, the primary Aboriginal peoples of Canada south of the Arctic. Carr's paintings of west coast forests capture the wild, energetic essence of this landscape. Her stirring record of disappearing First Nations villages, buildings, and totem poles reflect a profound understanding and respect for native people, their way of life and their spiritual connection to the land. Carr is considered a pioneer in the movement to conserve traditional First Nations art, culture, and the primordial forests of British Columbia.

Her work emanates from deeply personal beliefs, years of inner searching, an intense response to the natural world, and a fiercely unique and independent style. She painted abstracted emotional responses rather than detailed realism.

Emily Carr created a world where human and natural elements all swirled together in a beautiful, sensual, mystical dance. There is ethereal music in her skies and dreamy, moody magic in her trees and totem poles.

For much of her life, Carr's work was undervalued by a conservative art community, although she did participate in major international exhibits in Europe, the US, and Canada. In 1941 she wrote the book *Klee Wyck,* and it won the prestigious Governor General's Award. Her books are loosely autobiographical and tell of her adventures as an artist, landlady, potter, and dog breeder as she struggled to make a living. She died in 1945, shortly after the most successful show of her career, where fifty-seven of her sixty paintings sold.

Emily Carr is artist Maggie Vanderweit's favorite painter. She is moved to tears by Carr's understanding of a beautiful, sentient universe—alive, dancing, swirling, and breathing. Like her, Maggie feels a profound reverence for First Nations' art and culture. Maggie's children are Cree and Dutch-Canadian, and she has lived in Northern Canada. She deeply admires Emily's boldness, courage, talent, and uncompromising style.

Woman of the Deep Woods is based on a detail shot taken by Maggie of a feminine guardian of the deep woods, carved high into a totem pole. Maggie made her eyes stand out to honor Emily Carr's ability to see the world and create art in visionary new ways. Maggie wanted the forest to move and dance. On white cotton, she painted the figure using watercolors and the trees using Colour Vie Textile Medium. She machine quilted the outlines with black and invisible threads.

Rosalynn Carter (1927–)

. . . used her position to speak out for those who had no voice.

Rosalynn Carter Explains to the Senate

Luana Rubin

Boulder, Colorado

"I want people to know what I know—that today because of research and our knowledge of the brain, mental illnesses can be diagnosed and treated effectively, and the majority of those with these illnesses can recover and lead fulfilling lives . . . going to school, working, raising a family, and being productive citizens in their communities." —Rosalynn Carter

Rosalynn Carter rewrote the rules about what it meant to be a First Lady, the wife of a famous man, and a woman with a voice in the world. Wife of Jimmy Carter, the 39th president, Rosalynn was First Lady from 1977 to 1981. She was an activist who broke tradition and used her position to speak out for those who had no voice. She sat in on Cabinet and policy meetings and served as her husband's closest advisor. After her first two years as First Lady, *Time* magazine called her the "second most powerful person in the United States." Rosalynn was pleased that some considered her a demanding First Lady, not confined to being the official hostess.

As the daughter of a dressmaker, she had planned to become an interior designer before she met Jimmy Carter. While living at the White House, she accumulated American paintings to upgrade the appearance of the historic residence. Her creativity, her compassion, and her deep empathy came from an ability to see layers of truth and beauty and take effective action based on her deep understanding.

Rosalynn Carter showed us how to be compassionate activists who can give voice to those who cannot speak, and how to quietly and powerfully change the world in which we live.

This image shows her testifying to a Senate committee on behalf of the 1980 Mental Health System Bill. She was only the second First Lady to appear before Congress, the first being Eleanor Roosevelt. Mental health issues were her highest priority, and she worked to change the nature of government assistance to the mentally ill, to help remove the stigma so those affected could admit to their disability and seek help, without being labeled as "crazy." For those who have sought therapy for PTSD, abuse, grief, depression, or similar challenges, the ability to seek this help freely today is built on the foundation of Rosalynn Carter's passion for this issue.

One year after leaving the White House, Rosalynn Carter cofounded The Carter Center. She is on the center's Board of Trustees and is the chair of the Carter Center Mental Health Task Force. In 1987 she founded the Rosalynn Carter Institute for Caregiving to address issues related to caregiving both by family members and professionals.

Artist Luana Rubin considers it a privilege to know Rosalynn Carter through her work at the Carter Center. Luana particularly admires her unfailing advocacy for women and children, which is one of her own activist passions. She obtained an original historic black and white photo from Rosalynn Carter. Luana posterized it and translated it into a color fabric collage. She began with a drawing on a base cloth of muslin. Hand cut Bali batik and hand-dyed fabric pieces were fused over the drawing, using a lightbox. It was free-motion thread-painted and quilted.

Coco Chanel (1883–1971)

. . . freed women from corsets; created the most successful perfume in history; was an accomplished businesswoman.

LBD

Mary Kay Davis

Sunnyvale, California

"A girl should be two things: who and what she wants." —Coco Chanel

Gabrielle Bonheur "Coco" Chanel may not have cured cancer, flown into space, or written the great American novel, but she has probably done more for the independence of women than many other extraordinary people.

She was born into poverty in France in 1883. After her mother died, her father abandoned her to an orphanage. To sustain herself she worked as a shop girl and a café singer. With the financial assistance of one of her wealthy acquaintants, she opened a tiny millinery shop where she also sold simple sportswear made from jersey. Over time she was able to influence wealthy women, who were looking for relief from their corsets and crinolines, to wear her jersey creations.

Coco once said, "I wanted to give a woman comfortable clothes that would flow with her body. A woman is closest to being naked when she is well-dressed."

Her designs stressed simplicity and comfort and revolutionized the fashion industry. In the late 1920s, with the amazing success of her perfume, Chanel No. 5, Chanel had the financial capability to run a couture house, a textile business, perfume laboratories, and a workshop for costume jewelry.

Chanel is also known as one of the designers responsible for the Little Black Dress (LBD). The LBD is described as a black evening or cocktail dress that is often quite short. It is intended to be of simple, elegant, and classic design that can be worn for a number of years without going out of fashion. Everyone from Betty Boop to Audrey Hepburn in *Breakfast at Tiffany's* has worn a Little Black Dress.

Chanel closed her couture house in 1939 with the outbreak of World War II in Europe. When she reopened her business in 1954, she once again changed the fashion world by introducing the famous Chanel suit, which featured a collarless, wool tweed cardigan jacket and simple skirt that became known the world over as the uniform of the sophisticated and stylish woman.

Chanel died in 1971 after ruling the world of fashion for over six decades; her couture house, currently led by Karl Lagerfeld, is still a leader in the fashion world.

Artist Mary Kay Davis wanted to keep this design as sleek and simple as one of Chanel's LBDs. She has created this highly symbolic quilt in honor of Coco using cotton, faux leather, and metallic trim. The background is houndstooth representing the wool of her trademark Chanel suit. The LBD takes center stage, this time made of black leather, a material used successfully in her trademark purses. The gold chain that outlines her LBD was used as straps on her handbags, and also along the bottom hem of the jackets, causing them to hang exactly straight. Camellias adorn both sides of the piece. They were Coco Chanel's favorite flower partially because she could wear this flower, which lacked scent, without interfering with her signature scent, Chanel No. 5. The outline of the camellia often appeared on the LBD, in beading on Chanel's shoes, or embroidered on a blouse. Mary Kay's piece was machine appliquéd and machine quilted.

Julia Child (1912–2004)

. . . revolutionized American cuisine; hosted thirteen
different television series; published eighteen cookbooks.

Julia
Kathie Briggs
Asheville, North Carolina

*"Find something you're passionate about and keep
tremendously interested in it."* —Julia Child

Julia Child revolutionized American cuisine by introducing an
approachable version of French cooking. Her book and popular
television shows made the mysteries of fancy French cuisine
accessible, introducing gourmet ingredients, demonstrating
culinary techniques, and, encouraging everyday "home chefs"
to practice cooking as art, not to dread it as a chore.

During World War II Julia served the US as a typist and
a research assistant for the Office of Strategic Services (OSS),
the forerunner of the CIA. "I was too tall (6'2") for the WACs
and WAVES, but eventually joined the OSS, and set out into
the world looking for adventure." She communicated top secret
documents between US government officials and intelligence
officers, traveling around the world classified as a senior civilian
intelligence officer, a spy!

In Ceylon (now Sri Lanka), Julia met her future husband
Paul Child, a fellow OSS agent. Following the war, Paul was
assigned to the US Embassy in Paris where Julia enrolled in
the culinary arts institute Le Cordon Bleu, failing her first
attempt at the exam, but passing a year later.

Julia met two French women, Simone Beck and Louisette
Bertholle, who were collaborating on a cookbook and seeking
an American coauthor. The three women opened a cooking
school, L'Ecole des Trois Gourmandes (charging $5 per lesson),
and began working together on their book. After multiple
rejections from publishers, *Mastering the Art of French Cooking,
Volume One* was published in 1961.

While promoting the book, Julia gave an impromptu cooking
demo on TV which prompted Boston's PBS station to produce
three pilot episodes of *The French Chef*. The show debuted
nationally in February 1963 and aired through July 1966. In
1970 a new version of it debuted in color. The *French Chef*
series aired 200 episodes. Her lilting "Bon appetit!" brings Julia's
name to mind for anyone who watched her. Beginning in 1980
she was the cooking correspondent on *Good Morning America*,
teaching a new generation to cook.

Julia Child was a fixture on American TV, hosting thirteen
different series from 1963 to 2000 and winning three Emmy
Awards. She published eighteen cookbooks, one of which won a
National Book Award. In 2009 *Mastering the Art of French Cooking* appeared at #1 on the *New York Times* best sellers list for the
first time, catapulted to that position by the movie *Julie & Julia*.
In the movie, the character Julie blogs her way through making
all 524 of the recipes in *Mastering the Art of French Cooking*.

Artist Kathie Briggs grew up watching Julia Child on TV
with her mother. They enjoyed learning about new recipes and
techniques. Julia was never afraid to take a risk or even fail in
front of the camera. She believed that cooking and life should be
fun! It was a lesson that has stayed with Kathie. In 1997 she met
Julia at an event at Epcot. Julia was warm and gracious and signed
an apron for Kathie, which has become one of her prized possessions.

In addition to the TV set, featuring her signature blue apron,
and a small stack of cookbooks, Kathie chose to depict a few
of the tools of Julia's trade and some of the ingredients she used
to prepare the dishes she loved to demonstrate. The piece is
made of cotton, silk, and organza. It was created using raw-edge
appliqué and machine stitching.

Agatha Christie (1890–1976)

. . . the world's best-selling author of all time. Only the Bible and works by William Shakespeare have been more widely read.

Agatha Christie grew up homeschooled, socially isolated, and shy in southwest England. She had such an active mind that she began writing as early as twelve years old, stating "there's nothing like boredom to make you write." When her sister challenged Agatha to write a detective story, it sparked what would become her career. She published her first book, a Hercule Poirot mystery, *The Mysterious Affair at Styles*, at twenty-one.

Agatha had several difficult years starting in about 1925. Her marriage to Archie Christie was crumbling, and she was also mourning the loss of her mother. Consequently, Agatha became the center of her own personal mystery when she left her daughter and her house in the care of the maids and "disappeared" for a short time. This created a whirlwind of public speculation, but eventually, Agatha returned and recovered from this low point in her life.

She worked as a nurse during both World Wars, gaining medical and pharmacological knowledge that play important roles in her books. Dame Agatha and her second husband, archaeologist Max Mallowan, worked together on several digs and her experiences on them were woven into many of her mysteries.

One of Christie's few non-fiction works, *The Grand Tour: Around the World with the Queen of Mystery*, is a collection of her correspondence from her 1922 grand tour of the British empire. During the South Africa leg of her tour, Agatha became the first British woman to surf.

She became one of the top-selling authors in history, selling more books than all but the Bible and Shakespeare's works. She engineered the modern detective story, emphasizing logic and deduction. Her female characters are real and fleshed out and can be as villainous as any male. The detectives she invented are anything but ordinary. Spinster detective Miss Jane Marple is unprepossessing and non-threatening, but sharp as a tack; neither gender nor age is a deterrent. Hercule Poirot is not the typical dashing male hero type, but a funny little person whose reliance on "those little gray cells" is paramount. Complex and creative plots keep the reader enthralled and the detective characters mentally challenged.

Agatha went on to write over one hundred works including novels, short stories, and plays. Her mystery *And Then There Were None* was not only Agatha's favorite but also the public's, voted the "World's Favorite Christie" on the author's 125th birthday. Agatha said it was the most difficult book to write.

Agatha's most famous play, *The Mousetrap*, exceeded 25,000 performances in a London West End theater, becoming the longest running play. Agatha Christie also wrote six romantic pieces under the pen name Mary Westmacott.

Her works have been translated into 103 languages making her the most translated individual author. In 2013, *The Murder of Roger Ackroyd* was voted best crime novel ever by 600 fellow writers of the Crime Writers' Association. In 1971 she was promoted from Commander to Dame Commander of the Order of the British Empire in honor of her many literary works. Dame Agatha Christie, Lady Mallowan, has earned her crown as the Queen of Crime.

The Mind of Agatha Christie
Joanne Bast
Littlestown, Pennsylvania

"I'm sorry, but I do hate this differentiation between the sexes. 'The modern girl has a thoroughly businesslike attitude to life!' That sort of thing. It's not a bit true! Some girls are businesslike, and some aren't. Some men are sentimental and muddle-headed, others are clear-headed and logical. There are just different types of brains." —Agatha Christie's character Sarah King

Agatha Christie lives on through her books and plays as well as her subsequent movies and TV dramas. Artist Joanne Bast chose to emphasize her books, the products of her indomitable mind in a full-to-the-brim bookcase overlaid with sheers depicting visuals of three of her most popular stories: *Murder on the Orient Express, A Caribbean Mystery*, and *Death on the Nile*. Joanne enjoyed creating the contrast between the hardcover books and the photos through which the book spines can still be seen. Joanne printed photos on sheer silk organza to create the scenes from the novel. She machine embroidered the titles of the books. The piece was machine appliquéd and free-motion quilted.

Agatha Christie: The Queen of Crime
Lynn Randall
Dunlap, Iowa

"Women can accept the fact that a man is a rotter, a swindler, a drug-taker, a confirmed liar, and a general swine, without batting an eyelash, and without its impairing their affection for the brute in the least. Women are wonderful realists." —Agatha Christie

Agatha Christie's status as "The Queen of Crime" is reflected in the accolades artist Lynn Randall included in her quilt. Lynn wanted to present this tribute in the form of a mystery novel. Therefore, a few facts about Agatha and her characters are represented in ransom note form. Upon closer inspection of the quilt, you will find hidden clues in the quilting: a bottle of poison, footsteps, a fingerprint, a knife, a noose, a gun, and a body. It's a simple quilt in its design, but Lynn wanted to highlight the focus of the quilt, which is Agatha Christie. Computer printed photos and letters were used along with raw-edge fused appliqué.

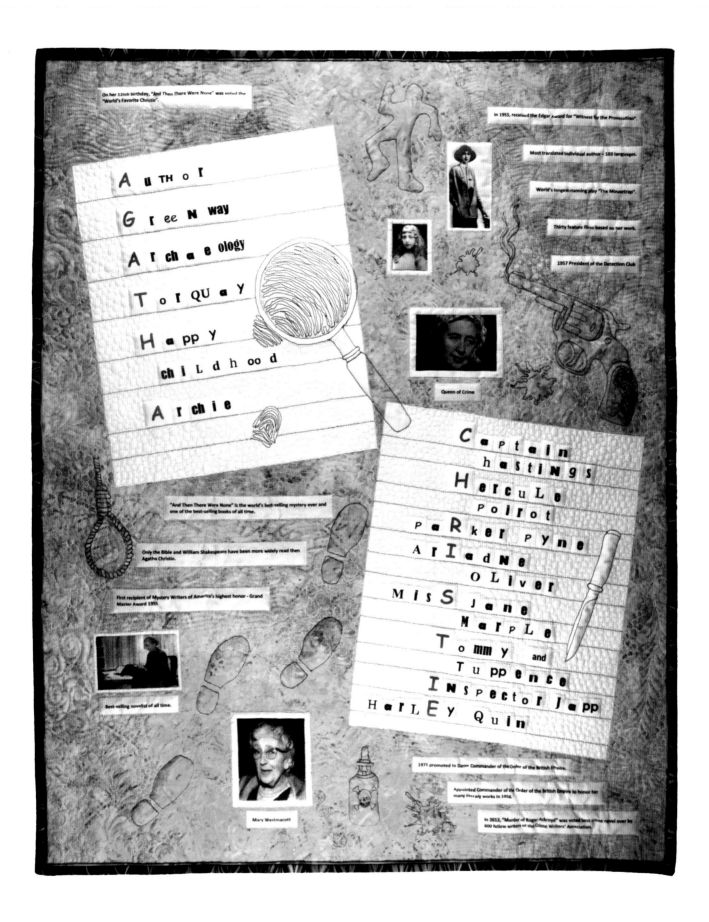

On her 125th birthday, "And Then There Were None" was voted the "World's Favorite Christie".

In 1955, received the Edgar Award for "Witness for the Prosecution"

Most translated individual author – 103 languages.

World's longest-running play "The Mousetrap".

Thirty feature films based on her work.

1957 President of the Detection Club

AUTHOR

GreeNway

Archaeology

TorQUay

Happy

chiLdhood

Archie

Queen of Crime

"And Then There Were None" is the world's best-selling mystery ever and one of the best-selling books of all time.

Only the Bible and William Shakespeare have been more widely read then Agatha Christie.

First recipient of Mystery Writers of America's highest honor - Grand Master Award 1955.

Captain hastings

HercuLe

Poirot

paRker pyne

ArIadNe

OLiver

MisS Jane

MarpLe

Tommy and

Tuppence

Inspector Japp

HarlEy Quin

Best-selling novelist of all time.

1971 promoted to Dame Commander of the Order of the British Empire.

Appointed Commander of the Order of the British Empire to honor her many literary works in 1956.

Mary Westmacott

In 2013, "Murder of Roger Ackroyd" was voted best crime novel ever by 600 fellow writers of the Crime Writers' Association

Hillary Rodham Clinton (1947–)

. . . first woman nominated by a major political party
as a candidate for president of the United States.

Hillary Rodham Clinton
Margaret Williams
Tucker, Georgia

"If a country doesn't recognize minority rights and human rights, including women's rights, you will not have the kind of stability and prosperity that is possible." —Hillary Clinton

Hillary Rodham Clinton was born and raised in Chicago, Illinois, the oldest of three children. She graduated from Wellesley College and Yale Law School, where she met Bill Clinton, and did further postgraduate work at the Yale Child Study Center. In 1974, Hillary became a member of the presidential impeachment inquiry staff, advising the Judiciary Committee of the House of Representatives during the Watergate Scandal. After Nixon resigned, she accepted a teaching position at the University of Arkansas Law School, where Bill Clinton was teaching. The two married in 1975. Bill won the governorship in Arkansas in 1978, serving a total of five terms, making Hillary the First Lady of Arkansas. She worked to improve the state's public schools and to help children. In 1988 and 1991, the *National Law Journal* named her one of the one hundred most powerful lawyers in America.

When Bill Clinton was elected President in 1992, Hillary became First Lady of the United States. She was pro-active in working for causes that she believed in, especially gender equality and health care reform. At the end of Bill Clinton's term, they established residency in New York, and Hillary ran for the US Senate while she was still First Lady. She won, becoming the first First Lady to have been elected to the Senate. In 2001 Hillary fought for and got federal funding for the first responders at Ground Zero after the 9/11 terrorist attack. In 2008 she ran an unsuccessful campaign for the Democratic nomination for President, losing the nod to Barack Obama.

During the Obama administration, she served as the US Secretary of State. In 2016, Hillary ran for the Democratic nomination for President. As the campaign began, Hillary was the clear leader. She overcame the strong competition from Senator Bernie Sanders. At the Democratic Convention, she was nominated as a candidate for President.

"It is with humility, determination, and boundless confidence in America's promise that I accept your nomination for President of the United States!" These were the words used by Hillary Rodham Clinton on July 28, 2016, in Philadelphia, as she became the first woman nominated by a major US political party. The evening of Hillary's nomination, she wore a white pantsuit in remembrance of the suffragists who fought to secure a woman's right to vote which became a reality with the ratification of the 19th Amendment in 1920. The election was bizarre, contentious, and in the end unpredictable. In a surprising turn of events, Hillary won the popular vote but lost the election by the Electoral College vote to Donald Trump.

In artist Margaret Williams' imagination, however, Hillary was literally clothed in the spirits of many women, men, and children who have worked to create an America that values freedom and justice for all human beings. They were right there with her on the podium as she made her acceptance speech. If you look closely, you can see many people and other images in this quilt. You might find the White House, the Capitol, the names of every state, the Statue of Liberty, a man playing saxophone, and several other surprises. The chain of her necklace is made up of tiny words that Margaret found in a number of commercial fabrics. Margaret calls her technique fusible mosaic. She used commercial fabrics enhanced with ProFab transparent fabric paints.

Jacqueline Cochran (1906?–1980)

. . . set more speed, distance, and altitude records than any other pilot.

With the Wind and the Stars
Ricki Selva
Fort Myer, Virginia

"I might have been born in a hovel, but I am determined to travel with the wind and the stars."
—Jacqueline Cochran

Savvy, ambitious Jacqueline Cochran holds more aviation records than anyone else, male or female, living or dead. She was an aviation pioneer and an undaunted advocate for women in military service.

Jackie was an intrepid aviator, striving tirelessly to reach new heights, at faster speeds. She was the first woman to take off from and land on an aircraft carrier, the first woman to fly a bomber across the Atlantic, the first woman to fly a jet across the Atlantic, the first woman to fly Mach 1, and the first woman to fly Mach 2. Jackie was the first pilot, male or female, to make an instrument landing, and the first pilot to fly above 20,000 feet with an oxygen mask. She was the fourteen-time winner of the Harmon Trophy for Outstanding Achievements in Aviation and the Associated Press's "Woman of the Year in Business" for 1953 and 1954.

Born Bessie Lee Pittman, she was orphaned at the age of four, and with no formal schooling, took a job in a mill to help support her foster family when she was only eight years old. With the money she saved from her wages, she bought her first pair of shoes. At fourteen, she became a wife and mother. After the death of their five-year-old son, she divorced her husband. She worked her way up from a shampoo girl in a beauty shop in Montgomery, Alabama, to a celebrated stylist at Saks Fifth Avenue in Manhattan, changing her name to Jacqueline Cochran along the way.

During a chance conversation with Floyd Odlum, whom she later married, Jackie revealed her dream of creating a cosmetics firm and selling her products on the road. He told her she needed to learn to fly to give her an edge over her competition. So Jackie did both. With Floyd's help, she launched her cosmetics firm, Wings, and earned her private pilot's license in less than three weeks. Enthusiastic about flying, Jackie and her close friend Amelia Earhart petitioned the 1935 Bendix Transcontinental Air Racers to allow females to compete and they became the first women to participate in that race. Three years later, Jackie won it.

Jackie traveled to Great Britain to serve as a ferry pilot with the Royal Air Force. Her advocacy of a similar program in the United States took wing at Avenger Field in 1942 when a highly select group of women began training to supplement the need for pilots during World War II. Over the following two years, 1102 women became Women's Airforce Service Pilots (WASP) under her direction.

Jackie Cochran is a personal talisman for artist Ricki Selva. Her piece depicts a single pivotal moment where Jackie tastes victory for the first time. She departed Burbank, California at three o'clock in the morning, and flew non-stop for over eight hours to land in Cleveland, Ohio. She has just landed. (She pauses to apply fresh lipstick, being the CEO of an up-and-coming cosmetics company.) She is climbing out of the cockpit after a physically demanding race. What she doesn't know, at that moment, is that she has won the 1938 Bendix Transcontinental Air Race. Ricki chose to work in an experimental way with the materials and techniques of this piece. The silk organza layers are a salute to early aviators and the trademark silk scarves, used to protect their skin from chafing in the open cockpits. Ricki created this tribute to Jackie by hand drawing and then hand painting Jackie.

Elizabeth "Bessie" Coleman (1892–1926)

. . . first African American woman to earn an international pilot's license.

Liberté de l'air
Ricki Selva
Fort Myer, Virginia

"The air is the only place free from prejudice."
—Elizabeth "Bessie" Coleman

When no one in the United States would teach a woman of color to fly, Elizabeth "Bessie" Coleman learned to speak French, moved to Le Crotoy, France and earned her international pilot's license, becoming the first African American woman to do so.

She was one of thirteen children born to sharecroppers in Texas, descendants of Native Americans and African American slaves. She worked hard as a child to try and earn an education. When she was old enough to pick cotton, she also worked to add to the family income. Her college hopes were dashed by financial constraints, so she quit after a single term to go back to work.

Her search for work took her from Waxahachie, Texas to Chicago, Illinois where she had the support of older brothers. While working as a manicurist in a barber shop, she began to hear stories from soldiers returning from Europe after World War I. They spoke of France and the opportunities enjoyed by French women. They spoke of flying.

A new path in life began to reveal itself to Bessie; she decided that becoming a pilot was her way to "amount to something." She enrolled in Chicago's Berlitz Language School and took French lessons. In 1921 she moved to France to attend Caudron Brothers School of Aviation. Seven months later she became the first African American to earn an international pilot's license and the first African American woman to earn a pilot's license at all.

After further instruction in acrobatics, she returned to the United States as "Queen Bess" or "Brave Bess" the barnstorming stunt pilot, performing with dignity, integrity, and grace and always holding on to a sense of responsibility for what her achievements meant for women and African Americans. When she couldn't fly, she gave lectures, inspiring thousands.

Her life as a barnstormer never brought her enough wealth to purchase a reliable aircraft. Her first aircraft was a World War I surplus Curtis JN-4 Jenny that crashed the first time Bessie flew it, due to its poor condition. Coleman was hospitalized for three months with her injuries, vowing to fly as soon as she could walk again.

Her next aircraft was even older and in worse condition. On April 30, 1926, while riding as an observer to survey a site for the next day's performance, the world's first African American woman pilot was killed in a tragic aircraft accident.

Bessie's dream of opening her own flight school, free of racism, was never realized. Nevertheless, she inspired thousands of people, especially women and people of color, to pursue a career in aviation.

To create this piece, artist Ricki Selva worked deliberately and diligently with her hands . . . drawing, painting, appliquéing, embroidering, and quilting all by hand. She thinks Bessie would have appreciated this loving effort. Clearly, Bessie was a very talented individual, but more important to her success was her willingness to work very hard and stay true to reaching her goals. Ricki used commercially printed cotton fabrics, hand painted cotton, Shantung silk, and recycled fabric from clothing. The Eiffel Tower was hand embroidered. She used Derwent Inktense pencils and sticks, Tsukineko All Purpose Inks and Pigma pens to add highlights.

Mary Colter (1869–1958)

. . . founded park-itecture, using on-site materials to build structures in our National Parks.

Mary Colter: Builder on the Desert
Karen Fisher
Tucson, Arizona

"Mary Colter was a female architect at a time when women were unknown to the profession, and she had the audacity to try to build structures along the rim of one of nature's greatest spectacles. Using local stones, and Native American themes and builders, Colter created buildings that stand today as the first examples of what would become known as 'National Park Service Rustic.'" —Susan Stamberg, NPR

Mary Colter's designs changed American architecture by honoring indigenous and historical Hispanic architecture and building with on-site materials. She worked with the Fred Harvey Company from 1902 to 1928, initially as an interior designer. In 1905, she was both architect and interior designer for Hopi House, a market for Native American crafts, and was interior designer for El Tovar Hotel, both at the Grand Canyon. She returned to the Canyon nine years later as architect and decorator of Lookout Studio, also known as The Lookout, which serves as an observation tower and gift shop. She also designed Hermit's Rest at the westernmost point of the Canyon's south rim. It was built as a rest area for tourists. These two structures appear to grow out of the very edge of the Canyon, a "natural" style of building that hadn't been seen before.

The 1920s found Ms. Colter back at the Canyon, building Phantom Ranch at the bottom. She built with on-site materials, which made sense for the location. In doing so, she created a new style that would become known as "park-itecture" or National Parks Rustic.

In 1930, she was architect and designer for La Posada Hotel in Winslow, Arizona. She considered it her masterpiece. She built a whole fictitious "history" for it, as was her custom, claiming it was the home of Spanish immigrants whose descendants had added to it over generations.

Mary later returned to the Grand Canyon to build the Watchtower, an homage to ancient pre-Puebloan towers all over the southwest and Bright Angel Lodge, designed with on-site materials to honor the first white settlers' log cabins.

Mary also designed the La Fonda Hotel in Santa Fe, the most successful of all the Harvey hotels. Throughout her career, she supervised all-male work crews to make sure everything was done just right. In an era when most women were still working at home, she was a powerhouse of creativity who changed the way we view the American landscape.

La Posada never prospered, and closed in 1957, shortly before Mary Colter's death at eighty-nine years old. She was devastated and remarked, "It's possible to live too long." In 1993, La Posada was scheduled to be torn down, but it survived. It was rescued in 1997 and is still undergoing restoration to make it, once again, a truly exceptional place to visit.

Artist Karen Fisher first became aware of Mary Colter when she purchased the biography *Mary Colter, Architect of the Southwest* by Arnold Berke. As an Arizona resident, Karen had visited the Grand Canyon more than once, and La Fonda hotel in Santa Fe, New Mexico, was one of her favorite places. As Karen learned more about Mary Colter, she was captivated by the way Mary had built interesting buildings and fit them into their settings so perfectly that she inspired a whole new style of architecture.

So Mary's "portrait" had to be about her work, which is her lasting, exceptional legacy. Karen drove through northern Arizona to photograph the Watchtower at the Grand Canyon, and La Posada Hotel in Winslow, along Interstate 40. Karen drew four buildings that show the breadth of Mary's work: the Watchtower and Bright Angel Lodge at the Grand Canyon, La Posada Hotel in Winslow, and La Fonda Hotel in Santa Fe, where she redesigned the interiors, relying on a mix of her photographs and multiple on-line images. Karen loved one photograph of Mary at the beginning of a workday, getting ready to descend into the Grand Canyon, so she made Mary's face near the top of the quilt, ghostlike among the clouds of a bright southwestern sky. Karen used curved piecing, broderie perse appliqué, reverse appliqué, and drawing with Derwent Inktense colored pencils. She embellished the quilt with hand applied buttons and hand lettering. It was made with commercial cotton and tulle.

Misty Copeland (1982–)

. . . first African American woman to be promoted to principal dancer in the American Ballet Theatre.

Misty in the Making
Nneka Gamble
Victoria, Texas

"You can do anything you want, even if you are being told negative things. Stay strong and find motivation." —Misty Copeland

Misty Copeland overcame a difficult childhood of poverty to become one of today's most recognized role models. Unlike most ballet dancers who are introduced to the art at a young age, Misty did not discover ballet until age thirteen. Her first ballet class was taught on a basketball court by a teacher looking to bring more diversity to her classes. Misty had a natural talent and made strides quickly. By the age of fifteen, Misty was already winning awards. She studied at the San Francisco Ballet School and had early affiliations with the American Ballet Theatre, being awarded a full scholarship to their intense summer program, later being named their American Ballet Theatre National Coca-Cola Scholar in 2000. One short year later she became a member of the corps de ballet of the company. In 2007, she was promoted to soloist—only the second African American woman to do so. Just eight years later, Misty Copeland became the first African American woman to be promoted to principal dancer in the American Ballet Theatre's seventy-five-year existence. She became a role model to girls and boys of all colors.

In her years as a ballet dancer, Misty has performed many traditional and contemporary productions including *Swan Lake, The Nutcracker, Firebird,* and *Romeo and Juliet.* She toured with musical artist Prince, thrusting her into the mainstream spotlight.

Misty has secured many endorsements during her career, and has been featured in numerous forms of media—magazine, newspaper, television and her own motion picture documentary, *A Ballerina's Tale.* With coauthor Charisse Jones, Misty penned a *New York Times* bestselling biography entitled *Life in Motion: An Unlikely Ballerina.* She even has a Barbie doll made in her likeness, wearing her *Firebird* costume.

When she is not on stage, she can be found mentoring youth and working with many charitable organizations. She serves as a role model for all and is a testament to the phrase: it doesn't matter where you start—determination, perseverance, and hard work can determine where you finish. She serves as an inspiration to all the ballerinas-in-the-making no matter their race, background, or age.

One morning, artist Nneka Gamble's daughter was watching one of her favorite programs, and a commercial came on with a ballerina in a graceful pose, spinning in a music box. Suddenly, the ballerina came to life and emerged as real life ballerina, Misty Copeland! Nneka's daughter immediately rose and did her best ballerina impression. From that moment on, her daughter wanted to know when she could begin taking ballet classes. Months later, Nneka found herself surrounded by little girls, in delightful little leotards and tutus, nervously and excitedly anticipating the moment they would be able to go on stage for the first time. Misty Copeland inspired more than Nneka's daughter; she inspired Nneka to make this quilt using raw-edge and fused appliqué. It shows Misty in an early dance class looking totally unlike the traditional ballet dancers. The images were hand drawn and painted with textile paint and gel pen. Nneka used commercial and hand-painted cotton fabrics. It is machine and free-motion quilted.

Marie Curie (1867–1934)

. . . first person to win two Nobel Prizes; first woman appointed to the French Academy of Medicine.

Marie Curie

Mirjam Aigner

Pambula, Australia

"Nothing in life is to be feared, it is only to be understood. Now is the time to understand more, so that we may fear less." —Marie Curie

Maria Salomea Sklodowska was born in Poland. She and her sister Bronya loved science, and their parents encouraged them to develop this interest. They moved to Paris where Maria, at age seventeen, became a governess to support Bronya through medical school. Maria studied too and joined her sister later at the Sorbonne changing her name to Marie. Marie finished at the top of her class, gaining a master's degree in physics in July 1893.

Marie met and married the brilliant researcher Pierre Curie. She borrowed a small space at Pierre's workplace, using his instruments to measure magnetic fields and electricity. She discovered that when uranium was present, she could measure faint electrical currents, which was the atomic property of uranium. Marie showed that the greater the percentage of uranium in the ore, the greater the radiation.

Working with Pierre, they found that chalcocite and pitchblende held a greater amount of radioactivity than uranium in its pure form. Their work led to the discovery of a previously unknown element which they named polonium after Marie's native country, Poland. They isolated a second element which they named radium, from the Latin for *ray*.

Marie was the first European woman to earn a doctorate in Physics. Her first Nobel Prize was shared with Pierre and Henri Becquerel for contributing to the scientific study of radiation and the understanding of atomic structure.

Sadly, Pierre was run over by a horse-drawn carriage and died, vacating the position of Chair of Physics. The University offered it to Marie, making her the first woman to be made a Professor at the University of Paris.

Marie's second Nobel Prize was for Chemistry, recognizing the discovery of polonium and radium. She is the only woman to receive the Nobel Prize twice.

With the support of her daughter Irene, Marie set up a medical unit in World War I. This unit x-rayed over one million wounded soldiers. In 1918, the Radium Institute, with Irene on staff, began to operate in earnest and became a universal center for nuclear physics and chemistry.

In 1921 Marie visited the United States, meeting with President Warren Harding at the White House where she was given one gram of radium, equipment, and financial support for her Radium Institute. It was a generous gift, given that one gram of radium cost $100,000. Subsequently, she was appointed to the French Academy of Medicine in 1922, the first woman ever so honored. In 1927, Marie was invited to a prestigious scientific conference on electrons and photons along with scientists like Max Planck, Albert Einstein, and other notables.

Marie never patented her findings and could not receive any profit. She worked tirelessly and selflessly on her scientific findings for the benefit of humankind. Marie Curie passed away from leukemia at the age of sixty-six in 1934 due to long exposure to radiation. In 1995, Pierre and Marie Curie's remains were taken from their burial place at Sceaux, outside of Paris, and interred under the dome of the Panthéon in Paris, making her the first woman to be so honored in her own right.

Mirjam Aigner was inspired in her dreams to make this quilt showing the radioactive rays discovered by Marie. In creating the piece, she used her husband's hand as the model for one hand and an x-ray of her hand for the other. Mirjam used layers of cotton, silk, and silk organza that she had monoprinted and screen-printed. She bonded them together with fine webbing. It was hand stitched through all three layers with embroidery thread.

Dorothy Day (1897–1980)

. . . founded the Catholic Worker movement and cofounded *The Catholic Worker* newspaper.

Dorothy Day
Diane Cadrain
West Hartford, Connecticut

"We must talk of poverty, because people insulated by their own comfort lose sight of it." —Dorothy Day

Dorothy Day, the founder of the Catholic Worker movement and a candidate for sainthood in the Catholic Church, spent her early years in Greenwich Village as a journalist, freelance writer, pacifist, and leftist radical. A chain-smoker and frequenter of saloons, who counted Eugene O'Neill among her friends, Day was also a seeker of quiet who would slip out to early mass after a night in a tavern. She was one of the suffragists who staged a hunger strike in front of the White House and was incarcerated at the Occoquan Workhouse, only one of the times that she was arrested at a protest.

In 1927, inspired by the beauty of nature and the birth of her daughter, Tamar, she underwent a conversion, turned to God in joy, and began living her life according to the teachings of Judeo-Christian heritage, to love God with your whole might and love one another.

In pursuit of that goal Day, who lived in the Bowery and saw the poor up close every day, embraced a life of voluntary poverty and began serving soup and coffee to the poor and unemployed in her neighborhood. During this time, she met Peter Maurin, and the two of them founded *The Catholic Worker*, a newspaper that focused on Catholic teachings and societal issues. She was often overwhelmed by what she saw as the hopelessness of the situation around her, which included hunger, violence, and addiction. Against these overwhelming needs, she built a life of prayer and persistence. Dorothy began a soup kitchen in New York, which ultimately became many soup kitchens and hospitality houses for the poor and marginalized. There are now 213 of them around the world, under the collective name Catholic Worker. Each is autonomous, providing clothing, food, and shelter to all who ask.

Dorothy wrote her autobiography twice; the first, *From Union Square to Rome,* was written in 1938 as a letter to her brother who was a staunch Communist. In 1952, she wrote a second autobiography, *The Long Loneliness*. Day, who has been called the conscience of American Catholicism, continued to live among the poor for the rest of her life, cooking, sorting clothes, and mopping floors while going on to write eight books and five collections of essays. Dorothy Day is known as a social activist, pacifist, and advocate for the poor.

To be considered for sainthood, a person must have exceptionally practiced three supernatural virtues: faith, hope, and charity; and the four cardinal moral virtues: prudence, justice, fortitude, and temperance. The Catholic Church now considers her on the path to sainthood and honors her with the title Servant of God as her canonization process continues. She will possibly be the first American saint canonized in the twenty-first century.

Dorothy Day lived the kind of life that artist Diane Cadrain idealized as a young woman. Indicative of the length of time that Diane has admired her is the price on her copy of Dorothy's biography, *The Long Loneliness*: $1.25. (It was purchased as a new release.) This dual portrait of Day is based on photographs of her as a young woman and again in the flowering of her age. The images are drawn with Derwent Inktense pencils on Pimatex cotton treated with GAC 900. In both the larger and smaller images, Diane used trapunto to raise and emphasize Day's silhouette.

Simone de Beauvoir (1908–1986)

. . . wrote *The Second Sex,* considered to be the philosophical seed of the second wave of feminism in the twentieth century.

Simone de Beauvoir
Yolanda Fundora
Summit, New Jersey

"Representation of the world, like the world itself, is the work of men; they describe it from their own point of view, which they confuse with absolute truth."
—Simone de Beauvoir

Simone de Beauvoir was born in Paris and raised in a Catholic family. At one point she was sure that she wanted to be a nun. In her teens, she had a crisis of faith and declared herself an atheist, a belief she maintained the rest of her life. Her focus then shifted to math, literature, and philosophy. She studied at the Sorbonne and met fellow student Jean-Paul Sartre. They formed a lasting relationship that would influence the rest of their lives. They remained together although they never lived under the same roof, never married, and were not monogamous. During World War II, they parted ways for a time, but both worked for the French Resistance. It was at this time that de Beauvoir began her literary career. Her first novel, *She Came to Stay*, published in 1943, used the real-life love triangle of Sartre, de Beauvoir, and a student named Olga to examine existential ideas regarding the complexity of relationships. She continued writing novels, essays, biographies, and monographs on politics, philosophy, and social issues. She also wrote her autobiography.

Simone de Beauvoir's writing, especially *The Second Sex*, published in 1949, influenced generations of young women all over the world. Its first sentence of the second part, "On ne naît pas femme, on le devient" (One is not born but rather becomes a woman), is regarded as one of the starting points of modern radical feminist thought. This is taken to mean that women are carefully constructed through social indoctrination to be "feminine" in ways that serve the establishment. In her book, de Beauvoir reflected upon the roles of wife, mother, and prostitute to show how women are forced into monotonous existences of keeping house, raising children, and keeping their men happy instead of becoming all that they could be through their own occupations and creativity. This book was considered so revolutionary and challenging to the established power systems of western culture when it was published that it was placed by the Vatican on its List of Prohibited Books in 1956.

One of artist Yolanda Fundora's favorite quotes from *The Second Sex* is "Representation of the world, like the world itself, is the work of men; they describe it from their own point of view, which they confuse with absolute truth." She feels that this quote addresses the need that this very collection, *HERstory*, has chosen to address directly.

Gloria Steinem said upon the death of de Beauvoir in 1986, "If any single human being can be credited with inspiring the current international woman's movement, it's Simone de Beauvoir."

In creating this tribute to Simone, Yolanda Fundora used her own fabric designs and two public domain images, a photograph of Simone, and the cover of her book to design the top for a whole cloth quilt in Photoshop which was printed through Spoonflower. Most of the fabrics used are from a fabric collection Yolanda was designing concurrently with her Simone quilt. There was a lot of cross-pollination going on between the two design activities. The backing fabric is also her design.

Phyllis Diller (1917–2012)

. . . first female comedian to become a
household name.

Humor Has It
Denise Currier
Mesa, Arizona

---

*"Always be nice to your children because they are
the ones who will choose your rest home."*
—Phyllis Diller

Phyllis Diller was a female pioneer in stand-up comedy. Born Phyllis Ada Driver on July 17, 1917, in Limo, Ohio, she lived to the age of ninety-five.

While raising six children, she started writing one-liners to share with family and friends. Phyllis was encouraged to start performing in nightclubs. Her career took off in the 1960s with special guest appearances on television series and comedy specials. Those appearances not only made Phyllis Diller a household name but opened many doors and created opportunities for women in comedy today.

Phyllis Diller married and divorced twice. As she began her stand-up career, she joked about what she knew: home, housework, and husbands. Her fictitious husband nicknamed "Fang" was the brunt of many of her jokes. Her sarcastic one-liners were appreciated by fans young and old. She was invited to share the stage with headliners George Burns, Red Skelton, and Jack Benny. She joined Bob Hope's USO tour in 1966 to perform for troops stationed in Vietnam.

Phyllis's creativity knew no bounds. She made her own cigarette holders as a stage prop but ironically was not a smoker. Her colorful and textured style choices included boas, teased up wigs, and ultra-long, thick false upper eyelashes. She wore short A-line sparkly dresses showing off her boney legs which she made fun of often. Phyllis Diller publicly acknowledged her face lifts and made fun of herself for it. Phyllis had a way of laughing at herself and taking audiences along with her. Self-deprecation was her hallmark. Her distinct contagious cackling laughter carried across any stadium, outdoor amphitheater or household living room.

Phyllis tried unsuccessfully to host her own comedy variety show. She appeared on Broadway and televised shows such as *Laugh-In, The Hollywood Squares*, and *The Gong Show*. People loved her humor, and it helped that she had good writers. Joan Rivers had written for Phyllis Diller before she became famous herself. Diller's comedy records were best sellers as were the humorous books she wrote. She did several voiceovers for cartoons, most notably *A Bug's Life* in 1998.

Some of Phillis Diller's famous one-liners:

"It's a good thing that beauty is only skin deep, or I'd be rotten to the core."

"'Fang' is permanent in my act, of course. Don't confuse him with my real husbands. They are temporary."

"I once wore a peekaboo blouse. People would peek, and then they'd boo."

"I still take the pill because I don't want any more grandchildren."

Artist Denise Currier rendered this image from a public domain photograph printed with archival Ultra-Chrome inks onto cotton sateen pretreated fabric. It was highlighted with Prisma color and graphite pencils. Denise hand-dyed pima and sateen cotton fabrics, using Procion reactive dyes. The quilt was pieced. It is free-motion quilted with cotton threads and was overcoated with spray fixative.

Marjorie Stoneman Douglas (1890–1998)

... defender of the Everglades, responsible for getting it reclassified as a valued river.

River of Grass
Polly Davis
Warrenton, Virginia

"It's a little bit late in the day for men to object that women are getting outside their proper sphere."
—Marjorie Stoneman Douglas

Marjorie Stoneman Douglas is best remembered for her relentless defense of the Everglades against the onslaught of business people trying to drain them for development. However, she was so much more! She started as a journalist after college and quickly added writer and environmentalist to her repertoire. Politically conscious, even as a young woman, civil rights and women's suffrage were issues in which she actively engaged.

In the 1940s, after five years of research, she verified with a geologist that the Biscayne Aquifer which was filled by the Everglades provided all of South Florida's fresh water and she could safely call this fresh water flowing from Lake Okeechobee a river of grass. This redefined the popular conception of the Everglades as a valued river instead of a worthless swamp, and the name River of Grass has since become interchangeable with the Everglades.

Published in 1947, the opening line of *The Everglades: River of Grass*, "There are no other Everglades in the world" has been called the "most famous passage ever written about the Everglades." The book galvanized people to protect this unique area and is often compared to Rachel Carson's *Silent Spring* in bringing environmental issues into the mainstream consciousness. In the 1960s she had to step back into the fray to save the Everglades from the imminent danger of disappearing forever in the name of progress. In 1969, at the age of seventy-nine, she founded Friends of the Everglades to protest the construction of a jet port in a section of the Everglades. Marjorie declared that "Conservation is now a dead word . . . You can't conserve what you haven't got."

Douglas traveled to speak in support of women's right to vote, lending her support to the Equal Rights Amendment and urging the legislature in Tallahassee to ratify it. She helped pass a law requiring all homes in Miami to have toilets and bathtubs after learning that no running water or sewers were connected in a racially segregated section. Along with Helen Muir, Douglas cofounded the Friends of the Miami-Dade Public Libraries and served as its first president.

Marjorie Stoneman Douglas was a feisty 5'2" dynamo. In 1993 President Bill Clinton awarded her the Presidential Medal of Freedom. She was inducted into the National Wildlife Federation Hall of Fame in 1999 and the National Women's Hall of Fame in 2000. Her reaction to the latter was, "Why should they have a Women's Hall of Fame? Why not a Citizen's Hall of Fame?" London's *The Independent* said upon her passing in 1998 at the age of 108, "In the history of the American environmental movement, there have been few more remarkable figures than Marjorie Stoneman Douglas."

When artist Polly Davis started drawing out her idea for this quilt, she wanted the river to be green, of course, but to also stand out from the river of water. So she placed the water blues horizontally and the flow of greens vertically, on the diagonal, to suggest movement. Because this area contains such a rich abundance of plant and animal life, Polly used many different fabrics as a base and then layered more fabric, different types of fiber and added bits and pieces of buttons and beads to be representative of this diversity. The Roseate Spoonbill is so unique that Polly wanted it to be a focal point. Polly put Marjorie as a spectator, an Everywoman if you will—viewing the miracle that is the River of Grass.

Amelia Earhart (1897–disappeared 1937–declared dead 1939)

. . . first woman to fly solo across the Atlantic, and the first woman to attempt to fly around the world.

Final Flight
Linda MacDonald
Powell, Wyoming

"Women, like men, should try to do the impossible. And when they fail, their failure should be a challenge to others." —Amelia Earhart

Amelia Earhart was one of the world's first female aviators, known as "Lady Lindy." She was a founding member of the Ninety-Nines, an organization of female aviators. On May 20/21, 1932 Amelia became a national hero by becoming the first woman to fly solo across the Atlantic Ocean. It took her fourteen hours and fifty-six minutes. She landed in Londonderry, Northern Ireland. President Hoover presented her with the Gold Medal from the National Geographic Society, and she was given the Distinguished Flying Cross by the US Congress. Subsequently, she set a record for flying coast to coast. Following that she flew solo from Hawaii to Oakland, California making her the first person to fly across both the Atlantic and Pacific oceans.

Not one to rest on her laurels, Amelia set out to fly around the world with only her navigator, Fred Noonan accompanying her. On May 20, 1937, they departed from Oakland, California, to begin their flight around the world, and chose a flight path near the Equator in an easterly direction. The world followed her progress as she made stops at Venezuela, Brazil, Senegal, Chad, Sudan, India, Burma, Thailand, Singapore, Australia and New Guinea. Amelia's plane disappeared from radar after leaving New Guinea on a heading for Howland Island. From the time her Lockheed Electra disappeared from radar on July 2, 1937, until July 6th there were more than 100 radio transmissions from Earhart calling for help. Radio operators from various locations including Australia, Texas, and Florida thought they heard her distress calls. While they recognized her voice, the signal was weak and unreadable. A teenage girl in Florida wrote down that she thought Amelia was saying New York City, which didn't seem to make any sense. While rescue planes were sent out, Amelia was not located.

The International Group for Historic Aircraft Recovery (TIGHAR) now believes Earhart landed her plane on Nikumaroro Atoll when she became low on fuel. Research shows that the SS *Norwich City* shipwrecked on this atoll in 1929. It is likely Amelia was saying Norwich City, which was misinterpreted as New York City in her distress calls. While it is believed the tide took the plane out to sea, there is evidence that Amelia Earhart died as a castaway on the small island. Small fire pits with bones of fish and birds were found, as well as a skeleton that may prove to belong to the famous aviatrix.

July 2017 marks the 80th anniversary since Amelia went missing. At this writing, TIGHAR has plans to use submarines to try to locate the Lockheed Electra debris underwater at Nikumaroro Atoll. Also, tests are being done on the bones found to determine if they are the remains of the famous Amelia Earhart.

Artist Linda MacDonald has been in contact with TIGHAR, which provided satellite photos of Nikumaroro Atoll. This art quilt uses both traditional piecing and appliqué in its construction. The checkerboard piecing represents the mix of ocean and islands, as Amelia made her way around the globe. The world map showing her flight path progress was made as a separate piece and added last.

Hand-dyed and commercial fabrics were used in this piece. Beading and hot-fix crystals depict Amelia's famous flight path around the world. A Photoshop sketch of Amelia was thread-sketched, while her hair and the airplane were thread-painted to add texture and interest.

Geraldine Ferraro (1935–2011)

. . . first female vice presidential candidate of a major US political party.

Shattering the Glass
Phyllis Cullen
Ninole, Hawaii

"By choosing a woman to run for your nation's second highest office, you send a powerful signal to all Americans. There are no doors we cannot unlock. We will place no limits on achievement."
—Geraldine Ferraro

Her college yearbook said "delights in the unexpected," and what happened in Geraldine Ferraro's life was certainly not what anyone would have expected. The daughter of immigrants, her story is that of the American dream. Geraldine lost her father to a heart attack when she was eight years old, a moment that she recalls as a dividing line in her life. She studied hard, made outstanding grades, and earned a scholarship to college where she majored in English and edited the school paper. She taught elementary school in Queens before applying to Fordham Law School. She passed the bar and married John Zaccaro the same week. After years spent raising her children, she began working in the district attorney's office. In New York's Queens County District Attorney's Office, Ferraro started the Special Victims Bureau, supervising the prosecution of sex crimes, child abuse, domestic violence, and violent crimes against senior citizens.

In 1978, she decided to run for Congress from New York's Ninth district. Speaker of the House Tip O'Neill was impressed with her, which helped her career. Her work in Congress included the Public Works Committee, Post Office and Civil Service Committee, and Budget Committee, where she was a strong voice against the Reagan Administration's economic policies. Ferraro also served on the Select Committee on Aging, where she was an advocate for the elderly, fighting proposed cuts in Social Security and Medicare. In Congress, Ferraro spearheaded efforts to achieve passage of the Equal Rights Amendment. She also sponsored the Women's Economic Equity Act in 1984, which ended pension discrimination against women, provided job options for displaced homemakers, and enabled homemakers to open IRAs.

Her job as chief of the Democratic Platform Committee helped win 1984 Democratic Presidential nominee Walter Mondale's confidence and placed her on the short list of those being considered for the Vice Presidential nomination. O'Neill endorsed her nomination before it was even made and the National Organization for Women delivered a strong message to the Democratic Party that it was time that a woman was on the ticket.

Walter Mondale nominated Geraldine Ferraro to be his running mate in July of 1984. They lost to Reagan in a landslide. It would be twenty-four years before another woman was on a major party's ticket. But Gerry Ferraro broke one glass ceiling, that of being nominated to the second highest office in the land.

After a hiatus from public life, she ran for the Senate and lost in 1992 and 1998. She was ambassador to the United Nations Human Rights Commission during the Clinton administration. From 1996 to 1998, she was cohost of CNN's *Crossfire*.

Gerry was diagnosed with multiple myeloma in 1998 and became one of the first cancer patients to be treated with thalidomide, the same drug that caused congenital disabilities in babies in the 1960s. She was amazed that a drug that had been so detrimental to fetuses would be so useful in fighting cancer. It was a battle she waged for over twelve years, dying in 2011.

Artist Phyllis Cullen chose to portray Geraldine Ferraro in the halls of Congress, overlooking her beloved New York City. It is a physically impossible view to have, but it is where her heart was. Isn't artistic license wonderful? Geraldine is pictured helping thread sketched immigrants and children in New York, and in the halls of justice, and breaking through a glass ceiling which Phyllis had fun creating with crystal embellishments, rhinestones, and glitter. Phyllis created this collage portrait by painting, appliquéing, thread-sketching, embellishing, and quilting.

Betty Ford (1918–2011)

. . . first prominent public figure to admit her alcoholism, drug addiction, and breast cancer, giving hope to millions.

Brave Betty
Janet Marney
Fairfax, Virginia

"A housewife deserves to be honored as much as a woman who earns a living in the marketplace."
—*Betty Ford*

Betty Ford, born Elizabeth Bloomer in 1918, was raised in an affluent home in Grand Rapids. To teach her social graces, Betty's mother enrolled her in a dance school at the age of eight. Following the death of her father, her mother worked as a real estate agent to support the family. Betty's awareness of her mother's struggles informed her opinions on women's rights and equal pay.

Dancing had become Betty's passion and studying with Martha Graham had a huge impact on Betty's life. To pay for dance lessons, Betty worked at a department store as a model and fashion director. She also performed and taught dance.

Betty married Gerald Ford following his election to the US Congress. It was a happy marriage, but from the first, it was stressful living in the public eye. She jumped into her responsibilities as a political wife. Since Gerald traveled frequently, she raised their four children virtually alone. Betty's health crisis began in 1964 opening a window, pinching a nerve in her neck, leading to severe inoperable pain, becoming addicted to the Valium she was prescribed. Eventually, she had a nervous breakdown and saw a psychiatrist, although her family remained in denial for years.

As Second Lady, she campaigned for women's rights and abortion rights as an alternative to "back-alley butcher jobs." When President Nixon was forced to resign due to the Watergate crisis, Ford became the thirty-eighth president, and Betty became the First Lady.

Thrust into the limelight with no time to prepare; Betty dove headlong into her duties at the White House. She maintained a good relationship with the press, freely expressing her views on issues, even if they disagreed with her husband's. When she was diagnosed with breast cancer and had a mastectomy, she informed the nation and became a role model for other women. The pink October movement was her idea. From dancer to cancer, she became a teacher again. She was the first First Lady to speak out on breast cancer.

She understood a woman's desire to have a career as well as a family life and tried to make that possible by fighting for equal pay. She used her position to lobby members of Congress and others for the amendment. In support of the ERA, she said, "a housewife deserves to be honored as much as a woman who earns a living in the marketplace." She was the first First Lady to have her own speechwriter.

In 1978, her daughter Susan initiated an intervention challenging Betty to get treatment for alcoholism and pain pill addiction. Betty realized very few recovery opportunities were geared toward the needs of women. Betty Ford Center became the first treatment center to reserve 50% of its beds for women. She became the nation's leading spokesperson for substance abuse. She also raised awareness for breast cancer, arthritis, and AIDS.

Artist Janet Marney cropped, posterized, and enlarged a public domain photo of Betty, then printed it out in color and black and white. Janet traced the main shapes of the face, hair, and dress twice: first in reverse onto Wonder Under, and second onto clear Quilter's Preview Paper with a Sharpie marker. Referring constantly to the original photo, Janet chose fabrics consistent with Betty's era. Pieces were cut from the shapes traced onto Wonder Under, then positioned on the background using the clear drawing. Janet quilted the portrait by machine using several different stitches. Quilting lines in the background echo Betty's form, reinforcing the idea of her radiant personality.

Dian Fossey (1932–1985)

. . . brought the plight and conservation of the mountain gorilla to the world through her work, loves, and loss.

Digit for Dian Fossey
Tracy Williams
Austin, Texas

"The more you learn about the dignity of the gorilla, the more you want to avoid people." —Dian Fossey

Dian Fossey was born in 1932 in San Francisco, California. She went to San Jose State College and earned her degree in occupational therapy.

On a visit to Africa in 1963, she met Dr. Louis Leakey at Olduvai Gorge. From then on, it was all about the gorillas for Fossey. Leakey encouraged her to embark on a long-term study of the mountain gorilla and lined up funding for her. She studied Swahili and primatology and relocated to Africa in 1966, beginning her study in the Congo in 1967 on the Rwandan side of the Virunga Mountains.

She set up a research station there and became a member of the mountain gorilla family using a method called habituation. She mimicked their actions, made grunting sounds, behaved in a submissive manner and ate the local celery plant. Fossey credited her success to her experience working with autistic children as an occupational therapist. It led the way for researchers to establish human gorilla relationships and friendships. In 1983, a gorilla named Peanuts reached out and touched Dian's finger. It was the first time any gorilla-initiated human contact had occurred and was photographed.

Dian had a special bond with a gorilla that she named Digit. Digit would come and sit beside her in the hills and touch her hands and face. They loved each other and played the way mothers and children do. Poachers murdered Digit, cutting off his hands which in some cultures are valued as collectible ashtrays. Dian never recovered from his loss. "The mutilated body, head, and hands hacked off for grisly trophies, lay limp in the brush like a bloody sack . . . For me, this killing was probably the saddest event in all my years of sharing the daily lives of mountain gorillas," Fossey wrote in a 1981 article in *National Geographic*.

After Digit's death, she spent more time on her own in her cabin, and rarely communicated with colleagues and friends. Her main focus remained on the plight of the mountain gorillas. There were about 475 of them in the early 1960s, but their numbers were decreasing rapidly due to poaching and habitat loss. In the early 1980s, the population dropped to about 254 individuals. Fossey vowed to protect the few remaining mountain gorillas before they disappeared. Digit's death raised awareness of the gorillas' plight, and it raised money. Dian fought governments and poachers and researchers and television crews. She never seemed to realize, however, that to save the gorillas; she would need all the help she could get, including help from the authorities she despised. In 1983, her autobiography, *Gorillas in the Mist*, became a best seller.

On December 26, 1985, Dian Fossey was hacked to death with a machete, dying before she could learn that her work had paved the way for mountain gorillas to begin recovery. Fossey was buried in the Virunga Mountains, resting beside her "beloved Digit." Following her death, her autobiography was made into an acclaimed movie in 1988.

Artist Tracy Williams sketched Digit in pencil on white fabric and thread scribbled him. Textile paints and acrylic paints thinned with water were added. Tracy then added more thread scribbling. She appliquéd the leaves and machine quilted the piece.

Aretha Franklin (1942–)

. . . first female artist to be inducted into the Rock and Roll Hall of Fame.

Aretha

Jeanne Knudsen

Cody, Wyoming

"We all require and want respect, man or woman, black or white. It's our basic human right."
—Aretha Franklin

Many of us learned to spell respect from Aretha: R-E-S-P-E-C-T, but that wasn't the beginning of her career. Aretha Franklin started her music career singing gospel in her father's church. Her father offered to get her piano lessons, but Aretha taught herself, regarded as a child prodigy.

By fourteen, she had recorded some of her earliest music tracks at her father's church. Aretha found her own style of playing secular love songs. Atlantic Records was stunned by these 1956 recordings saying, "The voice was not that of a child but rather of an ecstatic hierophant" (a priest in ancient Greece).

During the 1960s and 1970s, Franklin was viewed as a symbol of black advancement, often giving her talents to the Civil Rights' cause, performing publicly in support of Martin Luther King, Jr. When he died in 1968, Aretha sang a heartfelt rendition of "Precious Lord" at his funeral.

The 70s brought Franklin back to her musical origins with her album *Amazing Grace*. It sold more than two million copies and became the best-selling gospel album of all time. She dominated the Top 10 charts and soon earned the title of "Queen of Soul."

Throughout the 1980s Franklin had major hits; many of her biggest were collaborations with stars like Annie Lenox, James Brown, Whitney Houston, and George Michael. She also performed in the popular movie *The Blues Brothers*. In 1987 Franklin worked with Rolling Stones' Keith Richard. She recorded an amazing gospel album and was the first female to be inducted into the Rock and Roll Hall of Fame.

Franklin sang at the inaugurations of Presidents Bill Clinton and Barack Obama. Aretha received the Grammy Lifetime Achievement Award and the Kennedy Center Honors in 1994.

In 2005 President George W. Bush awarded her the Presidential Medal of Freedom. Aretha was awarded her eighteenth Grammy Award in 2008 making her one of the most honored artists in Grammy history.

Three years later, she released an album on her own label. To promote this album, she performed several concerts, including one in the famed Radio City Music Hall in New York City.

Over the last thirty years, Franklin has refused to fly. Instead, she travels by bus to her performances and venues. At the age of seventy-four, there is no doubt that Aretha Franklin still reigns as the Queen of Soul!

Artist Jeanne Knudsen had a public domain photo enlarged and posterized. Posterizing gives Jeanne a pattern for the portrait she is doing, helping her to make accurate fabric choices. Jeanne traced these shapes onto muslin and also onto a clear plastic sheeting to use as a pattern. She works with the muslin under the plastic, keeping the photo to the side for color reference. Once Jeanne gets many pieces on the muslin, the plastic shows her where those fabric pieces go. Jeanne lifts the plastic and places the fabric piece on the muslin, matching the placement on the plastic. Jeanne quilted and faced the piece.

Jeanne used 100% cotton fabric for Aretha's face, hands arms, and neck. Her dress is a nylon fabric to give the sheer illusion. The beads on Aretha's necklace were done with puff paint. Jeanne used crystals for her earrings and ring. The rose in her hair is made from silk wire ribbon. Jeanne painted her eyes with acrylic paints and thread.

Rosalind Franklin (1920–1958)

. . . made vital contributions to the understanding of the molecular structures of DNA.

Do You See What I See?

Marijke van Welzen

Vlaardingen, The Netherlands

"You look at science (or at least talk of it) as some sort of demoralizing invention of man, something apart from real life, and which must be cautiously guarded and kept separate from everyday existence. But science and everyday life cannot and should not be separated. Science, for me, gives a partial explanation for life. In so far as it goes, it is based on fact, experience and experiment." —Rosalind Franklin

Rosalind Franklin is best known for her work on the x-ray diffraction images of DNA which led to the discovery of the DNA double helix. In 1950 she joined a team at King's College in London as a research associate studying living cells. She worked with Maurice Wilkins. He assumed she was his assistant; she assumed she'd be working solo. Franklin was direct, quick, decisive, and Wilkins was shy, speculative, and passive. Their differences played a role as the race unfolded to find the structure of DNA.

Rosalind made incredible advances in x-ray diffraction techniques with DNA. She adjusted her equipment to produce an extremely fine beam of x-rays. She extracted finer DNA fibers than ever before and arranged them in parallel bundles, allowing her to discover crucial keys to DNA's structure. Her x-ray diffraction picture of the "B" form of DNA, Photograph 51, was acquired through 100 hours of x-ray exposure from a machine Rosalind herself had refined.

Wilkins shared her data, without her knowledge, with James Watson and Francis Crick, at Cambridge University, ultimately publishing the proposed structure of DNA in 1953.

Crick admitted that he and Watson had used Franklin's data to formulate their DNA structure hypothesis. Franklin's work was published third in the series of three DNA *Nature* articles, led by the paper of Watson and Crick which only hinted at her contribution to their hypothesis.

Due to disagreements with Wilkins, she moved to Birkbeck College. Rosalind led pioneering work on the tobacco mosaic and polio viruses. She died in 1958 at the age of thirty-seven from complications arising from ovarian cancer, certainly due to overexposure to radiation. During her lifetime the DNA structure was not considered fully proven. It took Maurice Wilkins and his colleagues about seven years to collect enough data to prove and refine the proposed DNA structure.

Rosalind Franklin was never nominated for a Nobel Prize although her work was a crucial part in the discovery of DNA, for which Crick, Watson, and Wilkins were awarded a Nobel Prize in 1962. Watson suggested that ideally Wilkins and Franklin should have been awarded the Nobel Prize in Chemistry. Unfortunately, the prize is not awarded posthumously.

Artist Marijke van Welzen honored Rosalind by creating a textile collage using commercial fabrics which she appliquéd. To find the right background fabric Marijke went to the farmers' market. Her eye landed on colorful bolts of fabric. She bought some, doubting that any of them would work for this quilt. When Marijke opened up the blue/pink piece, she couldn't believe her eyes! Marijke saw the shape of Rosalind's head, which Marijke had already created, in the pattern of the fabric. She posted a picture in the secret group for *HERstory* artists on Facebook and asked: "Do you see what I see?" Everyone thought that was the title of her quilt and as that was appropriate, Marijke used it. Convinced by fellow artists that the similarity in shape was real, she decided to use it as the background. You can see that shape as a shadow around her head. For the DNA structures, Marijke made a drawing and a simple paper stencil. She used black fabric paint to stencil them. The hexagons are stitched. Marijke finished the quilt with a lot of free-motion quilting.

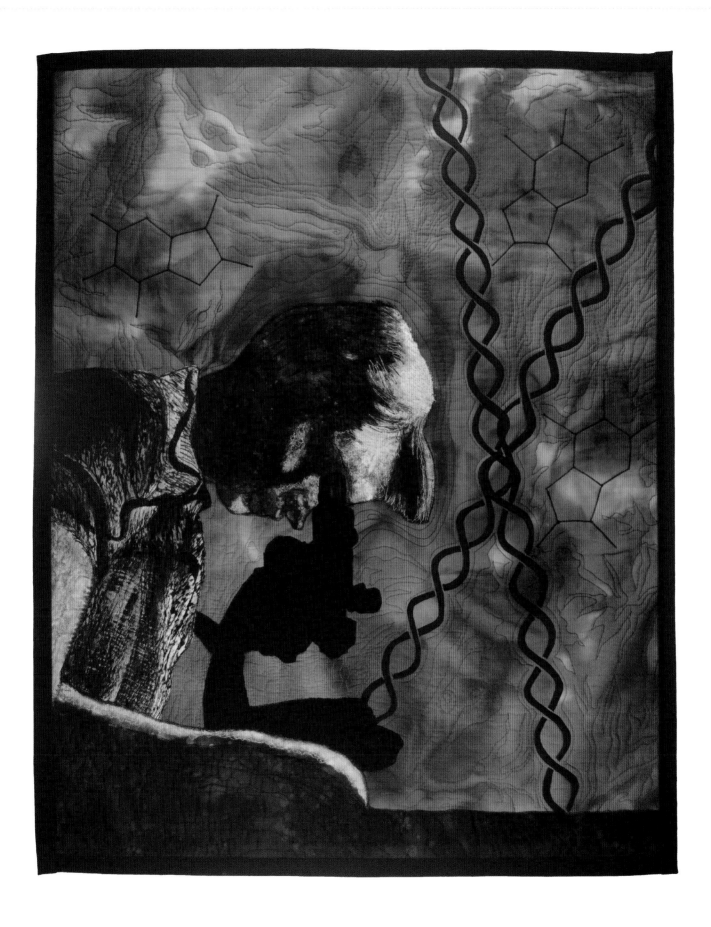

Betty Friedan (1921–2006)

. . . writer; feminist; cofounder of the National Organization of Women; author of *The Feminine Mystique*.

Is This All There Is?

Janice Paine-Dawes

Lakeview, Arizona

"Men are not the enemy, but the fellow victims. The real enemy is women's denigration of themselves."
—*Betty Friedan*

Betty Friedan was a pioneer for women's rights, a feminist, and activist for much of her life. She became a household name in the 1960s for her views on the plight of women, particularly depressed suburban homemakers who most likely gave up their college education to marry and raise a family. But her involvement in politics and rights of women did not start with her first published book, *The Feminine Mystique*, in 1963.

Born in Peoria, Illinois, in 1921, she became active in politics and what she felt was the injustice of anti-Semitism at an early age. She went to Smith College in 1938 as a psychology major.

As the editor-in-chief of the college newspaper, her editorials became politically charged. She had strong anti-war views and used the paper as a platform. After graduating summa cum laude from Smith, she spent a year at Berkeley where she continued to be politically involved and mixed with Marxist contemporaries.

After Berkeley, she became a journalist for leftist and labor journals. She was fired from one of the journals because she was pregnant. Consequently, she freelanced for other publications. She started writing articles about the plight of women who wanted more from life than being an extension of a husband or who found themselves unwillingly left alone after divorce.

The Feminine Mystique was published in 1963. Many credit Betty Friedan's book with spurring on the new wave of feminism which had been relatively quiet after the 19th Amendment passage and the "Rosie the Riveter" effort surrounding World War II. At the beginning of the book Ms. Friedan states, "The problem lay buried, unspoken, for many years in the minds of American women. It was a strange stirring, a sense of dissatisfaction, a yearning [that is, a longing] that women suffered in the middle of the twentieth century in the United States. Each suburban [house] wife struggled with it alone. As she made the beds, shopped for groceries . . . she was afraid to ask even of herself the silent question—'Is this all?'"

Betty cofounded the National Organization of Women (NOW), partly due to the Equal Employment Opportunity Commission's failure to enforce Title VII of the Civil Rights Act of 1964 to end sexual discrimination in employment. She stepped down as NOW president in 1969.

Ms. Friedan continued to be at the forefront of women's rights. She organized the Women's Strike for Equality on the 50th anniversary of the Women's Suffrage Amendment in 1970 and marched in New York City. She also organized the National Association for Repeal of Abortion Laws, renamed National Abortion Rights Action League in 1973 after abortion was legalized. Betty cofounded the National Political Women's Caucus in 1971 which vowed to make policy, not coffee. Betty continued to write about feminist issues until she died at eighty-five.

Beginning with a piece of fabric as her canvas, artist Janice Paine-Dawes sketched her design. Using textile paints or acrylic paints with textile medium, she painted the composition with a base coat of flat color. Janice sandwiched the top with batting and a backing, forming three layers in the style of a traditional quilt. It was stitched on a midarm quilting machine using a free-motion quilting technique. Multiple layers of paint were finally added to the stitched work to add depth and to accent the texture of the stitching.

Wally Funk (1939–)

. . . flight instructor and one of the Mercury 13, women who qualified for the early space programs.

Fly, Wally, Fly
Gay Young
Sweetwater, Texas

"The only thing a woman needs to compete in a man's world is ability." —Wally Funk

Wally Funk's optimistic outlook and "can-do" demeanor have taken her far. She earned her pilot's license at age sixteen and competed for the Flying Susies of Columbia, Missouri, and the Flying Aggies of Oklahoma State University. Wally has several "firsts" in aviation. "I was given the gift of great confidence and born with the ability to fly," stated Wally Funk. Indeed, Wally first "flew" at age five by jumping off the barn into the haystack wearing a Superman cape! She had her first plane ride at age fourteen and earned her private pilot's license when she was sixteen at Steven's College in Columbia, Missouri. She went to Oklahoma State University and joined their Flying Aggies, earning Outstanding Female Pilot, Flying Aggie Top Pilot, and the Alfred Adler Memorial Trophy. She was also a member of the Ninety-Nines, a female aviators group.

After college, Wally became the military's first female instructor, working with troops at Fort Sill, Oklahoma. While there, she heard of the program to test women to become astronauts. She applied for the program (with her mother's permission due to her young age) and was accepted. Thirteen women passed the initial testing and became known as the Mercury 13. All passed the physical and mental tests, scoring higher than some of the men who had tested. It was found there was no discernible difference between the genders in the performance on these rigorous tests. NASA and Congress were not impressed and turned a blind eye to their achievements. Consequently, none of the women became astronauts.

"These women known as Mercury 13 are pioneers in social and gender equality," said Martha Ackman, Professor of Gender Studies at Mount Holyoke College and a Fellow at the Radcliffe Institute at Harvard. "They forced NASA, the White House, and Congress to rethink what women were capable of doing and what women wanted to do."

Disappointed but undaunted, Wally became the first woman to complete the FAA's General Aviation Operations Inspector Academy courses covering pilot certification and flight testing procedures. After four years with the FAA, she was hired by the National Transportation Safety Board as its first female air safety investigator in 1974. She was chief pilot for five aviation schools across the country, captain for several small commercial airlines and logged over 19,400 hours of flight. Still teaching today, Wally Funk has stressed safe flying to over 3,000 students.

Wally is not a one-trick pony. She earned the Distinguished Rifleman Award at age fourteen, represented the Southwestern US as a top female skier in slalom and downhill races in US competition, and raced glider planes. Wally enjoys restoring automobiles. She is available for speaking engagements while she is waiting her turn to fly into space. Wally has her ticket!

Volunteering at the WASP Homecoming last year, artist Gay Young met Wally Funk. Wally selected the photo for the quilt, which set Gay's color scheme. The picture of Wally was digitally printed on fabric. Wally attributes her strength to Taos Mountain, having been brought up in Taos, New Mexico. She feels a spiritual connection to it, so Gay used it for the background using hand-dyed fabric. Wally's first plane was the Stearman, recreated and machine appliquéd in the foreground. Her "Go for It" attitude is a good model for all of us. All of this is important to Gay as a woman, but also as a grandmother. Her oldest granddaughter just entered the aerospace engineering program at the University of Texas. Wally Funk helped make this possible.

FLY WALLY FLY

THE ONLY THING A WOMAN NEEDS TO COMPETE IN A MANS WORLD IS ABILITY

FAA

NTSB

OK LA STATE

ARMY

STEVENS COLLEGE

FLYING SUSIE

22

19400 HOURS
3000 STUDENTS

Bobbi Gibb (1942–)

. . . first woman to run in the Boston Marathon.

Bobbi Gibb
Mary Ellen Simmons
Johnson City, Tennessee

"I thought about how many preconceived prejudices would crumble when I trotted right along for twenty-six miles." —Bobbi Gibb

In 1966 Roberta "Bobbi" Gibb became the first woman to run in the seventy-year-old Boston Marathon. Her courageous effort brought public awareness to the inequality and unfairness in the way women were viewed and treated.

Bobbi was raised near Boston, Massachusetts. She attended the University of California in La Jolla. She has written several books, earned a law degree, practiced law, worked in a neuroscience lab, married, and raised a family. She creates bronze sculptures of the human form. At the age of twenty-four in 1966, Bobbi became the first woman to run in the Boston Marathon. She wrote *Wind in the Fire* about her love of running and her personal journey to the Boston Marathon.

As a child, Bobbi loved to run. Her father took her to a park where she was allowed to run freely, enjoying nature and experiencing an amazing feeling of freedom. In April of 1964, Bobbi stood along the course of the Boston Marathon and watched the runners flying by with her father. The runners seemed powerful, beautiful, and almost mythical. Bobbi realized that she wanted to run in the Boston Marathon.

She began intensively training during the next two years. She didn't know how to train, and she didn't have a training book or a coach, but she began to run more and more every day, as much as forty miles some days. In 1964 no running shoes were available for women, so Bobbi trained in white leather nurse's shoes. On April 19, 1966, at the seventieth Boston Marathon, Bobbi hid in the bushes near the start of the race. Once the race started, Bobbi slipped into the race camouflaged as male. She wore a black tank-top bathing suit under a huge hoodie and a pair of her brother's Bermuda shorts. The runners realized that she was a woman and supported her. She shed the too warm hoodie and raced on in a new pair of men's running shoes. Her feet became blistered and burned, yet she continued. She completed the twenty-six-mile course, finishing before two-thirds of the other competitors. Crowds cheered her along the way, and at the finish line, Massachusetts Governor John Volpe shook her hand.

Bobbi ran again, as an unnumbered runner in the 1967 and 1968 Boston Marathons and was the female winner in both races. In 1972 female runners became officially sanctioned in the Boston Marathon. In 1996, the thirtieth anniversary of her first run and the 100th anniversary of the Boston Marathon, the Boston Athletic Association awarded her a medal, recognizing her wins in 1966, 1967, and 1968. She was the Grand Marshall of the 2016 Boston Marathon.

Artist Mary Ellen Simmons honored Bobbi Gibb because her youngest daughter Liane Jennings is a committed runner. She has completed thirty-five marathons. Her goal is to run in all fifty states and to run the Boston Marathon. Mary Ellen has never been to Boston, so her quilt is only representational. It is her graphic effort to translate the strength, endurance, perseverance, commitment, and determination of Bobbi Gibb and all women runners. Mary Ellen used commercial fabric. She made the templates from her own drawing. It is machine pieced, and hand and machine appliquéd. Mary Ellen machine quilted the piece and hand embroidered the letters.

Gabrielle Giffords (1970–)

. . . youngest woman in Arizona ever elected to the Arizona
State Senate; advocate for victims of gun violence.

Innocence Lost . . . Unfinished Business
Kathryn Wild
Tucson, Arizona

*"I'm fighting hard to make the world a better place,
and you can too. Get involved with your community,
be a leader, set an example, be passionate, be your
best." —Gabrielle Giffords*

Gabrielle Giffords grew up in Arizona. Awarded a Fulbright
Scholarship, she spent a year studying in Chihuahua, Mexico
before going to work at Price Waterhouse in New York City.
Her career was interrupted when assistance with the family
tire business was needed, so Gabby returned to Arizona and
became the president and CEO of El Campo Tire and remained
there until it was sold to Goodyear in 2000.

Gabby ran for a seat in the Arizona General Assembly and
won on her first try. Two years later she became the youngest
woman in Arizona ever elected to the Arizona State Senate. She
was re-elected in 2004. The following year she resigned to run
for Congress representing Arizona's Eighth District. She was
elected in 2006 and re-elected in 2008 and 2010. She served on
the Armed Services and Foreign Affairs Committee and participated
in the Science and Technology Committee. She chaired its Space
and Aeronautics subcommittee during her 2010 term, an
appropriate chairmanship since her husband, Mark Kelly, was
an astronaut. Representing a district that shares a one-hundred-
mile border with Mexico, Gabby was quite active in facilitating
discussions about what could be done to secure the borders and
to decrease drug trafficking and violence along the border.

On a balmy January morning in 2011, Gabrielle Giffords
was shot in the head, six constituents lay dead, and fifteen
others were injured in an upscale suburb of Tucson, and gun
violence took on a very personal meaning. At an innocent
"Congress on Your Corner" event, a madman brought horror
and death with a Glock purchased at a Walmart just down the
street. It took twelve seconds.

The University of Arizona Medical Center lawn became
a sea of best wishes and anguish for thousands of Arizona
residents. Candles, balloons, flowers, stuffed animals, canned
food, and well wishes mounted up while Arizonans kept vigil
for Gabby's recovery. She fought and she survived. Giving
one hundred percent has always been her way, and in 2011 she
gave her all to her rehab and recovery. But, when the debt
ceiling needed to be raised by congressional vote to avoid a
government shutdown, Gabby returned to the halls of Congress
for the first time since the shooting. When her voice rang out
with a vote to avoid the shutdown, there wasn't a dry eye in
the house. Following that vote, she resigned her seat in Congress
to continue to devote her attention to her recovery.

Gabrielle and Mark wrote *Gabby: A Story of Courage and
Hope*, a book about her recovery which was published in 2011.
She continues to advocate for victims of gun violence through
the organization Americans for Responsible Solutions which
she cofounded with Mark.

Artist Kathryn Wild painted the southern Arizona sunset
with watercolor pencils against the Tucson, Tumamoc Hill,
and San Xavier skylines. Gabby herself is represented as a
Western woman with leather gloves and boots, a neckerchief
and Concho belt. She has no facial features as the victims of
gun violence can be anyone.

The foreground of the piece is strewn with memorials of
flowers, candles, balloons, butterflies, food, flags, and messages
for Gabby's safe recovery. The flowers are ruched. A candle and
a personal item represent each of the six people who died. *Innocence
Lost . . . Unfinished Business* refers to the fact that in American
life we cannot anticipate the next victim: a child, a moviegoer, a
student, or a Congressperson. Kay painted this piece with watercolor
pencils. It was appliquéd using linen and cotton. She hand and
machine quilted it. It was embellished with ribbon.

Maria Goeppert-Mayer (1906–1972)

. . . theoretical physicist who won the Nobel Prize in 1963 for the shell model of the atomic nucleus.

Maria Goeppert-Mayer
Tanya Brown
Sunnyvale, California

"My father said, 'Don't grow up to be a woman,' and what he meant by that was, a housewife . . . without any interests." —Maria Goeppert-Mayer

Maria Goeppert-Mayer was born in 1906, attending university at a time when it was not easy for a woman to do so. Her parents expected her to acquire a higher education and, in the words of her father, "be more than a woman."

Toward that end, she attended a suffragist-run high school, the aptly-named "Frauenstudium," that prepared young women for university studies. When the school went bankrupt, she took the entrance exam a year early and was admitted to the University at Göttingen. She obtained her PhD in physics in 1930.

Shortly after that, she married a visiting Rockefeller Fellow in Chemistry, Joseph Mayer. The pair moved to the US where Joseph became an Associate Professor of Chemistry at Johns Hopkins University. Maria worked as an unpaid assistant in the Physics Department, assisting staff with German correspondence, doing research, and teaching some classes. When Joseph Mayer was fired from Johns Hopkins in 1937, he blamed it on the dean of physical sciences' hatred of women which, he thought was stirred up by his wife's presence in the laboratory.

From Johns Hopkins, the Mayers moved to Columbia University where, again, Maria received no salary. However, the chairman of the physics department did arrange for her to have an office. While at Columbia, she met Enrico Fermi and became part of his research team.

When the couple moved again, to the University of Chicago, Goeppert-Mayer was finally awarded the title of physics professor, albeit one of the unpaid variety. Her unpaid status continued until the end of 1941, when she attained her first paid professional position, teaching science part-time at Sarah Lawrence College.

In the late 1940s, while working part time at Argonne National Laboratory, she began puzzling over the fact that elements with certain numbers of nucleons (protons or neutrons) are particularly stable. Fermi, who was also at Argonne, suggested that there might be an indication of spin-orbit coupling. She realized that there was, and postulated that the nucleus is a series of closed shells and pairs of neutrons and protons tend to couple together. She poetically described the idea as follows:

"Think of a room full of waltzers. Suppose they go round the room in circles, each circle enclosed within another. Then imagine that in each circle, you can fit twice as many dancers by having one pair go clockwise and another pair go counterclockwise. Then add one more variation; all the dancers are spinning twirling round and round like tops as they circle the room, each pair both twirling and circling. But only some of those that go counterclockwise are twirling counterclockwise. The others are twirling clockwise while circling counterclockwise. The same is true of those that are dancing around clockwise: some twirl clockwise, others twirl counterclockwise."

Three German scientists, including Hans Jensen, were also working on the problem and independently reached the same conclusion. This work resulted in Goeppert-Mayer and Jensen winning the 1963 Nobel Prize in Physics for their work on the shell model. They shared it with Eugene Wigner, who'd performed unrelated work.

Goeppert-Mayer is still the only woman other than Marie Curie to be awarded a Nobel Prize in Physics.

Artist Tanya Brown's piece celebrates Maria Goeppert-Mayer gazing into the heart of an atom. The text from her elegant description is in the background. Visual elements were composited together in Photoshop to create the surface design for the fabric. The design was then printed on cotton fabric, batted, and densely stitched.

"Think of a room full of waltzers. Suppose they go round ... in circles, each circle ... another. Then i... circle, you can ... dancers by hav... wise and anoth... clockwise. Then ... ar... the dan... ning twirling 'run... tow... o they circl... pair both... only some... clockwise... wise. The... with which... The...

Maria Goeppert-Mayer

Physicist • Nobel Laureate • Nuclear Shell Model • Spin-orbit coupling

93

Jane Goodall (1934–)

. . . redefined the field of primatology through her observations of chimpanzees.

Jane Goodall
Kaylea Daubenspeck
Sherman, Texas

"Only if we understand, will we care. Only if we care, will we help. Only if we help shall all be saved."
—Jane Goodall

Jane Goodall observed animals even as a child, watching and sketching them and making notes on their behavior. She dreamed of traveling to Africa to see the animals in their natural habitats. On a visit to Kenya, she was introduced to anthropologist Louis Leakey, curator of the Coryndon Museum in Nairobi.

Jane was hired as Leakey's secretary and invited to participate in an anthropological dig at Olduvai Gorge. Her purpose was to study the velvet monkey on an island in Lake Victoria. Leakey believed that a long-term study of primates would yield interesting evolution information and he thought Jane had the proper temperament to endure the isolation that would be required. Goodall was sent to study the chimpanzees in the Gombe Stream Reserve. She established the "banana club" a systematic feeding system used to gain their trust and get a better understanding of their behavior. Skittish at first, the chimpanzees finally got so used to Jane's presence that they would often go looking for her for bananas. She imitated their behavior, climbed trees, ate their food, and made close relationships with about fifty of the one hundred chimps in the area. Through her observations, she discovered traits about the chimpanzees that revolutionized the field of primatology. The chimpanzees hunted and ate meat; they had previously been thought to be vegetarian. She discovered that they made tools, which was thought to be something only humans did. Jane discovered that they had a culture of their own, including a language containing more than twenty individual sounds. She made the first recording of chimps eating meat and making and using tools. Through her writings, she showed the world how humans and chimpanzees share many common traits.

In 1962, a *National Geographic* photographer/filmmaker, Baron Hugo Van Lawick, was sent to film Jane at work. They fell in love and married in 1964. Their honeymoon was one of the few times that Jane left the Gombe Stream. Her other absence was to fulfill the residency requirement for her PhD in Ethology from Cambridge University. She became the eighth person in Cambridge's history who was accepted to pursue a PhD without a baccalaureate degree.

Jane Goodall has not stopped fighting to protect chimpanzees from endangered habitat and lab testing. She stands up against the unethical treatment of all other animals and works to inspire others to preserve our planet for both humans and animals to coexist. In addition to being named a Messenger of Peace by the United Nations, Goodall has been awarded a multitude of honors.

Goodall's legacy has inspired numerous women to enter the field of primatology, resulting in long-term primate behavioral studies being dominated by women. She has had an impact all over the world. Today she is touring the globe giving lectures, and the Jane Goodall Institute has established many programs that teach how to conserve and encourage compassion towards all living things. Presently, she actively works to protect chimpanzees and promote environmental conservation.

Artist Kaylea Daubenspeck drew her design, then traced sections of it onto fusible paper and ironed that paper onto fabric. Jane's shirt, arms, face, and hair are all separate pieces of fabric as are the chimpanzee and the many leaves. All the pieces were ironed onto one large panel of fabric. Then Kaylea painted on highlights, shadows, and details with acrylic paint. Next, she adhered batting to the back of her panel and stitched around most of the fabric pieces. Lastly, Kaylea stitched the panel onto a second large piece of fabric, turned it right-side out, and made some finishing stitches around the leaves.

Virginia Hall (1906–1982)

. . . female spy most wanted by the Gestapo in World War II.

Virginia Hall

Charlie Hietala

Stafford Springs, Connecticut

"She is the most dangerous of all Allied spies. We must find and destroy her." —the Gestapo

"Virginia Hall is a true hero of the French Resistance." —Jacques Chirac (1995–2007), President of France

Ginger Rogers did everything Fred Astaire did, only backward and in high heels. Virginia Hall did everything with a wooden leg, nicknamed Cuthbert, and was the 007 of World War II. If anyone wanted to make a real life blockbuster movie, Virginia Hall's life would provide the perfect script! It would have everything to make it an action-packed thriller filled with selfless heroism: losing her leg in her twenties through a gun accident, surviving bomb raids, training to become a spy, and escaping on foot over the Pyrenees.

Virginia had dreamed of being in the Foreign Service since she was in secondary school. She began in a secretarial position working toward a Foreign Service appointment. She studied, passed the tests, even excelled at them, but would never be accepted for the appointment because she was a woman and an amputee.

Disillusioned she moved to France shortly before the war broke out. When the war moved into France, Virginia and a friend volunteered to drive ambulances, over dirt roads in rickety trucks, befriending the wounded soldiers and loading the vehicles on their own when necessary. When France was overrun by the Nazis, she moved to England.

Virginia, fluent in multiple languages, attended a dinner and was "discovered." Attendees included a few members of a newly formed spy organization who recruited her. After training, she was deployed to Nazi-occupied France, where Virginia posed as an American journalist. She instinctively made the right decisions on who to trust and developed a vast network of anti-Nazi supporters. She also submitted articles to the magazine that was her cover.

Virginia's network met in the woods to obtain vital air drop supplies, helped captured soldiers who were in hiding to escape, and transmitted intelligence to the Allies on the radio. The Gestapo became aware of her, nicknaming her "The Limping Lady." When the risk of discovery became too great, she escaped in a group with a scout traversing the Pyrenees Mountains on foot, sometimes walking in waist high snow, moving rapidly despite her disability. She could not tell her scout about her handicap fearing that the scout would refuse to take her. Virginia persisted and kept up the pace.

Back in England, she volunteered to return to the front in France after discovering that many of her friends were being held by the Nazis. Virginia organized a successful escape plan for them. She collected supplies, transmitted vital information and supported as many as she could. At the end of the war, she was recognized with awards by various nations. France awarded her the Croix de Guerre avec Palme. She was made a Member of the Empire by Great Britain. The United States presented Virginia Hall the Distinguished Service Award.

The United States planned to present Virginia's medal in a public ceremony, but Virginia wanted to continue to serve in the newly formed CIA, so she requested a private presentation. Virginia continued to be the unsung hero in the CIA until her retirement.

Artist Charlie Hietala created this quilt by fusing, piecing, and stuffing sections to create trapunto. She used recycled dryer sheets, recycled tea bags, batik, tulle, and handmade cording. Machine quilting represents prison bars and flowers while the quilt goes from the darkness of war on top to light representing the future. Wooden beads represent the mountain peaks she traversed as well as her prosthetic leg. Glass beads represent the lives she touched or saved.

Fannie Lou Hamer (1917–1977)

. . . known as "The Spirit of the Civil Rights Movement," risked her life demanding the right to vote in the Jim Crow South.

Fannie Lou Hamer
Carol Vinick
West Hartford, Connecticut

"Nobody's free until everybody's free."
—Fannie Lou Hamer

Fannie Lou Hamer, known as "The Spirit of the Civil Rights Movement," risked her life to fight for the right to vote in the Jim Crow South.

She was the granddaughter of slaves and the youngest of twenty children, born in Montgomery County, Mississippi on October 6, 1917. Her family worked the land as sharecroppers. They were poor and often hungry, so Hamer quit school after sixth grade to work in the fields to help support them. Fannie Lou was given a hysterectomy without her knowledge or consent when she was in the hospital for minor surgery, a procedure so common that it was known as a "Mississippi appendectomy." This experience led to her passion for the causes of the Civil Rights Movement. Unable to have children of her own, Fannie Lou and her husband adopted two daughters.

In 1962, she attended a church meeting where civil rights activists encouraged African American voter registration. When she filled out her application, Hamer was required to take a literacy test which she failed. The owner of the plantation learned of her attempt to register and demanded that she withdraw her application. She refused saying, "I didn't go down there to register for you. I went down to register for myself." Hamer personally registered thousands of black voters. In 1963 she sued Sunflower County for blocking black voter registration. She cofounded the Mississippi Freedom Democratic Party, established in opposition to her state's all-white delegation to the 1964 Democratic National Convention. Malcolm X called Hamer "the country's number one freedom-fighting woman."

She achieved this in spite her opponents' fear tactics. They evicted her from her home, offering to let her return if she withdrew her application to register to vote. Hamer received constant death threats. For attempting to integrate lunch counters, they jailed her and beat her senseless and then kept on beating her. She passed her time in jail singing the gospel song "Paul and Silas in Jail." When she continued to fight for freedom, they fired sixteen shots into the home where she was taking refuge. Even that failed to slow her down. She fought back, becoming known as "The Singing Freedom Fighter." In 1964, during the televised Democratic Convention, she brought the civil rights struggle in Mississippi to the attention of the entire nation.

Hamer dedicated the remainder of her life to helping the poor and needy in her Mississippi community. She founded a Freedom Farm and helped the people in her community get government childcare and housing loans. Hamer trained Freedom Summer Students for the Student Nonviolent Coordinating Committee, SNCC, and marched with Martin Luther King, Jr. in both Alabama and Mississippi.

Fannie Lou, who died at sixty in 1977, left a legacy of struggle for justice and equality. Her tenacious determination to ensure voting rights and desegregation changed history. Through it all, she kept her spirit high with song. "This Little Light of Mine" is still an inspiration for social justice movements today.

Artist Carol Vinick's method is fabric collage. She started with a sketch of her central image and transferred that image onto heavy muslin. Carol arranged tiny pieces of fabric to create the image, and then glued them down. Then she cut out the central figure and glued it onto the background. Carol hand painted the brick wall. She created the lunch counter using raw-edge appliqué. Finally, she used free-motion quilting to unify the image. Shadows were created by hand-painting silk organza. She used commercial, international, and hand-dyed cotton. Rick-rack and ribbon were used as embellishments. Paints used included Jacquard's Dye-Na-Flow, Lumiere, and Opaque.

Helen Hardin (1943–1984)

. . . changed the look of Native American painting by combining subjects from her heritage with modern techniques and materials.

Helen Hardin: Between Two Worlds
Karen Fisher
Tucson, Arizona

"Listening Woman is the woman I am only becoming now. She's the speaker, she's the person who's more objective, the listener, and the compassionate person."
—*Helen Hardin about her painting,* Listening Woman

Helen Hardin, Tsa-sah-wee-eh, "Little Standing Spruce" was born in Albuquerque, New Mexico, in 1943 to Pueblo artist Pablita Velarde and Herbert Hardin, an Anglo police officer. She grew up moving between her parents' very different lives. Yet throughout her life, she felt she never fully belonged in either world.

Within the Pueblo culture, conformity was very important. When Helen's mother married a white man and publicly sold her signed paintings, she was socially ostracized by the tribe. That separation applied to Helen as well, even though she lived in the traditional Pueblo community until she was six. She was not allowed to attend many of the sacred ceremonies, yet all around her were the visual elements of both ancient and modern Pueblo culture.

Helen began painting when she was very young. By her teens, she had broken with the so-called "traditional style" taught in the reservation schools to her mother's generation. Her work became more angular, more cubist in style. As a teenager, she attended the University of Arizona's Indian Art Project and was featured in *Seventeen* magazine. She had her first one-woman show at age nineteen.

Helen was the only woman among a group of young painters who were challenging the expectations Native American art should be. To achieve the geometric look she was striving for, she moved from tempera and casein paints to acrylics. She had taken drafting in high school, so she used drafting tools and airbrush to achieve the clean, geometric lines and richly layered colors that defined her complex paintings. The airbrush and spattering techniques that she employed gave her painted surfaces a subtle speckled finish.

She combined her modern style with imagery from her deep Native American spirituality. Motifs including the protective eagle curving around on itself, stepped designs, circles, linear patterns, and geometric faces came from the ancient ancestral peoples of New Mexico. Her work was a fusion of her deep Pueblo roots and her Catholic upbringing.

Helen Hardin died, too young, in 1984, from breast cancer. Her work stands as a brilliant and beautiful reminder of an exceptionally gifted artist. Many of her paintings are in the collections of major museums from Los Angeles to Washington, DC.

Artist Karen Fisher wanted to honor Helen Hardin's work because Karen and her husband owned one of her beautiful paintings and loved it for years. In Karen's piece the eagle and feathers that curve around her head repeat a symbol that appears over and again in Helen's work. Karen feels it is a symbol of both power and protection, as it is in many cultures. Karen used mostly paper piecing to achieve her precision, and she found perfect commercial fabrics to replicate her airbrush texture. Notice the Seminole patchwork, designs that are strip patterns, also called border or frieze patterns. The repeated design of strip patterns only occurs in one linear direction. She also used machine-appliqué, curved bias piecing, fussy cutting, and piecing of patterned fabrics. The piece was hand beaded with metal, stone, and glass beads. It was machine embroidered. Karen drew the face with Derwent Inktense pencils, and it was machine quilted.

Dorothy Hodgkin (1910–1994)

. . . discovered the structure of insulin, allowing millions of people to control the sugar levels in their bodies.

Injection Site
Colleen Ansbaugh
Manitowoc, Wisconsin

"I once wrote a lecture for Manchester University called 'Moments of Discovery' in which I said that there are two moments that are important. There's the moment when you know you can find out the answer and that's the period you are sleepless before you know what it is. When you've got it and know what it is, then you can rest easy." —Dorothy Hodgkin

Dorothy Hodgkin was born in Cairo where her father worked as an archaeologist. Her mother was also an archaeologist and an expert on Ancient Egyptian textiles. Her family lived in Egypt, returning to England a few months a year. When she was four, World War I began. Her parents returned to Egypt, but Dorothy was left with relatives in England where she went to boarding school starting in 1921. She studied at Oxford University and was awarded first class honors there, only the third woman to receive such. She studied for her PhD at Cambridge and earned a research fellowship at Somerville College. Somerville College made her its first fellow and tutor in chemistry, a position that she held from 1936 to 1977. She taught Margaret Roberts, the future Prime Minister of England, Maggie Thatcher. Theirs was a mutual admiration society, as Thatcher hung a portrait of Hodgkin at Number 10 Downing Street.

Hodgkin was noted for discovering 3-D biomolecular structures. In 1945, working with C. H. Carlisle, she published the first three-dimensional structure of a steroid, cholesteryl iodide. Dorothy and her colleagues confirmed the structure of penicillin. In 1948, Hodgkin first worked with vitamin B12 and created new crystals. Vitamin B12 had been discovered by Merck earlier that same year. Its structure was almost completely unknown at the time. Hodgkin discovered that B12 contained cobalt and became aware that the exact structure might be determined by x-ray crystallography analysis. From these crys-

tals, she discovered the presence of a ring structure because the crystals were pleochroic, a finding which she later confirmed using x-ray crystallography. As significant "as breaking the sound barrier" is the way physicist Lawrence Bragg described the B12 study published by Hodgkin. The final structure of B12 was published in 1955. Hodgkin was awarded the Nobel Prize for it in 1964.

In 1969, Dorothy utilized her advanced x-ray techniques in determining the molecular structure of insulin. A team collaborated with Dorothy doing further insulin research. After deciding to share her insights regarding insulin, Dorothy traveled around the world speaking about the importance of insulin and the relationship to diabetes.

Over a period of time, a diabetic coworker of artist Colleen Ansbaugh began losing body parts, a foot, the rest of the leg, then the other leg. His spirits were always positive, and he enjoyed each day even though bound to a wheelchair. Diabetes complications took over, and he passed away. Shortly after that one of Colleen's dear art quilter friends suffered a heart attack due to complications from diabetes. The seriousness of the disease loomed over Colleen; needing to express herself, *Injection Site* came forth.

The quilt intends to bring the viewer to the point where a needle would break the skin, bringing insulin to the body. Using stitch and tied resist techniques, the background fabric color was partially removed to conjure images of body parts and fluids. Later, the background fabric was over dyed several times to different "blood" shades, drawing the viewer in for closer inspection. In the center of the quilt, the fabric is hand dyed in fluid circle shapes representative of the punctures created by the injection needles. Needle users may need to use areas by old sites or sometimes on the same site, hence the proximity of one circle to another. Fresh injection sites may be a different shade or color than older, healing sites. The hand stitching inside the circles is to show the cuts made for daily blood level checks.

Grace Hopper (1906–1992)

. . . first woman coder on the Harvard Mark I;
wrote the first computer compiler.

Amazing Grace
Dena Brannen
Reston, Virginia

*"Humans are allergic to change. They love to say, 'We've
always done it this way.' I try to fight that. That's why
I have a clock on my wall that runs counter-clockwise."*
—Grace Hopper

When Grace Murray Hopper was a young girl, she dismantled
alarm clocks to try to figure out how they worked. Her parents
encouraged her curiosity. Luckily for the computing world,
they believed girls should be taught just the same as the boys.
That young girl grew up to be a pioneer in computers, achieving
such firsts as: being the first woman to code on the Mark I
computer at Harvard in 1944, and writing the first compiler
for a computer in 1952.

Grace was an academic first. She received a BA in
Mathematics and Physics from Vassar College in 1920, then
an MA and PhD in Mathematics from Yale in 1930 and 1934,
respectively. She taught at Vassar until she joined the United
States Naval Reserves in 1943 and was assigned to the Bureau
of Ordinance Computation Project at Harvard University.

She was recalled to active duty in 1967 to help the Navy
with computing problems and was given repeated extensions
to stay on active duty once she turned sixty-two, the mandatory
retirement age. She retired in 1986 at the age of eighty as a
Rear Admiral. Of her love of the Navy, she said, "I've received
many honors, and I'm grateful for them, but I've already
received the highest award I'll ever receive, and that has been
the privilege and honor of serving very proudly in the United
States Navy."

She was nicknamed "Amazing Grace" as was the destroyer
named after her, the USS *Hopper*. Hopper will be the first
woman to have a building at a US military academy named
after her; the US Naval Academy's new cybersecurity building
will be named Hopper Hall.

She loved mentoring younger staff as much as coding a
computer. "We've always done it that way," was never acceptable
to her. She taught all of the young people that she mentored
to do what they thought was necessary and apologize later.
She admonished all she supervised to "Dare and do."

Grace was also a great storyteller and speaker. She loved
to use visuals that would make an impression on those in her
audience. She used to hand out pieces of plastic-coated wire
about 30 cm (11.8") long to show the distance that an electric
signal travels in a nanosecond, one billionth of a second.

Artist Dena Brannen used fabric with the green and white
stripes symbolizing the computer paper she used to print her
programs on when she was a young programmer. The anchor
fabric was used to symbolize Grace's love of the Navy. All of
the straight line quilting in the piece goes 11.8" in one direction
then changes direction for another 11.8", a nod to the wire
lengths that she handed out at lectures. Dena quilted the shape
of the USS *Hopper* at the bottom of the piece. The center
portion of the seal of the ship is also quilted on the upper left
of the piece, with several references to Admiral Hopper. The
lion references the USS *Hopper*'s survivability and the motto
"Dare and Do." It is based on the coat of arms of Scotland
referencing Admiral Hopper's heritage. The lozenge shape is
typical of crests for women. Finally, the laurel and oak that
make up the wreath represent honor and strength. The three
stars quilted in the upper right portion represent Admiral
Hopper's one-star rank, her contributions to computing and
her dedication to educating younger generations.

Grace Hudowalski (1906–2004)

. . . ninth person and first woman to scale all forty-six peaks of the Adirondack Mountains.

Good Climbing
Sue Rook Nichols
Riverside, California

"It is not important whether you make the summit; it is important how you make the climb."
—Grace Hudowalski

In 1906, Grace Hudowalski was born in New York. She spent her childhood in the shadows of the Adirondack Mountains. Her love affair with them began when she was fifteen years old. On August 2, 1922, she climbed to the peak of Mt. Marcy, the state's highest mountain. She said, "that did something to me. I had seen something. I felt it. I never forgot that mountain and I never forgot that trip."

Grace married Ed Hudowalski in 1926, and the two of them became champions of the Adirondack Mountains. They led climbing trips to encourage children to get outdoors. Grace was a founding member of the "Forty-Sixers Club," which encouraged people to climb the forty-six peaks of the Adirondacks. Members were expected to climb one peak per year. Grace wrote letters of encouragement to other climbers as they challenged the forty-six peaks. She also expected them to write about their experiences as well.

Grace achieved her goal of climbing all forty-six peaks on August 26, 1937, when she reached the summit of Mt. Esther. She was one of only nine people and the first woman to climb all forty-six.

As editor of *The Cloudsplitter*, the journal of the Albany Chapter of the Adirondack Mountain Club, she had a chance to comment on the threats to the wild mountains from logging and pollution. Advocating for the wilderness had been dominated by men, but Grace became a leading proponent of Article 14 of the New York Constitution, the "forever wild" clause. It helped to protect the pristine wilderness. Grace accepted a position with the State of New York Commerce Department, promoting tourism in the region. She held this position from 1948 until her retirement in 1961.

Grace had three loves: the mountains, good writing, and young people. She sponsored an essay contest at Schroon Lake High School from 1957 to 1974. She encouraged women to experience the outdoors, "It's good to get out of doors, to get lots of fresh air to bring color to your cheeks and zest to your step."

Her contributions to the Adirondacks were recognized by the Adirondack Mountain Club on March 13, 2004, when they conferred on her their highest honor, the Trail Blazer Award. Grace passed away that evening at the age of 98. In 2014, the 4,012-foot mountain previously called East Dix was renamed Grace Peak in her honor.

Artist Sue Rook Nichols loves to hike and recently completed her first long distance hike, 103 miles on Cotswold Way in 11 days. Sue is a self-taught artist, and she likes to work in a whimsical style. She drew Grace's features with Prismacolor pencils and used her finished drawing as a pattern which was traced onto freezer paper, then ironed onto fabric pre-fused with Mistyfuse. After Grace had been fused together, she resembled a fabric version of a paper doll. Sue was able to move her around the background, and make any needed adjustments to the design. She quilted the background first, fused Grace onto it, and appliquéd around all pieces using invisible thread. Finally, Sue added the details, straight stitching lapels, pockets, and the fly front on her shorts. She used tulle on some of the mountains to give an illusion of distance. The last step was adding a few beads for buttons and hand stitching around her "46" patch that marked her as a member of that elite group who has climbed all forty-six peaks of the Adirondacks.

107

Amy Johnson (1903–1941)

... first woman pilot to fly solo from London, England, to Darwin, Australia.

Aviatrix Amy
Sue de Vanny
Greenvale, Australia

"I think it is a pity to lose the romantic side of flying and simply to accept it as a common means of transport, although that end is what we have all ostensibly been striving to attain." —Amy Johnson

What could be more romantic than flying through the air from England to Australia? Flying solo in an open cockpit, that's what! Well, if it wasn't romantic, it was certainly cold and thrilling! Amy Johnson was the first woman pilot, or aviatrix, to fly solo from London, England to Darwin, Australia. She only had eighty-five hours of flying experience before she attempted this feat. Amy was also the first woman in the United Kingdom to become an Air Ministry qualified ground engineer in 1929.

The famous flight from England to Australia was in May 1930 and was completed in nineteen and a half days, flying 11,000 miles (18,000 km). The aircraft was a Gipsy Moth plane nicknamed "Jason" after her father's business and is in the Science Museum in London. Amy received a Harmon Trophy as well as a Commander of the Most Excellent Order of the British Empire (CBE) in recognition of her achievement.

The following year Amy and her copilot Jack Humphreys became the first pilots to fly from London to Moscow, completing the 1,760 miles (2,830 km) in about twenty-one hours. Then they continued across Siberia and on to Tokyo, setting another record time for the entire flight from Britain to Japan.

Amy married Jim Mollison whom she met when they flew together in 1932. That same year she flew solo from London to Cape Town in South Africa, breaking Jim's previous record by eleven hours. Subsequently, they flew together from Britain to India, as part of the Britain to Australia MacRobertson Air Race. Even though they set a record on the Britain to India portion, Jim and Amy were not able to finish the race due to engine trouble. In 1936, Amy regained her record for the same flight, which turned out to be her last long-distance flight.

Amy Johnson Mollison was the President of the Women's Engineering Society from 1935 to 1937. In 1938, she divorced her husband and took back her maiden name. She looked for opportunities to demonstrate for women's rights. Amy wanted to show that women were as capable as men in what many considered masculine activities.

Mystery surrounded Amy's death in 1941. Apparently, after flying off course in terrible weather, she ran out of fuel and bailed out landing in the Thames Estuary. Her body was never recovered.

Artist Sue de Vanny created this tribute to British aviatrix Amy Johnson. Most of the background is paper-pieced drawn by Sue in a computer program. Amy's face and goggles were fabric collaged separately then laid on the background and appliquéd. Sue thread-sketched the details of the eyes and finer features. Sue then followed up with quilting. The aircraft and map were quilted first then the remainder. The quilted aircraft and map were subtlety painted in with Tsukineko ink. The piece is faced.

Lady Bird Johnson (1912–2007)

. . . left an enduring environmental legacy through the Highway Beautification Act and National Wildflower Research Center.

Field of Hope
Sarah Entsminger
Ashburn, Virginia

"Some may wonder why I chose wildflowers when there are hunger and unemployment and the big bomb in the world. Well, I, for one, think we will survive, and I hope that along the way we can keep alive our experience with the flowering earth. For the bounty of nature is also one of the deep needs of man." —Lady Bird Johnson

Drive through Washington, DC, in the spring, and you will see beds of seasonal flowers that are constantly in bloom, replaced with the next season's flowers before the last petal of the previous variety can fall to the soil. Her beautification program became Lady Bird's legacy.

Claudia Alta Taylor was nicknamed "Lady Bird" by a family nurse who said she was as "pretty as a ladybird." She found her love for the natural world nurtured as a child walking in the woods, looking for the blooms of spring, running barefoot in the sand, listening to the wind whispering through leaves and exploring each season's beauty. Traveling with Lyndon Baines Johnson on the campaign trail, she thought a great deal about what they could do to preserve our country's natural heritage and heighten the beauty that surrounds all of its citizens.

LBJ was elected as Kennedy's vice president and served as the thirty-sixth president of the United States, following Kennedy's assassination. Lady Bird believed that as First Lady she could make an impact on the environment. She called her efforts "beautification," defined as "the whole effort to bring the natural world and manmade world to harmony—to bring order, usefulness, and delight to our whole environment —and that, of course, only begins with trees and flowers and landscaping." Lady Bird created the First Lady's Committee for a More Beautiful Capital, to initiate efforts within the District of Columbia to clean, plant, and care for common areas.

Beautification included clean water, clean air, clean roadsides, safe waste disposal and the preservation of valued old landmarks, national parks, and public wilderness areas. Legislation during LBJ's term included water and air pollution cleanup, preservation of wilderness areas, and highway beautification. She worked tirelessly for the passage of these legislative initiatives, coordinating with business leaders, legislators, activists, civic leaders, employees of various state and national agencies, and as many citizens as she could recruit.

Passage of the Highway Beautification Act in 1965 put programs in place that changed the face of public lands and roadsides throughout the country. Thank Lady Bird each time you drive down a billboard-free byway, enjoy flower-planted medians or visit public parkland and wilderness areas. Lady Bird believed that a person's enjoyment of their surroundings contributed to improving their overall health and welfare.

When the Johnsons returned to Texas, Lady Bird continued her efforts to improve the natural world. She believed that there were impressive reasons to use native plants, especially wildflowers, in landscape preservation projects. On her seventieth birthday in 1982, she celebrated by giving sixty acres of land on the Colorado River, just outside Austin Texas, and enough seed money to found the National Wildlife Research Center. The center was later renamed the Lady Bird Johnson Wildflower Center. In 1977, President Ford awarded Lady Bird the Medal of Freedom; and eleven years later, President Reagan awarded her the Congressional Gold Medal for her environmental preservation work.

Artist Sarah Entsminger found that many of Lady Bird's statements about why she concentrated her work on environmental issues echoed her own thoughts. In particular, "My heart found its home long ago in the beauty, mystery, order, and disorder of the flowering earth," and the quote Sarah quilted into the sky over a meadow much like one of hers in Texas, "Where flowers bloom, so does hope." Sarah's art quilt is machine pieced, machine appliquéd, beaded, and machine quilted. She used commercial cotton, hand-dyed fabric, colored pencils, and beads.

Barbara Jordan (1936–1996)

. . . first African American woman elected to the US Congress from the Deep South.

Barbara Jordan
Julie Hallquist
Tucson, Arizona

"I felt somehow for many years that George Washington and Alexander Hamilton just left me out by mistake. But through the process of amendment, interpretation, and court decision, I have finally been included in 'We, the people.'" —Barbara Jordan

When Barbara Jordan was born in Houston, Texas, no one would have predicted all that she would achieve. She was educated in segregated schools and went to Texas Southern University. She earned her law degree at Boston University, one of only two black women in her class. Returning to Texas to practice law, she first became involved in politics volunteering for John F. Kennedy's 1960 presidential campaign. After two unsuccessful campaigns for the Texas House, she became the first black woman elected to the Texas Senate. During her final year in the Senate, she was elected president pro tem, allowing her to serve as governor for a day, June 10, 1972, per state tradition.

She was elected to represent Texas in the US House of Representatives, becoming the first black woman to represent the Deep South since Reconstruction. Through the influence of her friend, President Lyndon Johnson, she was appointed to the House Judiciary Committee. In 1974, she made the opening statement in the Judiciary Committee's impeachment hearing for Richard Nixon. That speech helped lead to Nixon's resignation over the Watergate scandal and won Jordan national recognition for her rhetoric, her ethics, and her intellect. Two years later, she became the first woman to give the keynote address at the Democratic National Convention. Those two speeches are recognized in American Rhetoric's Top 100 Speeches of the Twentieth Century.

Barbara was diagnosed with multiple sclerosis and retired from public service in 1979. During this time of reflection following her political career, she wrote her autobiography, *Barbara Jordan: A Self-Portrait*. She accepted a position at the University of Texas at Austin and became the Lyndon B. Johnson Centennial Chair of Public Policy in 1982. In 1992 she was again asked to address the Democratic National Convention. This time she did it from a wheelchair as her health was in decline. President Clinton awarded her the Presidential Medal of Freedom in 1994. She passed away in 1996 from pneumonia, a complication of her battle with leukemia.

Artist Julie Hallquist loves the challenge of using commercially printed fabrics and threads to paint a picture and tell a story in her art quilts. She enjoys surface design techniques such as stamping and screen printing to add texture to fabrics. Printing on fabric can communicate a phrase or idea directly. Barbara Jordan's era was reliant on the written word and print media such as newspapers and magazines. Twenty-four-hour news channels didn't exist. Julie wanted to communicate this, and the fact that her strong oratory skills would be a significant advantage, through the use of excerpts of her speeches and textual embellishments in the background, suggesting newspaper stories. Barbara's home state figures prominently in the quilt, represented by the state flag overlaid on the silhouette of Texas. Barbara's Presidential Medal of Freedom, was printed directly on fabric and enhanced with fabric markers. Julie printed excerpts of speeches on fabric to include in the quilt. The other text is a combination of stamping, stitching, or fused appliqué. She used fused raw-edge appliqué to create her face from her black and white Congressional photo. Julie's hope is that people who view this quilt and are unfamiliar with Barbara Jordan's life story and achievements, would become curious enough to explore further and learn more about a very powerful woman of conviction.

Frida Kahlo (1907–1954)

. . . opened doors for female artists and profoundly influenced feminist studies.

Frida Kahlo
Marisela Rumberg
Annandale, Virginia

"I paint self-portraits because I am so often alone, because I am the person I know best." —Frida Kahlo

Passionate, talented Frida Kahlo is one of the most important Mexican artists. She opened doors for generations of female artists. At age six, Frida was bedridden with polio that gave her a permanent limp. At eighteen, she suffered a broken back in a bus crash and was impaled by a steel pole that smashed through her pelvis. She wore surgical braces, corsets, and endured surgeries on her spine trying to relieve her pain. Frida suffered substance abuse, infections, lengthy hospitalizations, and an amputation due to gangrene.

She met muralist Diego Rivera when she was fifteen as he was painting *Creation* at her high school. In 1928, she met Diego again, and a year later they married. The marriage was untraditional. They lived in separate but adjoining houses and were frequently estranged. Frida said her heart loved Diego so much that it hurt. She endured his perpetual infidelities, including one with her sister. After divorcing him, she remarried him. She desperately wanted children but never had any. Frida went through bouts of severe depression, including suicide attempts.

Frida, fifteen, was among the first young women enrolled in the elite National Preparatory School. She joined a rebellious group, "Cachuchas"; became involved in socialism and Mexican nationalism; protested against the government; and joined the Young Communist League and the Mexican Communist Party. Frida and Diego successfully petitioned Mexico to grant asylum to Leon Trotsky and his wife during their exile from Communist Russia. She hosted them in her home for several years and had an affair with Trotsky.

Frida took up painting during her recovery from the bus crash. Confined to bed, she had a special easel built and a mirror installed on the ceiling so she could paint reclining. Her early work was heavily influenced by Renaissance and Cubist styles. When she and Diego moved to Cuernavaca, Frida changed to a folk art style that incorporated her passion for native mestiza culture. She began to wear indigenous peasant clothing, huipiles, rebozos, headdresses, and jewelry. It allowed her to express her feminist ideals, anti-capitalist politics, and feel ever more connected with the "regular" Mexican people.

During the 1930s Frida's art came into its own. Her painting, *Frida and Diego Rivera*, was well received when it was shown in San Francisco. In New York, half of the paintings on exhibit sold, and she received a commission from Clare Boothe Luce to paint a portrait as a gift to the grieving mother of a friend who had committed suicide. Frida instead painted the friend's suicide. Her other works frequently included gore, pain, and suffering, causing at least one gallery in Paris to label them too shocking to be exhibited. She received much critical success in Europe culminating with her painting *The Frame* being purchased by the Louvre, making her the first Mexican artist to be featured in their collection.

When Frida had her first solo show in Mexico, she found herself bedridden under doctors' orders, so she attended the show in her bed! When her leg was amputated that August, she said, "Feet, why do I need you when I have wings to fly?"

Artist Marisela Rumberg was born in Mexico and says that every Mexican knows about Frida. Marisela painted her face with textile paint then she stitched this whole cloth quilt very densely. Marisela free-motion quilted all the Zentangle designs in the body and around the head. She used Fabrico markers and textile paint to create the gray tones for shading. Finally, she painted the background and filled it with free-motion hearts.

Frances Oldham Kelsey (1914–2015)

. . . stopped the approval of thalidomide by the FDA,
preventing widespread birth defects in the US.

Integrity: Frances Oldham Kelsey, PhD, MD
Bobbe Shapiro Nolan
Eagle Lake, Texas

*"When a woman took a job in those days, she was
made to feel as if she was depriving a man of the
ability to support his wife and child. But my professor
said: 'Don't be stupid. Accept the job, sign your name
and put "Miss" in brackets afterward.'"*
—Frances Oldham Kelsey

"Civil Servant Prevents Widespread Birth Defects" never headlined the newspaper, but it should have. Frances Oldham was born in 1914 in Canada. She received a PhD from the University of Chicago and studied drugs that crossed the placental barrier, causing serious impacts on unborn babies, earning her MD in 1950.

In 1960 Frances began working at the Food and Drug Administration as a medical officer reviewing newly submitted drugs. Her first assignment was approval of Kevadon (thalidomide), an over-the-counter sedative sold in Europe since 1956 which relieved morning sickness and insomnia in pregnant women. Its approval was considered a "slam dunk." Kelsey's review noted the drug's popularity and the evidence provided enthusiastic testimonials unsupported by clinical data. Lack of FDA action within sixty days would trigger automatic approval, so she returned the application, requesting chronic toxicity data.

The company responded that such data was unnecessary and unavailable. They approached her superiors, demanding that they override her, and threatened to go to the FDA Commissioner. Kelsey's colleagues supported her.

More than 2.5 million doses of the drug had been distributed to over one thousand doctors in the US as part of its "investigational period." Thalidomide was prescribed to nearly 20,000 patients, including several hundred pregnant women. In 1961, a British medical journal reported that peripheral neuritis, a serious side effect, was noted in some women who took thalidomide. Frances again requested evidence of safe use during pregnancy. The company increased its pressure for approval.

Later that year, a German pediatrician and an Australian gynecologist recognized a link between phocomelia, a serious congenital disability, and the use of thalidomide during the first trimester. The German report concluded that fifty percent of mothers of children with this deformity had used the drug. Thousands of babies were born in Europe with: missing limbs, fingers attached at the shoulder, deformed ears, and impaired vision. There were untold miscarriages. Many babies did not live to see their first birthday. Kevadon was withdrawn from the European market in 1961. A Johns Hopkins pediatric cardiologist, Dr. Helen Taussig, visited Europe and saw the severe congenital disabilities caused by the drug. She conferred with the FDA and informed Congress. There was little reaction.

Senator Estes Kefauver had been laboring for years to pass improved regulations governing new drug licensing. Information leaked to the *Washington Post* was published in a front-page story about the tragedy and Kelsey's role in preventing the drug's distribution in the US. The Drug Amendments of 1962, the Kefauver Amendments, became law on October 10, 1962.

There were seventeen officially recognized cases of thalidomide-related phocomelia in the United States. There were probably more, given the distribution of the drug and its availability to women who visited Europe in the years before its toxicity was recognized. A widespread tragedy was averted by the integrity of Dr. Frances Oldham Kelsey.

President Kennedy awarded her the US President's Award for Distinguished Federal Civilian Service in 1962. She continued to work for the FDA for forty-five years, retiring at ninety. Frances was loved and respected at the agency, which named its new headquarters in her honor.

In 2015 she was appointed to the Order of Canada, the nation's highest civilian award. She died a month later at the age of 101.

Artist Bobbe Nolan created this art quilt by making a photo transfer of copyright-free text of federal statutes on fabric. She stamped tiny feet on the piece to represent the innocent victims of thalidomide. It was hand quilted with Perle cotton and machine quilted. The brightly colored diagonals are appliquéd.

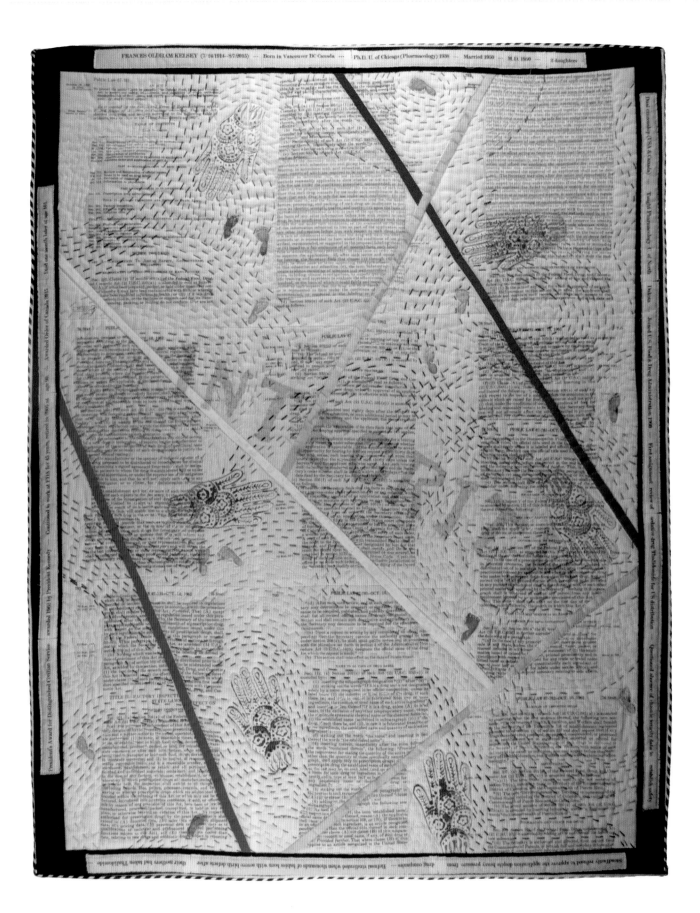

FRANCES OLDHAM KELSEY (7/24/1914–8/7/2015) · · · Born in Vancouver BC Canada · · · Ph.D. U. of Chicago (Pharmacology) 1938 · · · Married 1950 · · · M.D. 1950 · · · 2 daughters

Billie Jean King (1943–)

. . . formed the Women's Tennis Association; famously defeated Bobby Riggs in the "Battle of the Sexes."

She Is King

Karla Vernon

Vienna, Virginia

"That's the way I want the world to look: men and women working together, championing each other, helping each other, promoting each other—we're all in this world together." —Billie Jean King

Billie Jean King is a champion both on and off the court. She couldn't help it. It was in her genes. Her father tried out for the NBA; her mom was an excellent swimmer; and her brother Randy Moffitt grew up to be a Major League Baseball pitcher. Originally Billie Jean pursued softball until her parents encouraged her to try a more ladylike sport. So at the age of eleven, she started playing tennis. Just seven years later she and partner Karen Hantze Susman became the youngest pair ever to win the Wimbledon women's doubles title. As a player from the early 1960s to the early 1980s, Billie Jean won thirty-nine Grand Slam singles, doubles, and mixed doubles tennis titles, including wins at Wimbledon, a record twenty career titles there: six singles, ten women's doubles, and four mixed doubles. She is an author and is the cofounder, with her ex-husband Larry King, of World Team Tennis and founder of the Women's Tennis Association.

In 1968 the "open era" in tennis began. All players could compete in all tournaments, and top players were able to make their living from tennis. King crusaded for equal prize money in men's and women's games. In 1973, Bobby Riggs, a former world champion tennis player, taunted female tennis players to challenge him in a tennis match. Billie Jean King played him in a nationally televised "Battle of the Sexes." Billie Jean King beat him 6-4, 6-3, 6-3. That same year the US Open became the first major tournament to offer equal prize money for men and women. Other major tournaments followed suit.

Billie Jean spent her tennis career trying to make the tennis prize money for women equal to that of men. Many, but not all, of the tennis tournaments now have equal prizes. Even to this day, although tennis offers prize money equality more than any other major sport, the pay gap roughly matches that seen in American workplaces.

She was named one of the "100 Most Important Americans of the 20th Century" by *Life* magazine in 1990. The USTA National Tennis Center in Flushing Meadows–Corona Park was rededicated as the USTA Billie Jean King National Tennis Center on August 28, 2006.

Billie Jean's life has been spent empowering women and fighting for gender equality. She was the first prominent female athlete to announce her homosexuality. She is actively involved with the USTA and LGBT organizations. She chairs or serves on the boards of several committees and foundations which promote compassion and women's rights.

Being a tennis player all her life, it seemed fitting that artist Karla Vernon would honor Billie Jean King as an accomplished tennis player, as well as an advocate for gender equality. Karla is not a portrait artist, so she decided a beautiful "fantasy tennis court" with a side view of a tennis player would fit her style. Karla put short phrases attributed to King on oversized tennis balls. The audience was created with chopped up bits of fabric, fused, and then overlaid with tulle. One hundred twelve beads were sewn on to represent faces. Her figure was appliquéd using the Apliquick method.

Stephanie Kwolek (1923–2014)

. . . inventor of Kevlar®, the main component
in bulletproof vests.

Stephanie Kwolek
Mary Tims
Oakton, Virginia

"I tell young people to reach for the stars. And I can't think of a greater high than you could possibly get than by inventing something." —Stephanie Kwolek

Stephanie Kwolek dreamed of becoming a doctor, but ended up saving more lives as a chemist. After college, she took a job with DuPont doing research. There, in 1964, she made a discovery that ultimately saved countless lives. Tasked with creating a high performance fiber to replace steel in racing tires, Kwolek formed a cloudy solution of liquid crystals and proceeded to test its properties. The lab technician in charge of the spinneret needed convincing to process this cloudy liquid for fear of clogging the equipment. After much persistence on Kwolek's part, the liquid was spun and showed the characteristics of a very stiff, strong fiber which came to be called Kevlar®. This lightweight, heat resistant fiber which is five times stronger than steel has since been used in a wide range of products including tires, helmets, flame-resistant fabrics and ropes, fiber-optic cables, and aircraft and armored vehicle panels. It is, most notably, the main component of bulletproof vests which have become invaluable to legions of soldiers and law enforcement officers.

A native of New Kensington, Pennsylvania, Kwolek graduated in 1946 with a bachelor of science in chemistry from Margaret Morrison Carnegie College (Carnegie Mellon University), during a time when women were encouraged to be homemakers instead of going to school. Inspired and supported by her parents to pursue this route, Kwolek commented, "I recommend that parents encourage their daughters to pursue scientific careers, if they are so inclined, in the same way, they would their sons. The opportunities for both sexes are far more equal now." Though she faced gender discrimination as she rose to the top, she paved the way for other aspiring female scientists and came to serve as a mentor to other women scientists. After retirement, Ms. Kwolek tutored high school students in chemistry, paying particular attention to grooming young women for work in the sciences.

Stephanie Kwolek is a role model for all that women can achieve in science and technology. She won many patents and awards including the 1999 Lemelson-MIT Lifetime Achievement Award for her technological invention of Kevlar®.

Artist Mary Tims has always loved fabric and thread. She is fascinated by how the world works. So this chance to combine her love of quilting with a world-changing invention was something Mary couldn't pass up. She used both old-fashioned hand embroidery and computerized machine quilting to create this tribute to a woman whose work has made such a difference in so many lives. This piece shows a small but oh-so-important part of the results of her work and allowed Mary to contribute to her memory. It was created using cotton and Kevlar® fabric. It was machine quilted and hand embroidered. Mary used Inktense pencils and Paintstiks to fill in the words. Thanks to DuPont and Pelican Rope for their donations of Kevlar® products.

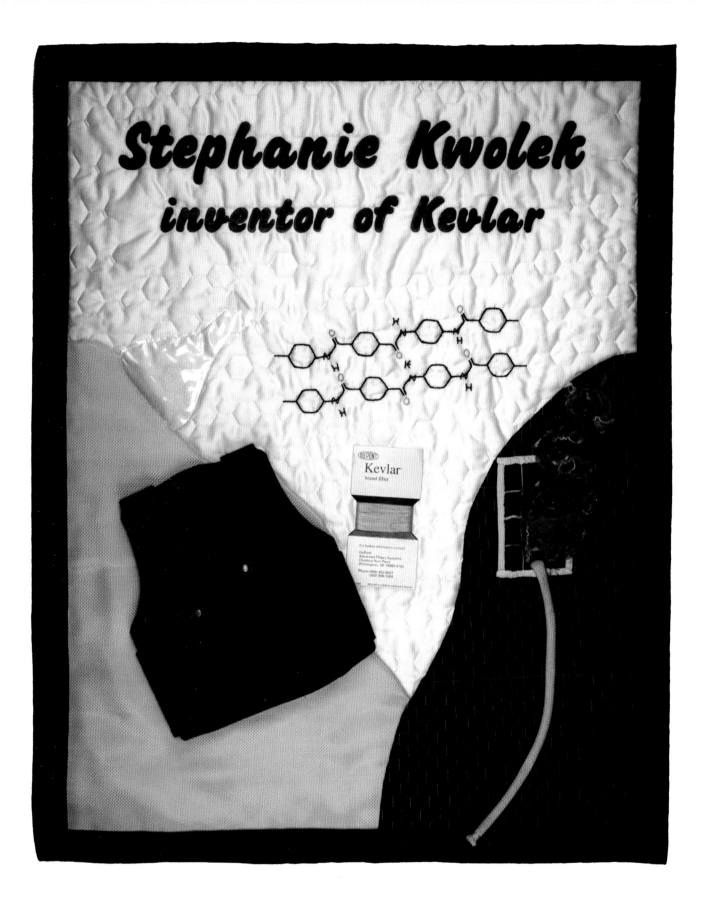

Henrietta Lacks (1920–1951)

. . . supplied the first immortal cells ever grown in a laboratory, used in ongoing groundbreaking medical research.

HeLa Cells
Joyce Carrier
Bluemont, Virginia

"Henrietta's were different: they reproduced an entire generation every twenty-four hours, and they never stopped. They became the first immortal human cells ever grown in a laboratory." —Rebecca Skloot, The Immortal Life of Henrietta Lacks

In the early 1950s, African American housewife Henrietta Lacks, mother of five and a poor tobacco farmer from Virginia, went to Johns Hopkins Medical Center in Baltimore to have treatments for something she described as a knot. She could feel it. She knew something was wrong. The knot was diagnosed as cervical cancer. A doctor at Johns Hopkins took a sample of her tumor and sent it, without her consent, to scientists there who had been trying to grow tissues in culture for decades without success. Unfortunately, the cancer was too advanced to save Henrietta's life. She died at the age of thirty-one.

Mysteriously Henrietta's cells never died, even though she did. Her cells were the first immortal human cells ever grown in a culture. The cells have been used in countless tests and research studies. They were an integral part of developing the polio vaccine. They were sent up in the first space missions to find out what would happen to cells in zero gravity. Henrietta's cells have been used in research about cloning, gene mapping, and in vitro fertilization. They continue to aggressively divide and reproduce and are known to scientists and medical researchers as HeLa.

The code name HeLa was used based on the first two letters in Henrietta and Lacks. Today a code for samples would have been made so that the donor would have been anonymous. Personal privacy wasn't an issue in the 1950s, so they weren't careful about her identity. When the press got close to finding Henrietta's family, the researcher who had grown the cells in a culture made up a pseudonym—Helen Lane—to throw them off the track. Other fake names like Helen Larsen were floated to the press as well. Her real name wasn't made public until the 1970s. It was twenty years after her death that Henrietta's family, poor and lacking health care of their own, discovered that their mother's cells are still living and being used in research all over the world. These cells have spawned a billion dollar industry in medical research and are still being used today in laboratories all over the world. Yet her family has been without insurance and health care that they needed.

Henrietta's unwitting contribution of these immortal cells resulted in medical breakthroughs that have benefited us for over 60 years. The prolific growth and reproduction of the HeLa cells have been an important biomedical tool in finding cures or treatments for many illnesses such as AIDs, polio, and cancer.

Her tombstone in Lacktown, Virginia, reads:

Henrietta Lacks, August 1, 1920 – October 4, 1951
In loving memory of a phenomenal woman,
wife and mother who touched the lives of many.
Here lies Henrietta Lacks (HeLa). Her immortal
cells will continue to help mankind forever.
Eternal Love and Admiration, From Your Family

Artist Joyce Carrier layered two cotton fabrics: black over teal. After sandwiching the batting and heavyweight interfacing, black shapes were cut away to reveal the teal layer. Joyce used two shades of rayon thread in the upper needle at the same time to create a more textured feel to the piece. Red rayon thread was used to fill in the black areas, and the edges of each shape were finished with cotton cording.

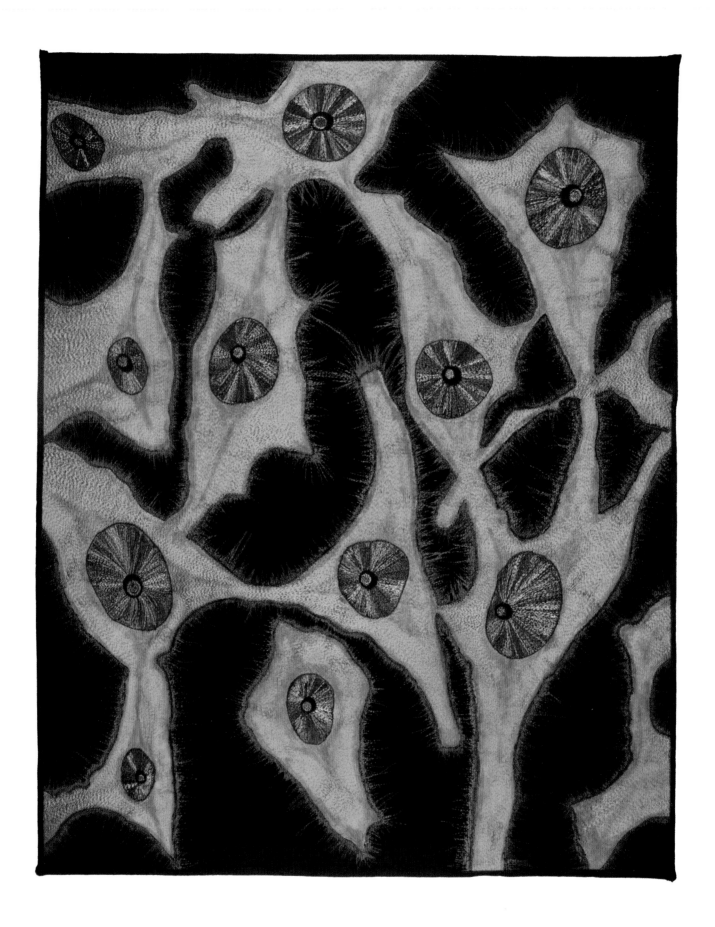

Hedy Lamarr (1914–2000)

. . . invented technology that is used in Wi-Fi and Bluetooth.

Hedy Lamarr
Kerry Faraone
Purcellville, Virginia

"The world isn't getting any easier. With all these new inventions I believe that people are hurried more and pushed more . . . The hurried way is not the right way; you need time for everything—time to work, time to play, time to rest." —Hedy Lamarr

One of Hollywood's glamour gals was smarter than she was glamorous and she was responsible for many of the devices that keep us connected to the rest of the world. Hedy Lamarr once said, "Any girl can be glamorous, all you have to do is stand still and look stupid." It was impossible for Hedy Lamarr to look stupid. Naturally beautiful, she also had brains.

Born in Austria, she began her film career in Czechoslovakia. She married Friedrich Mandl when she was eighteen. He had ties to fascist leader Mussolini and German leader Hitler as well. Both were guests in the Mandl home. Hedy went with her husband to business meetings where he met with scientists involved in military technology. Those meetings were Hedy's introduction to applied science. She divorced Friedrich, who sold arms to the Nazis, and fled alone to the US. Securing a contract with Metro-Goldwyn-Mayer, she became a box office sensation following her first film's release.

When other Hollywood dinner parties simply shimmered in sequins, she had scientists and other thinkers at her dinner table. In 1942, Hedy and her friend, composer George Antheil, patented a way of "hop-skipping" radio signals, blocking the radio signals which sent torpedoes off course. The hop-skipped radio signals could not be blocked, so torpedoes hit targets more reliably. The signals used the syncopated rhythms similar to those used when multiple pianos played the same tune, but just slightly differed in timing. Their "Secret Communications System" also kept enemies from decoding secret messages. It was originally designed to defeat the Nazis. The system was an important step in the development of technology to maintain the security of both military communications and cellular phones. She was a pioneer of wireless technology which has given birth to GPS, Blue Tooth, Wi-Fi, and cell phones. Thank you, Hedy!

Lamarr and Antheil weren't instantly recognized for their invention since its impact wasn't understood until decades later. In 1997 they were honored with the Electronic Frontier Foundation (EFF) Pioneer Award, and that same year Hedy received the BULBIE Gnass Spirit of Achievement Award, the "Oscar" of inventing, becoming the first female to do so.

She married six times, had three children, and became a naturalized US citizen. She made her last movie in 1958. She spent her final days in seclusion in a community near Orlando where she died at the age of eighty-six.

Artist Kerry Faraone is fascinated with art quilts. Creating them allows her to use skills and techniques that she learned in paper maché and photography. To create this piece Kerry printed organza overlays describing Hedy's patent and its practical application. There are also overlays of photos from her film career. Kerry chose to make a fabric portrait of her to highlight her beauty. Kerry wanted to show the juxtaposition between the stunningly gorgeous woman and her phenomenal, scientific mind.

Ann Landers (1918–2002)

. . . wrote a popular advice column read by
approximately ninety million people daily.

Eppie Lederer: Wake Up and Smell the Coffee
Sally Harcum Maxwell
Poquoson, Virginia

*"Let this coming year be better than all the others.
Vow to do some of the things you have always wanted
to do but could not find the time. Call up a forgotten
friend. Drop an old grudge, and replace it with some
pleasant memories. Vow not to make a promise you
do not think you can keep. Walk tall, and smile more.
You will look ten years younger. Do not be afraid to
say, I love you. Say it again. They are the sweetest
words in the world." —Ann Landers*

Although the name Eppie Lederer may not spark recognition, Eppie's pen name Ann Landers is very familiar. At the end of her career in 2002, approximately ninety million people read her daily advice column. For forty-seven years she had helped readers learn how to cope with modern society and its problems, from desegregation to homosexuality, SIDS to AIDS. Ann cared about her readers. Her advice in the column was honest, direct, and usually helpful. Her frequent admonition to "wake up and smell the coffee" was a typical piece of advice to someone in a state of denial.

Eppie Lederer began writing the "Ann Landers" column upon the death of the original writer of the column in 1955. She used her connections within the community to get expert advice for her column. Over time, society changed and Ann Landers changed with the times. In fact, sociologists say her column both reflected and informed the nation's moral compass.

Eppie was involved in the Jewish community, active in the Democratic Party and fundraised for many charities. In 1971 Ann urged readers to write to their congressional representatives and the resulting 300,000 letters delivered to Congress convinced them to enact the National Cancer Act and allocate one hundred million dollars for cancer research. In an ironic twist, Eppie Lederer died of multiple myeloma, a cancer of the bone marrow. Although her daughter continued the column as the author, there was no replacing Eppie. Ann Landers was without a doubt an outstanding and beloved national treasure.

Artist Sally Maxwell began with a foundation, Eppie's foundation, of newsprint. Sally was not able to use wording from actual "Ann Landers" columns because of copyright issues, so she substituted her own words on different, related topics organized in straight columns, designing and printing her own fabric to resemble the newspaper. The straight lines of the copy and the quilting are in direct contrast to the more organic and circular forms of the coffee stains, superimposed on the newsprint, as well as the free-motion quilting around her names—both Eppie and Ann. Her bouffant-style hair typical of the 1960s changed little over the years and was fun to create. One thing that never changed was the slightly asymmetrical smile with the deep dimples. It's an open, honest face that mirrors her straightforward advice. Admittedly, Sally's interpretation of Eppie Lederer is more of a caricature than a realistic portrait, but if you see this work and leave with the idea that she is a straightforward and caring woman of her era, Sally will feel that she has done her job. The entire composition is in black and white, except for the brown coffee spilled over the background—a direct reference to the quote "wake up and smell the coffee," a favorite of Ann Landers. Commercial inks and dye were used to print the coffee rings and spatters.

Dorothea Lange (1895–1965)

. . . documentary photographer of Depression Era Americans and the internment of Japanese Americans.

Through the Lens

Jeanne Knudsen

Cody, Wyoming

"Seeing is more than a physiological phenomenon . . . We see not only with our eyes but with all that we are and all that our culture is. The artist is a professional see-er." —Dorothea Lange

Dorothea Lange has been called the greatest documentary photographer of twentieth-century America. She is well known for her photographs, although many who recognize her work are not always familiar with her name. Lange's recognizable images have documented much of the history of the early twentieth century of the US.

Lange, who was born in New Jersey, and her mother were abandoned by her father. At the age of seven, she contracted polio which left her with a permanent limp in her left leg. Following high school graduation, she informed her mother that she was going to be a photographer. She took a course at Clarence White, the best photography school in New York. Lange moved to San Francisco in 1918 and opened a successful portrait studio. Dorothea found this work very unsatisfying and took her camera to the city's streets.

Lange's photographs of migrant workers, the poor, and the homeless brought her the opportunity to be employed by the Farm Security Administration (FSA). She was assigned to document rural poverty in California: the migrant farm workers and the Dust Bowl refugees. She used her camera to photograph the poor in the fields just as she had done portraits of the wealthy in the studio. Her photos peeled back the layers and revealed a dignity in the images of the poor that had never been seen before. Dorothea had never considered herself an artist, but people who saw her work did. One of her most moving photos of that period was called *Migrant Mother*. It was a thirty-two-year-old mother who was living in a lean-to with her children. They existed on frozen vegetables from the fields and on birds that the children killed. The photo had a haunting quality. The FSA photos that Lange took influenced the growth of documentary photography.

Soon after the Japanese bombed Pearl Harbor in 1941 Lange was hired by the government to document the internment of Japanese and Japanese Americans living on the West Coast of the United States. Because she humanized these photographs, the government considered them "sympathetic" to the internees. All of her photographs, taken to document this horrific time in American history, were impounded by the US Army. These historic photographs were not viewed by anyone, including Lange, for over twenty years. Before her most impactful work was made public Dorothea Lange died in San Francisco on October 11, 1965.

Artist Jeanne Knudsen posterized and enlarged a public domain photo and traced it onto a muslin foundation and clear plastic sheeting. From those tracings, Jeanne made the pattern, and then placed those pieces onto the muslin and under the plastic. Once she put lots of the pieces on the muslin, the plastic showed where those pattern pieces actually were to go. Lift, place the pattern piece on the muslin, and check the placement against the plastic. Once all that was done, she sewed the pieces down with her regular sewing machine, and then longarm quilted it.

Mary Leakey (1913–1996)

**. . . discovered the oldest hominid skull and
fossilized footprints from the first bipedal hominid.**

Mary Leakey, Paleoanthropologist
Betty Hahn
Sun City, Arizona

*"There were details like clothing, hairstyles and the
fragile objects that hardly ever survive for the
archaeologist—musical instruments, bows and arrows,
and body ornaments depicted as they were worn . . .
No amounts of stone and bone could yield the kinds
of information that the paintings gave so freely."*
—Mary Leakey

Mary Leakey was a self-described failure at school. She claimed she had never passed a test and never would. Having traveled with her parents, she was taught some math and reading by her father, but formal schooling was not successful. She became interested in archeology while traveling with her dad and she loved to draw. It formed the basis of her career.

After her father died, she returned to England with her mother and was enrolled in several convents from which she was expelled for spirited behavior. She participated in excavations in Devon and attended lectures in geology and archeology, and began drawing stone tools for publication.

In the 1930s, Mary began auditing archaeology and geology classes. She became quite an expert in flint points and was renowned for her abilities in scientific illustration. Mary was introduced to Louis Leakey, an archaeologist and anthropologist, in 1933. He asked her to come to Africa to draw stone tools that he had found. Mary and Louis got along immediately and developed a personal relationship. They married in 1937, becoming one of science's most famous husband-wife teams. They moved to Africa when Louis started an excavation project at the Olduvai Gorge, a steep ravine in present-day Tanzania, East Africa.

Despite Mary's primary interest in art and artifacts, she had an amazing talent for discovering fossils. In 1948 Mary discovered Proconsul africanus which was an ape that lived twenty-three to fourteen million years ago. She found a skull in 1959 that became known as Zinjanthropus, whom she and her husband called Zinj or Nut Cracker Man because of his massive jaws and molars. It was believed to be 1.75 million years old. Mary discovered Homo habilis in 1960. It was estimated to have lived 2.4 to 1.4 million years ago and is thought to be the species that was the first maker of tools.

In 1974 she began excavations at Laetoli, which produced Australopithecine skeletal remains. It was there that Mary discovered the first set of bipedal footprints in 1979, dating from 3.8 million years ago. These were the earliest definite hominid samples known at the time. When she left the site, she buried the footprints under sand and boulders. Trees grew and now obscure the site.

As she aged, she spent more time studying cave art from a nearby region. She said she couldn't get nearly the information from stones and bones that she could get from the cave paintings. Mary raised three sons who all became involved in anthropology. She continued her research and wrote manuscripts until her death in 1996.

Artist Betty Hahn loves to paint a story. When Betty researched Mary Leakey, she discovered many photos that seemed to tell the story of her exciting life. Betty printed the photos in various sizes and arranged them under silk. Using a permanent fine line pen, Betty drew and then painted the images with permanent Tsukineko ink in sepia, brown, black, and gray tones. She left open areas between images to allow space to quilt phrases and quotes relating to the pictures. The pictures show Leakey working alone and with her family, and identifying her discoveries.

Wangari Maathai (1940–2011)

. . . founded the Green Belt Movement; first African woman and first environmentalist to receive the Nobel Peace Prize.

I Will Be a Hummingbird
Lisa Arthaud
Warrenton, Virginia

"We are called to assist the Earth to heal her wounds and in the process heal our own—indeed, to embrace the whole creation in all its diversity, beauty, and wonder. This will happen if we see the need to revive our sense of belonging to a larger family of life, with which we have shared our evolutionary process."
—Wangari Maathai

Wangari's eyes grow big. Her voice lifts with excitement, and she begins to tell a folktale about a raging fire consuming the African forests. The large animals are overwhelmed, powerless, paralyzed with fear, and watching in disbelief. The small hummingbird rushes in to "do something." Little by little the hummingbird carries drops of water to help extinguish the fire. She expresses her truth: "I may be small, but I can do something! I am doing the best that I can." As the story ends, Wangari affirms her role in changing the world . . . "I will be a hummingbird." Listen to Wangari tell the story using the code reader on your phone to access the QR code below.

Wangari Maathai was born in a rural area of Kenya, Africa, in 1940. She was the first woman in Eastern and Central Africa to earn a PhD. Returning to her village, she was devastated to see deforestation's effect on her community. Rural Kenyan women reported that streams were drying up, food supply was less secure, and they had to walk further to get firewood. Through the Green Belt Movement, Wangari encouraged women to work together to grow seedlings and plant trees to bind the soil, store rainwater, provide food and firewood, and receive a small monetary token for their work. Since 1977, over fifty-one million trees have been planted. Wangari has improved the lives of over 900,000 women. She was known as "Mama Trees."

Sadly, Wangari passed away in 2011. Her work in conjunction with the Green Belt Movement continues to stand as a testament to the power of grassroots organizing, proof that one person's simple idea can make a difference.

Artist Lisa Arthaud envisioned Wangari's portrait in the upper corner of the layout beaming above the women who continue to do her work with a "Green Belt" of trees being planted honoring the movement.

Lisa posterized her favorite image into five layers, numbering each section one through five, taped the paper onto her light box, and taped good quality, neutral muslin over the paper image. Lisa chose Shiva Paintstiks as her painting medium, picking three primary skin tone hues ranging from light to dark and added in a tint and tone. To make the Paintstiks more fluid, Lisa modified them by crumbling a small bit of each color into a set of five shallow dishes and added a bit of linseed based gel to thin each hue. Starting from light to dark, Lisa began adding paint onto each area of the piece using a small paintbrush. She blended the layers with her Paintstik blender stick. Lisa added Inktense charcoal gray and black colored pencils for a few details near Wangari's eyes. She appliquéd the image onto a beautiful hand-dyed fabric that reminded her of the Earth, trees, sun, and sky.

Lisa found an unusual, elegant fabric that reminded her of the garment that Wangari wore when receiving the 2004 Noble Peace Prize. Lisa made Wangari's 3-D hair and adorned her image with beautiful silks, rayon, cotton, and embellished trim. She twisted and turned bits of fabric until she was pleased with the look of her headpiece.

Lisa added the hummingbird last. As the larger, strong animals looked on, the hummingbird pronounced, "I may be small, but I can do something!" For Lisa, that quote symbolized Wangari's life work. She started out small with only her voice . . . but eventually her mission grew into an International Green Belt Movement.

Hattie McDaniel (1895–1952)

. . . first African American to win an Academy Award.

To Play One or To Be One, That Is the Question!

Nneka Gamble

Victoria, Texas

"The only choice permitted us is either to be servants for $7 a week or to portray them for $700 per week."
—Hattie McDaniel

Born in 1895 in Wichita, Kansas, Hattie McDaniel enjoyed singing at home, school, and church. She sang, danced, and acted professionally as a part of "The Mighty Minstrels" when she was in high school. She dropped out of school to pursue her passion. After touring with an orchestra and Vaudeville troops, Hattie was invited to perform on a Denver radio station, becoming the first African American woman to perform on the radio. Hattie began writing and singing blues music. She returned to the radio as "Hi-Hat Hattie" around 1930 and soon landed her first small film role. Roles for black actors were few and far between. In the next few years, Hattie landed bigger roles with prominent actors such as Will Rogers, Shirley Temple, and Lionel Barrymore.

In 1939, she was given the most significant role of her career, Mammy, the house servant in *Gone with the Wind*. This performance earned her the 1940 Academy Award for Best Supporting Actress—the first African American to ever win an Oscar in any category. McDaniel was not treated with the respect she deserved by the Academy and some members of the African American community. Neither she nor her black castmates were allowed to attend the premiere of the movie. The venue for the Academy Awards ceremony, the Ambassador Hotel's Cocoanut Grove nightclub, was for whites only, and she was permitted to attend only after studio executives pleaded with the establishment. Sadly, she was only allowed to sit in the back. Some members of the black community criticized McDaniel for playing a role that was considered old-fashioned and portrayed African Americans in a negative, stereotypical way, a mammy. McDaniel continued to play maids and slaves, stating that she "would rather play one than be one."

As the Civil Rights Movement made progress, she began to be viewed as someone helping to break down racial stereotypes. Returning to her radio roots, Hattie starred in *The Beulah Show*, once again as a maid. Shortly after it transitioned to television, McDaniel was diagnosed with breast cancer. She quickly succumbed to the disease. McDaniel had left instructions for her remains to be buried in Hollywood Memorial Cemetery. Her final wish was denied due to the cemetery being for whites only at the time, but in 1999, a marble cenotaph was placed there in her honor.

McDaniel has been honored in many ways, including two stars on the Hollywood Walk of Fame and a commemorative US postage stamp. Every year during October, Sigma Gamma Rho Sorority, Inc., a service organization that Hattie belonged to, honors her through various breast cancer awareness efforts.

In artist Nneka Gamble's quilt honoring McDaniel, the spotlight is not only on her but on the roles that she so frequently portrayed: that of a slave and maid. Hattie is wearing a suit in lavender, a color which represents something special or unique, and her hair is adorned with a white gardenia similar to one she wore when she accepted the Academy Award. In the background, Aya, an Adinkra symbol that resembles the fern, has been quilted. The fern, like Hattie, grows in harsh and challenging terrain, but still, flourishes and survives. McDaniel had to endure tremendous prejudice and judgment throughout her career, and even after her death. Because she was a pillar of strength, she paved the way for people of color to be accepted and recognized in the radio, television, and film industry. The quilt was created using raw-edge and fusible appliqué. Nneka drew and painted the images.

Golda Meir (1898–1978)

. . . cofounded the Jewish state of Israel and
served as its first female prime minister.

Golda, Leader of Men

Phyllis Cullen

Ninole, Hawaii

*"Trust yourself. Create the kind of self that you will
be happy to live with all your life. Make the most of
yourself by fanning the tiny, inner sparks of possibility
into flames of achievement." —Golda Meir*

On a list of illustrious national leaders who are female and
Jewish, Golda Meir stands alone. She served as the Prime
Minister of Israel from 1969 to 1973. She was a pioneer,
visionary, risk-taker, tireless fundraiser, advocate for the Jewish
people, and one of the founders of the Jewish state of Israel.

Born in Kiev, Russia, Golda remembered hiding from
Cossacks during constant pogroms as a child. Her family had
lived in poverty before immigrating to the US. She became a
teacher and married. Golda and her husband immigrated to
Palestine, where they joined a kibbutz. Golda flourished there.
Her husband Morris felt useless as he watched Golda take on
leadership roles in the kibbutz. Morris insisted that they shouldn't
have the family that they both wanted unless Golda agreed to
be a traditional stay-at-home mom. They had a son and a daughter.
Golda tried to be that traditional mom. But it wasn't for her.

She became active in the government, and moved quickly
through the ranks, holding several ministry positions, confounding
the religious male elements.

When the State of Israel was established in 1948, it became apparent that armed confrontation with the Arabs was
inevitable. An enormous amount of money was necessary to
equip Israel's newly formed military. Golda spoke perfect
English, so she volunteered to go to the US to raise twenty-
five million dollars from the American Jewish community.
Others had tried and failed, but Golda succeeded beyond their
wildest expectations, raising twice the amount of money that
they expected, fifty million dollars. She did this by commu-
nicating to the American Jewish citizenry a sense of shared
mission and a compelling urgency.

Her courage took many forms. In May 1948, with five
Arab armies poised on Israel's borders, Golda disguised herself
as an Arab woman and went to Amman for a secret meeting
with King Abdullah of Transjordan, to try to persuade him to
stay out of the war.

Golda was the only female foreign minister in the world.
Foreign dignitaries were invited to her home where Golda,
wearing an apron, served them homemade pastry with a lecture
on Israel's security on the side. She refused to obey the color
line in Rhodesia, inspiring other dignitaries to follow her lead.
Her proudest accomplishment was the export of Israeli technical
and agricultural expertise to Africa.

At age sixty-eight when she was tired and ill and ready to
retire, she was drafted to be Prime Minister of Israel, serving in
that position from 1969 to 1973. She was tough. When confronted
with difficult issues, she told it like it was. Israel went through
an epidemic of violent rapes. A cabinet member suggested that
women be put under curfew until the rapists were caught. Meir
immediately put a kibosh on that: "Men are committing the
rapes. Let them be put under curfew." When asked to estimate
when the Arab problem would be resolved, she said, "When the
Arabs love their children more than they hate us."

As a tribute to Israel's great pioneer, leader, and advocate
for her people, artist Phyllis Cullen chose to depict her as the
larger than life "Iron Lady" that she was. Golda devoted her
life to the creation, development, and security of the state of
Israel, so Phyllis included the iconic symbols of the state, the
Wailing Wall, Israel's flag, and the legions of women pioneer
kibbutzniks with farm implements. This collage portrait was
created using thread sketching and actual painting, embellishments, and elements from printed fabrics.

Angela Merkel (1954–)

. . . first female chancellor of Germany.

Angela Merkel, World Leader
Kat Campau
The Villages, Florida

"To exclude groups of people because of their faith, this isn't worthy of the free state in which we live. It isn't compatible with our essential values. And it's humanly reprehensible, xenophobia, racism, extremism have no place here. We are fighting to ensure that they don't have a place elsewhere either."
—Angela Merkel

At this time Angela Merkel is arguably the most powerful woman in the world. She speaks for moderation on the world stage. The European Union has her to thank for its stability and continuation. Germany has a healthy economy and a strong middle class, largely due to her influence. She is known for her understated authority.

Angela Kasner Merkel was the child of a Lutheran pastor and an English teacher. Her father moved his family east from Hamburg to the German Democratic Republic. Angela grew up in East Germany. Her early life was concerned with not antagonizing the repressive government in which she lived, so she could continue to pursue her studies. She studied at the University of Leipzig, earning a doctorate in physics and working as a chemist. Angela is fluent in English and Russian. She was a voracious student, striving to learn and excel all her life.

After Germany had reunited, Angela's struggle to gain knowledge and control continued. Her first political appointment was by Helmut Kohl, as a minister for women and youth. She was able to escape untarnished from the financial scandal that later embroiled Helmut Kohl. Her rise to Chancellor was relatively rapid. The skills in diplomacy she had gained while trying to educate herself without causing repercussions from those in authority, serves her well in all the roles she plays.

Artist Kat Campau's interest in making art usually concerns color. She has a visceral reaction to it, in all combinations. She thinks of fabric as a painting medium when she is making a quilt. When Kat turned forty, it seemed to her that she became invisible. It was harder to attract the attention of clerks in stores, waiters in restaurants, and people in general. In reaction to that feeling of invisibility, she made a series of art quilts expressing this feeling of being ignored. The quilt she made for *HERstory* is part of her effort to give courage to the gray-haired ladies who are the underlying structure of society.

The doll-like figure on this quilt is shown climbing the Berlin Wall. It's a way of expressing the obstacles Angela Merkel had to overcome on her way to ruling reunited Germany. The misty building in the distance is the traditional seat of power, the Reichstag. The overall drab color of the scene represents the deprivation people endured under Communist control. The separated coil of barbed wire is symbolic of the beginning of reunification that allowed Ms. Merkel to come to the attention of people in the west. The art quilt was created using hand appliqué, and hand and machine embroidery. It was machine quilted. Inktense colored pencils were used to highlight the piece.

139

Lee Miller (1907–1977)

. . . only female combat photographer in
Europe during World War II.

Lee Miller

Jim Smith and Andy Brunhammer

Tampa, Florida

*"No question that German civilians knew what went
on. Railway into Dachau camp runs past villas, with
trains of dead or semi-dead deportees. I usually don't
take pictures of horrors. But don't think that every
town and every area isn't rich with them. I hope* Vogue
will feel it can publish these pictures." —Lee Miller

Elizabeth Miller was a model, photographer, war correspondent,
actor, photojournalist, and gourmet cook. She was born April 23,
1907, in Poughkeepsie, New York. Her father, Theodore, used
his children, especially Lee, pursuing his photographic hobby,
often photographing Lee in the nude starting about age twelve.

Lee Miller's entrance into the world of modeling began
by accident when she was prevented from being hit by a car
by Condé Nast, the publisher of *Vogue*. Awed by her looks,
Nast gave her a job modeling. Bored with modeling Lee
journeyed to Paris and convinced photographer Man Ray to
teach her photography. She became his lover, muse, and
collaborator. During that time, Lee met many famous artists,
including Picasso and Max Ernst. She became an exceptional
photographer composing her own self-portraits. She began
doing fashion shoots for French *Vogue*. When Lee and Ray
split up, she moved back to New York and opened her own
portrait studio. She married an Egyptian and moved to Cairo.

Bored again, she returned to Paris, where she met surrealist
artist Roland Penrose. Still married to the Egyptian, she was
living with Penrose when World War II broke out. She reinvented
herself as a photojournalist and documented the London Blitz.
After the US entered the war, she became a war correspondent.
On April 29, 1945, she walked with American forces entering
Dachau to liberate those still there. She took photos of the
atrocities. Later in the day, she went to Munich and entered

Hitler's apartment. She posed in his bathtub for a photo, with
her boots and a military uniform positioned carefully on the
floor and a chair. Hours later Hitler and Eva Braun killed
themselves in their bunker.

Following the war, she divorced her husband and married
Penrose. She became pregnant at forty and gave birth to her
only son Antony. Unable to forget the sights she had seen during
the Liberation, she became depressed and an alcoholic. She
moved to a farmhouse in East Sussex where she filled her days
cooking elaborate gourmet meals for her guests. She lived there
until her death at age seventy in Chiddingly, United Kingdom.

Her son knew nothing of her war correspondent days until
after she died when he found about six thousand of her photos
hidden away. Antony spent much of his time after that trying
to honor her work and her memory.

Many of her wartime photos achieve a surrealist perspective
and acumen: "a bombed chapel, with bricks pouring from its
door, resembles a mouth with a tongue hanging out; a grounded,
air balloon, with two geese in the foreground, is titled *Egg-
ceptional Achievement*."

This quote from Liz Byrski's novel *Gang of Four* says
it all: "'She was some woman that Lee Miller,' said Steve,
leaning across from her. 'She did what she wanted to do and
damn the conventions.'"

Artists Jim Smith and Andy Brunhammer pieced and
appliquéd this quilt and overlaid it with tulle. The artists call
this a mashup of several elements of Lee's life and work. They
used Miller's 1937 *Portrait of Space*, a picture she took in Nr
Siwa, Egypt for inspiration. The German Rolleiflex in the
hanging mirror is the camera she used. The lettering of *Vogue*
honors her years as a model and war correspondent. Lee Miller's
lips were superimposed on the piece in homage to Man Ray's
1934 *Observatory Time—The Lovers* and were photo-transferred
to the fabric.

Mother Teresa (1910–1997)

. . . founded the Missionaries of Charity,
a Roman Catholic congregation of women
dedicated to helping the poor.

A Loving Tribute to Mother Teresa: Turning Negatives into Positives
Meena Schaldenbrand
Plymouth, Michigan

"We think sometimes that poverty is only being hungry, naked and homeless. The poverty of being unwanted, unloved and uncared for is the greatest poverty. We must start in our own homes to remedy this kind of poverty." —Mother Teresa

Mother Teresa was an Albanian born Indian citizen. Christened Gonxha Agnes, she received her First Communion at the age of five and a half and was confirmed when she was six. Her father died when she was eight, and she was raised by her loving mother until she decided at eighteen to become a nun. She joined the Institute of the Virgin Mary, known as the Sisters of Loreto, in Ireland. Gonxha received the name, Sister Mary Teresa. In 1929, she arrived in India to join the Sisters of Loreto Entally where she taught at St. Mary's School for Girls. In 1937, Sister Mary Teresa made her Final Profession of Vows becoming known as Mother Teresa from then on. She continued teaching at the school and became the principal.

In 1946 she heard a call that she was convinced came from Jesus himself. He asked Mother Teresa to establish the Missionaries of Charity to minister to the poorest of the poor. After two years of discernment and testing, she was given permission to proceed.

Mother Teresa dressed in her blue and white sari for the first time in 1948 and went to live among the poor, taking up residence with the Little Sisters of the Poor. Daily she ministered to the poor and downtrodden.

She founded the Missionaries of Charity, a Roman Catholic congregation of women dedicated to helping the poor in 1950. They opened their first house outside of India in Venezuela in 1965 with five sisters. The first Missionaries of Charity home in the United States was established in the South Bronx, New York. By 2012, they had grown to 4,500 sisters, in 133 countries.

Mother Teresa worked with orphanages, hospices, and charity centers and cared for the poor, orphans, homeless, lepers, refugees, the blind, disabled, aged, alcoholics, and victims of floods, epidemics, and famine. She championed the unborn and cared for unwanted children.

In 1971, she was the first recipient of the Pope John XXIII Peace Prize for her work with the poor, display of Christian charity, and efforts for peace. She was awarded the Nobel Peace Prize "for work undertaken in the struggle to overcome poverty and distress, which also constitutes a threat to peace" in 1979. She lived a simple life by her values and principles and is considered one of the greatest humanitarians of the twentieth century. Mother Teresa died in 1997 and was canonized as Saint Teresa of Calcutta in 2016.

Artist Meena Schaldenbrand, born in India, created this piece to honor Mother Teresa, amazed to see someone become a saint in her lifetime. The quilt is blue and white as they are the colors of her convent's saris. Meena printed out the text and the heart on a home printer, traced it onto fabric with a lightbox and Frixion pen and hand embroidered the text using the chain stitch because that is a common embroidery stitch in India. She used positive and negative images throughout the design as symbols of Mother Teresa turning negative circumstances into positive results. Meena painted the white lace to blue for the center heart. The piece was created using machine-appliqué. It is free-motion quilted. Meena embellished it using beads, a cross charm, lace, painted lace, ribbons, rickrack, and trims.

Louise Nevelson (1899–1988)

. . . challenged the dominant stereotype of the male sculptor, opening doors for women in sculpture and installation art.

Channeling Nevelson: Mostly Gray
Pauline Salzman
Gulfport, Florida

"I believe in my work and the joy of it. You have to be with the work and the work has to be with you. It absorbs you totally and you absorb it totally. Everything must fall by the wayside by comparison."
—Louise Nevelson

Leah Berliawsky was born in Russia. Her family immigrated to the US when she was six because of cultural strains between the Jewish community and the Tsarist Russians, changing her name to Louise so she would be more American. Louise dreamed of going to New York to study art. When she married Charles Nevelson in 1920, the two of them moved there. She had a son in 1922. From 1928 to 1930 she studied at the Art Students League. In 1931 she left her son with her parents, divorced Charles, and went to Munich to study with Hans Hofmann. She returned to New York in 1932 where she met Frida Kahlo and Diego Rivera, eventually helping the muralist with his paintings for the New York Workers' School. She worked for the Works Progress Administration, WPA, through the Federal Art Project. One critic wrote, "We learned the artist is a woman, in time to check our enthusiasm . . . otherwise we might have hailed these sculptural expressions as by surely a great figure among moderns."

Louise Nevelson emerged in an art world of sculptors dominated by men. She paved the way for the Feminist Art movement of the 1970s. She proved that women's artwork could be done on a large-scale. Arranging objects found in debris piles, she created large assemblages then spray painted them gray or white. She later included Plexiglas, aluminum, and steel in her works, allowing her to expand the size and complexity of her work. She is considered one of America's most innovative sculptors.

Winifred Klarin, artist Pauline Salzman's husband's aunt, knew Louise. Winifred was the first woman invited to be a member of an all men's art society called the Hylozoists. They called themselves junk painters. They used wood chips, glass, cement, wire, and whatever they could find.

Louise Nevelson holds a special place in Pauline's heart because she helped women like Pauline's Aunt Win achieve their destiny. She carved a place for women in the art world. Pauline is continuing the tradition of Harriet Powers, creator of the hand appliquéd *Bible Quilt*. As Harriet did, Pauline wants her quilts to tell a story. She loves to work with textiles; the touch and the feel of fabric and thread are powerful. Each quilt is different and poses new challenges. More often than not Pauline's quilts make you smile. Quilting is therapy. Pauline gets lost in the making of each piece. She wants her quilts to appeal on a few levels: the overall image, the stitching, and the story. The overall image should pull the viewer in to get a closer look. The stitching sculpts the object forming the shape, the roundness, and the movement. The quilting should not just lay there and be flat. It should complete the image.

Channeling Nevelson: Mostly Gray is a sculpture of boxes stacked and filled with the debris found in a woman's world; the kitchen. It was created in fabric and thread. Using a mostly gray palette with a little bit of color was a challenge. Pauline added the small bit of color that every woman needs. Her piece was created using blind-stitch appliqué. Dense quilting gave it the feel of movement. Fabric pens were used to create the plate and the casserole. Each box was built separately and then put together.

Nichelle Nichols (1932–)

. . . groundbreaking role as Lt. Uhura, first non-stereotypical role portrayed by a black woman in television history.

Nichelle Nichols: The Next Generation
Joanne Bast
Littlestown, Pennsylvania

"All the people in Star Trek *will always be known as those characters. And what characters to have attached to your name in life! The show is such a phenomenon all over the world." —Nichelle Nichols*

Nichelle Nichols's parents encouraged her talent in singing and dancing. She studied dance at the Chicago Ballet Academy and hoped to someday perform on Broadway. She sang with the Duke Ellington Orchestra and danced with Sammy Davis, Jr. in the movie *Porgy & Bess*. But it was a guest appearance on a short-lived TV series that gave her the break that would make her career. The creator of that series, Gene Roddenberry, was the creator of *Star Trek*, a science fiction TV series about a space exploration vehicle and its crew. It premiered in 1966 and ran for three seasons. He offered Nichelle the role of Lt. Uhura, the bridge communications officer, saying that he would like to "add a little color to the bridge." *Star Trek* went on to break many barriers both technological and social. Many taboo subjects got past the censors by being staged on other worlds, not the least of which was the first televised interracial kiss between Captain Kirk and Lieutenant Uhura.

As Lt. Uhura, Nichols appeared professional, competent, in charge, and accepted as an equal by other bridge staff. It was not so behind the scenes. Nichelle persevered through much bias and discrimination, even having her fan mail withheld. She became a role model for the next generation of girls of all colors.

Nichelle almost quit the show but was encouraged to continue by Martin Luther King, Jr., who called her "the first non-stereotypical role portrayed by a black woman in television history" and impressed on her the impact her character was having on the next generation of girls—all girls but especially those of color. What a loss it would have been if she had let personal slights discourage her. The next generation would not have been the same.

Nichelle Nichols has continued to support girls entering the sciences and has assisted in recruiting minority and female personnel into NASA. Nichelle found and recruited five women, three African American men, and one Asian American. Her recruits include Sally Ride, Mae Jemison, and former NASA administrator Charles Bolden. Actress Whoopi Goldberg is one of her most famous fans. Whoopi credits the role of Uhura on *Star Trek* with convincing her nine-year-old self that she could be anything she wanted to be. Nichols continues to raise funds for charities through StarPower, which encourages celebrities to become involved in worthwhile causes.

Artist Joanne Bast chose to portray Nichelle Nichols as both a young Lt. Uhura and as a mature advocate for NASA. The quilt plays black on white against white on black. She decided to use the balance of black and white to represent the confidence of command, authority, and equality. Joanne used X's and O's to commemorate the first interracial kiss on TV—only one of *Star Trek*'s groundbreaking firsts. Joanne also paid tribute to Nichols' vocal background by incorporating music-inspired fabrics as well as a black glittery knit (interfaced and stitched for stability) that just cried "space." The children represent the ongoing reach of inspiring the next generation.

Michelle Obama (1964–)

. . . first African American First Lady; advocated for healthy families and girls' education.

Michelle Obama
Julie Hallquist
Tucson, Arizona

"We learned about gratitude and humility—that so many people had a hand in our success, from the teachers who inspired us to the janitors who kept our school clean . . . and we were taught to value everyone's contribution and treat everyone with respect." —Michelle Obama

A Chicago native, Michelle Obama was raised in a close-knit family. She went to Princeton and majored in sociology. She earned her JD from Harvard Law School in 1988. Michelle worked as an associate at Sidley Austin, where she was assigned an intern, Barack Obama. Believing that coworkers should not date, Michelle initially turned down Barack's invitations. Eventually, she relented, and they married in 1992. She decided to pursue a career in public service and worked as an assistant to Mayor Richard Daley, as an assistant commissioner of planning and development, and as an executive director of a nonprofit leadership-training program. Michelle held several positions at the University of Chicago where she continued to work part-time until shortly before her husband's inauguration.

Although she continued to work throughout Barack's campaigns for Senate and the Presidency, she was actively involved in his campaign, attracting the attention of the American public.

When Michelle became First Lady, she reminded everyone that her first responsibility was to be a mom to her two daughters. She planted a vegetable garden at the White House to promote healthy eating of locally grown food. Next, she launched Let's Move!, a program dedicated to solving the problem of childhood obesity within a generation. As a result of Michelle's super-mothering, fifty million children now have healthier meal and snack choices in their schools and eleven million kids in Let's Move! "Active Schools" have sixty minutes of physical activity each day.

Because doors were opened to Michelle as a result of her own education, she believes that "knowledge is power." That conviction and the opportunity to meet Malala Yousafzai caused the Obamas to launch Let Girls Learn. Sixty-two million girls worldwide are not in school or face other educational challenges so Let Girls Learn works to change the perception of the value of girls at the individual, community, and institutional levels. Let Girls Learn fosters an environment which enables girls' education and equips girls to make life decisions and significant contributions to society. Michelle Obama has said that girls' education is an issue that is personal to her, and one she intends to work on for the rest of her life.

Artist Julie Hallquist loves the challenge of using commercially printed fabrics to paint a scene or tell a story. Julie enjoys digging through her stash and finding just the right color and texture to evoke woodgrain or water gives her a feeling of deep satisfaction. Julie also loves thread—both using it in a decorative stitch to draw attention to an area, or provide a touch of contrast, and to have it melt into the fabric and simply provide texture. As an art quilter, most of her work is representational, but Julie usually includes some bit of traditional technique in the design to honor her grandmother and the other women who kept the quilting tradition alive and passed it on to her. In this quilt, the patchwork of different ethnic fabrics represents the different cultures worldwide where adolescent girls are deprived of an education and benefit from the Let Girls Learn program. Julie chose the royal purple color for her dress and the background of the First Lady block to designate the position and the grace with which she conducted herself. Julie used fused raw-edge appliqué to create the face, arms, and hands. It is also machine pieced, free-motion embroidered, and thread-painted. It involves bobbin work where the stitching is done on the wrong side of the piece so that the bobbin threads end up on the front of the quilt.

Mary Oliver (1935–)

. . . won the Pulitzer Prize for Poetry in 1984 and the National Book Award in 1992; best-selling poet in recent times.

Mary Oliver: Poetic Inspirations
Barbara Dove
Alexandria, Virginia

"When it's over, I want to say: all my life I was a bride married to amazement. I was the bridegroom, taking the world into my arms." —Mary Oliver

Born in Ohio in 1935 and living much of her adult life in Provincetown, Massachusetts, Mary Oliver began writing poetry at age fourteen. Her first book was published when she was twenty-eight. She won the Pulitzer Prize for Poetry in 1984 for her fourth book, *American Primitive*. Her latest book, *Upstream: Selected Essays* was published in October 2016.

Mary Oliver is fascinated with the natural world and interprets it with empathy and powerful imagery through writing. She creates thought-provoking poetry that contemplates how precious and short our life on Earth is. In many poems, she encourages us to slow down and go for a soulful walk in nature—indicating that this uplifting accomplishment does more to nourish our spirit than anything in our fast-paced modern life. She carefully observes nature and uses it metaphorically to express facets of the human condition, including emotional themes like faith, joy, love, loss, aging, and the search for the true meaning of life. Her poems are short, story-like, and humorous at times, while her words are full of imagery, making the universal truths easier to understand.

Some of her books include *Red Bird*, *Dog Songs*, and *Blue Horses*. In *Blue Horses*, in a poem called "Drifting," she talks about walking along a path in the rain and how a feeling of holiness unexpectedly swept over her as she weightlessly drifted along not unlike a cloud. Here, Barbara believes, Mary emphasizes the importance of a cloud as the metaphor for nourishing the beauty of the Earth with rain, as well as infusing her spirit with gratefulness for being alive.

In one of her most famous poems called "The Summer Day," she presents the idea that a simple day of walking in the woods can help put your life into perspective. Her message is that listening, closely observing, and learning from nature is the true gift of life. Her poetic messages are a reminder to the reader to actively experience the gift of being and especially feeling alive, through the power of paying attention to the simple beauty in life, and further, to consider its contrast to today's modern world, complex as it is. While the messages she delivers are powerful, the words are simple, uplifting, and a joy to read.

Pictorial art quilts are exciting because of the creative freedom and opportunities afforded during the process. Barbara enjoys selecting the fabric and designing the initial idea with paper and pencil, although the idea may change as the process unfolds. Barbara selected the poet Mary Oliver as she is inspired by the imagery of her poetry. Barbara decided to make a quilt about what inspired her many poems—the woods and pond near her home in New England. She selected one of her most famous poems with a profound message to depict in the scene, called "The Summer Day." This poem appeared in volume one of *New and Selected Poems*, for which she won the National Book Award in 1992. Barbara added her own twist on the meaning of Mary's message through the use of fabric color, whereby the warm foreground colors represent Mary's visual clarity and love of life, while the foggy background connotes an individual's uncertain but hopefully uplifting future, upon heeding her words. It is machine appliquéd, machine quilted, and stuffed to create dimension through the use of trapunto.

Jacqueline Kennedy Onassis (1929–1994)

. . . restored the White House to its original elegance, and became the only First Lady to win an Emmy Award.

Jackie
Susan Lenz
Columbia, South Carolina

"You have to be doing something you enjoy. That is a definition of happiness: Complete use of one's faculties along lines leading to excellence in a life affording them scope. It applies to women as well as to men. We can't all reach it, but we can try to reach it to some degree." —Jacqueline Kennedy Onassis

Jacqueline Bouvier was born with a silver spoon in her mouth, daughter of a wealthy stockbroker. She enjoyed horseback riding, French, and ballet lessons. She attended the prestigious Miss Porter's School and was named Debutante of the Year. She went to Vassar, spending her junior year in France. Returning to the States, she transferred to George Washington University, earning her BA in French literature.

She met senator-elect John F. Kennedy, and they married in 1953. Jackie gave birth to Caroline in 1957. Jackie encouraged her husband to write *Profiles in Courage*, about US senators' acts of bravery and integrity, and subsequently helped edit it. John F. Kennedy ran for president in 1960, narrowly defeating Nixon to become the thirty-fifth president of the United States. Less than three weeks later, Jackie gave birth to their son, John Fitzgerald Kennedy Jr. known to all as John-John. The Kennedys' third child, Patrick Bouvier Kennedy, would be born prematurely on August 7, 1963, and die two days later.

Jackie was appalled at the White House décor. She transformed the White House into a museum of American history and culture, going to extraordinary lengths to find art and furniture owned by past presidents, including George Washington, James Madison, and Abraham Lincoln. Jackie gave a televised tour of the restored White House on February 14, 1962. Fifty-six million viewers watched it, and Mrs. Kennedy won an honorary Emmy Award for her performance.

As a patron of the arts, Jackie invited the nation's leading writers, artists, musicians, and scientists to dine at the White House with the officials, diplomats, and statesmen. Jackie frequently traveled abroad. Her knowledge of foreign cultures and her ability to speak three foreign languages fostered international goodwill. She was received so well in France that President Kennedy introduced himself as "the man who accompanied Jacqueline Kennedy to Paris."

On November 22, 1963, Jackie was waving to the crowds alongside the president in a Lincoln Continental convertible in Dallas, Texas, when he was shot and killed by Lee Harvey Oswald, making her a widow at the age of thirty-four.

Jacqueline Kennedy became Mrs. Aristotle Onassis in 1968 when she married the Greek shipping magnate. He died seven years later, making Jackie a widow for the second time. She went to work as an editor at Viking Press in New York City, then moved to Doubleday, where she served as senior editor. Jacqueline Bouvier Kennedy Onassis died on May 19, 1994, at the age of sixty-four. She was buried beside President John F. Kennedy at Arlington National Cemetery.

Jackie was a fashion icon. This art quilt was inspired by her impeccable taste in fashion, in particular her triple strand simulated pearl necklace, white gloves, and the classic pink Chanel suit and matching pillbox hat that were captured in the images taken after her husband's assassination.

Artist Susan Lenz used several public domain images and altered them significantly, using photo manipulation to draw attention to the faux-pearl necklace. Most of the White House images of Jackie are in black-and-white. Susan made her piece in black and pink, the color of the outfit Jackie wore on the day of JFK's assassination. Susan added black millinery netting symbolizing the black chiffon veil she wore for JFK's funeral because it is iconic of hats from that era. Susan created Jackie's portrait using three things that are in our collective memories: her pearls, her pink suit, and a mourning headpiece. It is a whole cloth quilt. It was embellished using free-motion machine embroidery and hand beading.

Rosa Parks (1913–2005)

. . . refused to surrender her seat on an Alabama bus, igniting the Civil Rights movement in the United States.

It All Started on a Bus
Carole Nicholas
Oakton, Virginia

"I don't think well of people who are prejudiced against people because of race. The only way for prejudiced people to change is for them to decide for themselves that all human beings should be treated fairly. We can't force them to think that way." —Rosa Parks

Rosa Parks was born in 1913, in Tuskegee, Alabama, and went to Montgomery Industrial School for Girls. Rosa was encouraged to take advantage of any opportunity that came her way, and they were very few. Mrs. Parks said in an interview, "Back then we didn't have any civil rights. I remember going to sleep hearing the Klan ride at night and hearing a lynching and being afraid the house would burn down."

After attending Alabama State Teachers College, Rosa and her husband, Raymond settled in Montgomery where they joined the local chapter of the NAACP and worked hard to improve the lives of African Americans.

On December 1, 1955, Rosa Parks was returning home from working as a seamstress when she refused to give up her seat to a white man on a public bus. She was arrested and fined. This event led to the formation of the Montgomery Improvement Association, led by a young pastor, Dr. Martin Luther King, Jr. A bus boycott was called for which lasted 382 days and attracted international attention. The subsequent US Supreme Court decision struck down the Montgomery ordinance and outlawed racial segregation on public transportation.

In 1957, Rosa and Raymond moved to Detroit. The actions of Rosa Parks, Dr. Martin Luther King, Jr., and others led to the passing of the Civil Rights Act of 1964. It banned racial segregation in public places; outlawed job discrimination on the basis of race, religion, sex, and national origin; and established fair uniform voting standards.

After Raymond died in 1977, Rosa founded the Rosa and Raymond Parks Institute for Self-Development which sponsors Pathways to Freedom, an annual summer program for teenagers. Her courage, determination, and strength changed the course of history and transformed the lives of millions. President Clinton awarded Rosa Parks the Presidential Medal of Freedom in 1996. She received a Congressional Gold Medal in 1999.

Mrs. Parks died in Detroit on October 24, 2005, at age ninety-two. Her casket was placed in the Rotunda of the United States Capitol for two days so the nation could pay respect to this extraordinary woman. She is the only woman and the second African American to lie in state at the Capitol, an honor usually reserved for American Presidents.

The words on artist Carole Nicholas' quilt were written by Kiari Day, a single mom living near Pittsburgh, Pennsylvania, in 2008, on a bedsheet banner for Barack Obama's first Presidential campaign. Ms. Day rightfully credits Rosa Parks with being the person on whose shoulders Martin and Obama stood. Her "poem" was incorporated into a rap song by Jay-Z and was quoted by Hillary Clinton at a 2016 campaign concert in Cleveland, Ohio.

Carole hand embroidered words using silk twist between the quilting lines. The two quotes that she embroidered and that were attributed to Rosa are: "The only tired I was, was tired of giving in" and "Nah," a pop-culture version of what she actually said which was a very clear, "No." She also embroidered the titles bestowed on Rosa by the United States Congress, "First Lady of Civil Rights" and "Mother of the Freedom Movement." The design and words were drawn on this quilt with Sharpie permanent marker and Identipen. The bus was filled in with fabric paint and Inktense watercolor pencils. The bus was machine appliquéd. Carole's piece was machine and hand quilted.

Rosa sat

so Martin could walk,
Martin walked
so Obama could run,
Obama ran
so our children can fly.

Nancy Pelosi (1940–)

. . . first woman to be elected as speaker of the US House of Representatives.

Madame Speaker

Shoshana Spiegel

Herndon, Virginia

"Let's just do what is right for the American people. And those of us who are involved in politics and government know that our responsibility is to the American people, that we have a responsibility to find our common ground, to seek it and to find it."
—*Nancy Pelosi*

Nancy D'Alesandro was born into an Italian-American family in Baltimore on March 26, 1940. She was the sixth child and the only girl. Her father, Thomas, was a well-known Democratic politician. He served as a member of the Maryland State of Delegates, the US House of Representatives, and later as mayor of Baltimore. Nancy was constantly exposed to the comings and goings of constituents and politicians at home and often accompanied her father to Democratic gatherings.

She attended Trinity Washington University in Washington, DC, and graduated with a degree in political science. She met Paul Pelosi there, and they married in 1963. When they moved from New York City to Northern California in 1969, she became involved in the Democratic Party as a volunteer. During this time Mrs. Pelosi was raising five children. She did not aspire to hold office, but she was excellent at fundraising. In 1976 she was elected to be a member of the Democratic National Committee from California, a position that she held for thirty years. She

also served shorter terms as party chair for Northern California and then for all of California. When a friend who was a member of the House of Representatives passed away, Nancy was encouraged to succeed her. She won the election and has represented what is now California's Twelfth District since 1987. It encompasses most of the city and county of San Francisco.

Nancy Pelosi took on the AIDS crisis, which affected many of her constituents. She was also concerned about US relations with China and maintaining the status quo of Social Security. Nancy served on the Appropriations and Intelligence committees in the House. She was elected as House Minority Whip in 2001, becoming the first woman to hold that position. She moved up to Minority Leader in 2004 when Dick Gephardt resigned. In 2006, when the Democrats achieved a majority in the House of Representatives, Mrs. Pelosi was elected the Speaker of the House, the first woman to hold the position. She served in that capacity from 2007 to 2011. She resumed the position of Minority Leader in 2011.

Artist Shoshana Spiegel is amazed at Nancy Pelosi's commitment to public service and the energy that she brings to her many roles. Shana wanted to express this by having her assume a dynamic pose that demonstrates her passion. She chose colors to portray her vibrant personality and embellished with beads, which are her trademark accessory. The piece is machine appliquéd and machine quilted. Shana hand embellished it with grosgrain ribbon, cording, buttons, and beads.

Frances Perkins (1880–1965)

. . . first woman to hold a US Cabinet post;
author of much of FDR's New Deal.

Frances Perkins
Betsy True
Alexandria, Virginia

*"The door might not be opened to a woman again
for a long, long time, and I had a kind of duty to other
women to walk in and sit down on the chair that was
offered, and so establish the right of others long hence
and far distant in geography to sit in the high seats."*
—Frances Perkins

Fannie Coralie Perkins' parents taught her how to work hard
and expected her to study and go to college. After graduating
from Mount Holyoke with a degree in chemistry and physics,
Fannie's parents encouraged her to be a teacher and find a nice
man to marry. She had other ideas. She moved to Illinois,
changed her name to Frances and began looking for a job in
social work. Unable to do so, she started teaching and volunteering
at Hull House, founded by Jane Addams. While working there
with the poor and unemployed, she discovered her passion and
life's calling. She moved to Philadelphia and worked with
immigrant girls, then moved on to New York City where she
had a fellowship at the New York School of Philanthropy to
investigate malnutrition in children living in Hell's Kitchen.
Frances earned her master's degree at Columbia University.

In 1910 she became head of the New York Consumers
League. The following year Frances witnessed the Triangle
Shirtwaist Factory Fire of 1911 in New York City. It was the
worst industrial disaster of its time. One hundred forty-six
died, mostly young women, many of them immigrants. Doors
to the fire escapes were locked to keep the workers in place,
so they could not escape, and the fire wagon ladders didn't
reach to the top floors. Some jumped out the windows of the
building to their deaths. It was a pivotal event in Frances' life.
It inspired her to quit her job as a professor and begin working
to improve workers' lives. The tragedy initiated many changes
in working conditions. Through her efforts, New York was at
the forefront of reform.

Frances began working with Roosevelt in 1929 when,
newly elected as governor of New York, FDR appointed her
as the first Commissioner of the New York State Department
of Labor.

During Roosevelt's presidency, Frances served as Secretary
of Labor, the first woman to serve in a cabinet position. She
initiated the Civilian Conservation Corps, the Public Works
Administration, the Social Security Act, and the Fair Labor
Standards Act. Frances was responsible for establishing
unemployment benefits and other benefits for the elderly and
the poor. She established the first minimum wage and overtime
laws for American workers, laws regulating child labor, and
was largely responsible for the adoption of the standard forty-
hour work week. Frances was the author of much of the New
Deal under FDR, failing only in securing universal access to
health care.

She is the longest serving Labor Secretary, serving from
1933 to 1945 under Presidents Roosevelt and Harry Truman.
Being in the Cabinet, she was also the first woman to be in the
Presidential line of succession. The Department of Labor
headquarters is named the Frances Perkins Building.

The Triangle Shirtwaist Factory Fire of 1911 is depicted
in the background of this quilt. Two shadowy figures are shown
against the building, and one on the next to top floor is getting
ready to jump. Artist Betsy True wanted to give the feel of the
black and white pictures of the fire, but she also wanted Frances
to come alive, so she is shown in color. Betsy used commercial
cotton prints, batiks, and sheer fabrics. It was created with
fusible machine-appliqué and machine quilted. Detail was
added using pen and ink.

born 1880, died 1965
Secretary of Labor
1933-1945 (longest
serving in that position)
under Roosevelt and
Truman. After she
witnessed the Triangle
Shirtwaist Factory fire in
1911, she dedicated herself
to improving the lives of
workers.

Perkins was the principal
architect of the New Deal,
the Social Security Act and
the Fair Labor Standards
Act. She also advocated
for universal access to
health care.

FRANCES PERKINS

1ST WOMAN IN CABINET

Queen Elizabeth II (1926–)

. . . longest serving monarch in British history.

Her Majesty

Susan Auden Wood

Croydon South, Victoria, Australia

"The upward course of a nation's history is due in the long run to the soundness of heart of its average men and women." —Elizabeth II

Elizabeth Alexandra Mary (known to her family as Lilibet) was born to the second son of King George V. After the abdication of her uncle, King Edward VIII, her father became King George VI, and she became next in line to the throne. She spent a quiet and relatively normal childhood with her parents and sister Margaret. Both girls were tutored at home. During World War II she joined the Auxiliary Territorial Service and became an expert driver as well as an auto mechanic, a skill that in later life proved extraneous. She loved riding horses, and certainly, the Queen of England never needed to fix her own automobile. When the war was over, she and her sister Margaret were allowed to mingle anonymously amongst the public on Victory in Europe Day (VE Day).

Princess Elizabeth met her future husband, Prince Philip when she was thirteen. They eventually married in 1947 when she was twenty-one. Since her wedding took place on the heels of World War II, Princess Elizabeth collected ration coupons to get fabrics for her gown. Queen Elizabeth's coronation was held on June 2, 1953, sixteen months after she ascended the throne following the death of her father. She wore the St. Edward's Crown which is only worn once by a monarch at the moment of Coronation. The King George IV State Diadem was worn by her during the Coronation procession. It is worn to and from the State Opening of Parliament and appears on all stamps. As a Constitutional Monarch, Queen Elizabeth doesn't get involved in political matters or reveal her political views. She has worked with thirteen prime ministers during her reign. In 1965 she made a groundbreaking trip to Germany, the first British Monarch to tour there in more than five decades. In 2011 she became the first British Monarch to visit Ireland since 1911. Queen Elizabeth has modernized the monarchy and welcomed the elimination of the Civil List, which was a public funding system of the monarchy dating back about 250 years. The Royal Family still receives some government support. Queen Elizabeth has headed a total of thirty-two independent countries during her reign. This number has been reduced to sixteen, known as Commonwealth realms. Queen Elizabeth II has dedicated her adult life as Queen to being there for the British people.

When artist Susan Auden Wood was deciding on a design for her quilt to honor Queen Elizabeth II, there were just too many possible scenarios to include in her ninety years of life. Sue decided to depict her in a postage stamp. Throughout the Commonwealth, all countries have had numerous stamps over the years honoring Her Majesty. Sue's childhood stamp albums finally had a chance to shine, and she managed to source the perfect background fabric in the London map design. There were many famous and well-known landmarks, streets, buildings, and parks. Queen Elizabeth's face was made using a technique mixing four to five shades of fabric coloring to make her features realistic, then appliquéd. Sue made this piece using a combination of piecing plus a method of quilting she learned in a class with Anna Williams from New Zealand which she used for the face and crown. Her quilt honoring Queen Elizabeth was made using all cotton fabrics and various threads for embroidery.

Ann Richards (1933–2006)

. . . as governor of Texas she opened the doors of government to women and minorities.

Texas Governor Ann Richards
Teresa Bristow
Springfield, Virginia

"I did not want my tombstone to read, 'She kept a really clean house.' I think I'd like them to remember me by saying, 'She opened government to everyone.'"
—Ann Richards

Texas Governor Ann Richards was admired for her quick wit, feisty attitude, strong personality, and a passion for the rights of all.

Dorothy Ann Willis was born in Lakeview, Texas. Participation in the Girls State mock-government assembly of students piqued her interest in government. Ann received her BA from Baylor University in 1953. She married David Richards, and they had four children. Ann volunteered on political campaigns and taught junior high school, later saying it was the hardest job she ever had.

In 1976 Ann Richards became the first woman elected County Commissioner and elected to a second term. She was the first woman elected State Treasurer and the first female to win a statewide office in Texas. Ann was the first woman elected Governor of Texas in her own right.

Not all went well. She and David Richards divorced, and she was treated for alcoholism. She later said that she had seen the bottom of life at that point and was afraid that she would lose her zaniness and sense of humor. Thankfully she remained the sharp-witted, strong, charismatic person that was loved by so many.

Her speech at the 1988 Democratic National Convention in Atlanta brought her national attention. It was one of the highlights of the convention. One of artist Teresa Bristow's favorite quotes from that speech was "Ginger Rogers did everything Fred Astaire did, she just did it backwards and in high heels." (Note the high heels in the top right-hand corner of the quilt.)

In 1990, Ann Richards became the Governor of Texas. She was passionate about the rights of women and minorities. She believed in open government and appointed more women and minorities than any of her predecessors. She added the first African Americans and females to the Texas Rangers, keeping a campaign promise.

She believed political appointments should reflect the state demographics and that there was a disparity between what government was intended to be and what it was. Confronting and winning over the "good ol' boy system" was an uphill battle. She expanded the state's prison system, cracking down on the number of prisoners being paroled, and instituting a substance abuse program. She supported the creation of the Texas lottery using funds to help finance public schools. She vetoed a bill that would have allowed the destruction of the Edwards Aquifer, a major underground water system, wishing she could have preserved more parklands.

Ann started the Ann Richards School for Young Women Leaders located in Austin, Texas, ranked one of the best schools in Texas and nationwide. It prepares secondary school girls for college studies. The students develop real-world service projects, developing leadership and problem-solving skills.

Artist Teresa Bristow knew that she wanted to show some of Ann's history on the quilt. She included the Texas flag, state seal, and capitol. Teresa created each section of the background as an individual piece using a mixture of piecing and appliqué. She placed them on the design wall to determine placement in the overall design and relationship and pieced border portions to bring it all together. The portrait of Ms. Richards was created separately using a layered appliqué technique and then placed on top of the background. Ann's portrait is covered in bridal tulle. The portrait, state seal, capitol, and high heels are raw-edge appliquéd.

Sally Ride (1951–2012)

. . . first female astronaut to go into space.

Ride Sally Ride
Deb Berkebile
Conneaut, Ohio

"I think it's important for little girls growing up, and young women, to have one in every walk of life. So from that point of view, I'm proud to be a role model!"
—Sally Ride

Sally Ride was highly educated, so it was no surprise when she joined NASA as the first female American astronaut. She earned a bachelor of science, a bachelor of English, a master of science, and a doctorate in physics. Ride joined NASA in 1978, after answering an advertisement, and became the first American woman in space in 1983. Ride remains the youngest American astronaut to have traveled to space, having done so at the age of thirty-two.

Before her first space flight, she was subjected to media attention due to her gender. No other astronaut was ever asked questions like these: "Will the flight affect your reproductive organs?" and "Do you weep when things go wrong on the job?" Her response was genuine: she saw herself in only one way—as an astronaut. She overcame adversity in dealing with the press and becoming a role model to women everywhere, which helped to usher in an era of equality in human spaceflight. She was on the crew of three Space Shuttle missions. Following her career at NASA, she joined the faculty of the University of California at San Diego as a professor, teaching physics and directing their California Space Institute. She cofounded Sally Ride Science, a company which encourages young girls and women to take science as career options. She authored five science books for children.

Sally Ride served on the President's Committee of Advisors on Science and Technology and served on many boards. She is the only person to have served on the commissions investigating the tragedies of both the Challenger and the Columbia space shuttles.

Sally died of pancreatic cancer on July 23, 2012. President Obama said soon after her death "She inspires generations of young girls to reach for the stars (for she) showed us that there are no limits to what we can achieve."

Sally Ride was Deb's first subject choice because she stood for women achieving their dreams and boldly going places where no woman had gone before. In that spirit, artist Deb Berkebile took great joy in using a technique that she had never tried. Deb loves trying out new techniques, pushing herself to new levels. The construction of her piece started with two images, one of Ride and one of the shuttle. Deb manipulated them in Photoshop, using special filters, to make one image. The image then was printed on fabric. After the image was transferred onto fabric Deb began using the new technique of "flinging paint." She used Dye-Na-Flow paints in all colors of the spectrum. Each color was applied separately. The piece was then quilted on a longarm machine to add unique details of the launch pad, shuttle exhaust plumes, shuttle body/ wings, and of Sally herself—hair, clothing, and facial features. The NASA logo was sponge painted on for a graffiti effect.

Eleanor Roosevelt (1884–1962)

. . . cowrote the Universal Declaration of
Human Rights.

Eleanor Roosevelt

Nancy Hershberger

Breezewood, Pennsylvania

*"A woman is like a tea bag—you can't tell how strong
she is until you put her in hot water."*
—*Eleanor Roosevelt*

Eleanor was always a Roosevelt. Born Anna Eleanor Roosevelt, she was the niece of Theodore Roosevelt, twenty-sixth president of the United States. Having lost both of her parents by the time she was ten, she was raised by her maternal grandmother and attended a finishing school in London. Returning home to make her debut following the ascendancy of her uncle to the Presidency, she ran into her father's cousin, Sara Roosevelt and her son Franklin on a train. Friendship blossomed, and three years later they were married, with President Theodore Roosevelt giving away the bride. As a wife and mother of five children, she chose to remain in the marriage despite infidelities. Eleanor worked for him, with him, and sometimes against him, redefining the role of First Lady. She vowed to reduce the White House budget by twenty-five percent, simplify the calendar, and be the President's eyes and ears. She held her own Press Conferences, the first and only First Lady to ever do so. She invited citizens to write to her about their concerns, and they did.

Eleanor listened to their concerns and fought for civil rights twenty years before the Civil Rights movement. The Southern Conference for Human Welfare took place in Birmingham, Alabama in 1938 and Eleanor attended. It was fully integrated on the first day. When the city commissioner, Bull Connor, enforced segregation regulations on the second day, Eleanor parked her chair in the middle of the aisle between the white and black sections, refusing to sit on the white side. She traveled on behalf of her husband, reporting to him on the human condition during the Great Depression. During the war, she traveled the world inspecting hospitals and visiting wounded soldiers, reporting to the President on conditions overseas. Following the death of FDR and the end of World War II, President Harry Truman appointed her to the US delegation to the United Nations. Eleanor was unanimously elected Chair of the UN Commission on Human Rights. She proved a fearless leader, corralling members to write the Universal Declaration of Human Rights, which she considered her greatest accomplishment. Among her other achievements, she was the first chair of the Presidential Commission on the Status of Women, the first US Representative to the UN Commission on Human Rights, and the first chair of the UN Commission on Human Rights.

Artist Nancy Hershberger considers Eleanor the greatest First Lady our country has ever had. Nancy decided to portray Eleanor's self-proclaimed greatest accomplishment, The Universal Declaration of Human Rights, adopted by the United Nations in Paris in 1948. Nancy also included the segregated event in Birmingham, Alabama, and the concert by contralto Marian Anderson on the steps of the Lincoln Memorial in 1939, since Eleanor was instrumental in arranging Marian's performance there.

Nancy knew that an abstract design would not deliver the message that she intended. It had to be a portrait, and it had to be simple. Since the events in Birmingham and Washington, DC, were about color, Nancy used very little color to portray them. The Universal Declaration of Human Rights was about basic rights, so color became meaningless. Sepia tones resonated with Nancy and they worked. The public domain image of Mrs. Roosevelt that Nancy used was found in the FDR Library photo archives. Her piece honoring Eleanor was made of cotton fabric and was made using fusible machine-appliqué. It is machine quilted and painted using Shiva Paintstiks.

Rosie the Riveter (1940–1945)

. . . icon of women's accomplishment in working outside the home, particularly in factories and shipyards during World War II.

Rosie the Riveter
Linda MacDonald
Powell, Wyoming

"All the day long, whether rain or shine,

She's a part of the assembly line.

She's making history, working for victory,

Rosie the Riveter."

—*"Rosie the Riveter" by Redd Evans and John Jacob Loeb*

"Rosie" is the name given to women whose work helped to win World War II. These women filled the many factory jobs left vacant when the men went to fight the war. The history of remarkable women would not be complete without mentioning Rosie the Riveter since she is the embodiment of so many women during World War II. After Rosie, women were in the workforce to stay.

The term "Rosie the Riveter" first appeared in a song composed by Redd Evans and John Jacob Loeb. "Rosies" became the term identified with women who worked with rivets, and any woman whose work helped to win World War II. The famous "We Can Do It!" poster, produced by J. Howard Miller in 1942, was meant to inspire women to work outside the home. The following year, Norman Rockwell painted a piece for the cover of the *Saturday Evening Post* featuring a "Rosie."

The government encouraged women to fill vacant positions, as their way to help the war effort and bring the men home sooner. In addition to working in factories, women of this period were encouraged to grow Victory Gardens and to preserve and can their produce as a means to provide for their families during a time of increasing food shortages. Urban women could grow Victory Gardens in small yards, while rural women took on more responsibility for raising crops as well as the feed needed for farm animals while their men were away in the war. Rosie is a celebration of women and their ability to adapt to and conquer any situation that came along. They accomplished this additional workload and still provided for their children and kept households intact.

In 2015, a Seton Hall University professor, James J. Kimble, began researching the famous poster's origins and he found the original photo of Naomi Parker-Fraley, age twenty, who worked at a machine factory at the Naval Air Station in Alameda, California. She is now ninety-five years old and living in Redding, California. Her photo was taken again, with the signature red bandana, and published in *People* magazine in September 2016.

Artist Linda MacDonald chose to depict Rosie in a factory setting, using commercial gray fabrics for the background. The cloth-painted "Rosie" was purchased from a custom fabric website. Her image was cut out, quilted to wool batting, and then appliquéd onto the background which Linda had previously quilted. Her iconic red dotted head-scarf was made from another piece of fabric. The textile art piece is adorned with Hot Fix rivets in keeping with the theme. Beads were used to add depth and texture to the name. Some of the lyrics to the "Rosie the Riveter" song were printed onto an organza overlay. The verse tells the story of the women who helped win the war.

J.K. Rowling (1965–)

... wrote the bestselling *Harry Potter* series;
created a parallel wizarding world.

The Brilliant Creation of J.K. Rowling
Rosanne Williamson
Warrenton, Virginia

"I was set free because my greatest fear had been realized, and I still had a daughter who I adored, and I had an old typewriter and a big idea. And so rock bottom became a solid foundation on which I rebuilt my life." —J.K. Rowling

Joanne Rowling reportedly got the initial idea for *Harry Potter* while sitting on a delayed train in 1990. Upon returning home, she drafted an outline for the series and began writing. The books tell of the life of Harry Potter, a young wizard, and his classmates at the Hogwarts School of Witchcraft and Wizardry. This writing process took five years, during which she struggled emotionally and financially. In 1997, *Harry Potter and the Philosopher's Stone* by J.K. Rowling, not Joanne Rowling, was finally published. The publisher had suggested initials: *J* for Joanne and *K* for Kathleen, her paternal grandmother because they were worried that the boys, the target audience, wouldn't want to read a book by a female author. The British Children's Book of the Year Award was given to Rowling in 1998 with Warner Brothers getting rights for the first film. When it was published in the US, the title was changed to *Harry Potter and the Sorcerer's Stone*. The record-breaking response to Rowling's books continued, with sales from the books and films totaling more than fifteen billion dollars.

Adults who read crime novels might be surprised that the books that they enjoy by Robert Galbraith are also penned by Rowling. She continues to write fantasy that appeals to her Harry Potter fans, recently collaborating on a story for the stage, *Harry Potter and the Cursed Child Parts One and Two*. She has also made her screenwriting debut with the film *Fantastic Beasts and Where to Find Them* which premiered in 2016.

J.K. Rowling wrote stories that children loved, gave birth to a whole world immortalized in film and a theme park, and captured our imaginations. Indeed she founded an entire empire both fictionally and financially. She was awarded the Order of the British Empire (OBE) in 2001.

Artist Rosanne Williamson created this scene of the children during their third year at Hogwarts which is in *The Prisoner of Azkaban*. Perhaps they are going to visit Hagrid at dusk—breaking school rules. The children, Ron, Harry, and Hermione, are in the foreground in Gryffindor robes. J.K. Rowling's signature, in the lower left-hand corner, is quilted in silver metallic thread coming from a quill to complete the scene.

Hand-dyed ombre fabric was used for the sky. The moon is made of several layers of semi-sheer metallic fabric. *Starry Night* by Van Gogh was the inspiration for the blue iridescent swirly quilting in the sky. The castle is silhouetted against the night sky in three purple fabrics with shadows for a more magical feeling. The front parts of the castle, as well as the cliffs down to the lake, are shaded with Inktense Paintstiks. Lilac tulle makes the reflection of the castle on the darker tulle water of the Black Lake. Hedwig, Harry's owl, is flying over the lake. The Quidditch pitch, with its three rings, is just visible over the hill. All appliqué is raw-edge with machine quilting to secure. The front part of the castle is thread-painted with variegated purple. The little pines are thread-painted.

Hannie Schaft (1920–1945)

. . . Dutch resistance fighter during World War II.

The Girl with the Red Hair
Marijke van Welzen
Vlaardingen, The Netherlands

"I could shoot better!" —Hannie Schaft (last words spoken to a German soldier after having been shot in her execution; the soldier subsequently emptied his machine gun into her)

Hannie Schaft was born as Jannetje Johanna (Jo or Jopie) Schaft in Haarlem, the Netherlands. Her mother was a Mennonite, and her father was a member of the Social Democratic Workers' Party. During World War II, the Netherlands were occupied by the German Nazis from May 10, 1940, until May 5, 1945. Even though most Dutch people were anti-German during the war, only a few people offered active resistance. Schaft studied law at the University of Amsterdam and became friends with Jewish students. Consequently, she developed very intense feelings about the Nazi actions against Jews. She became very active in the resistance movement and helped people who were hiding from the Germans by giving them stolen identification cards and food coupons. During this time she was known as "the girl with the red hair" (in Dutch: *Het meisje met het rode haar*). The name Hannie was given to her as a secret name by the movement. To help the resistance, Hannie gave out illegal newspapers, transported weapons, disguised herself as a German girl to get information from German soldiers, and brought Jewish children to hiding places. Hannie also killed several members of the German secret police and Dutch collaborators.

She had to be very careful, and she couldn't tell anyone about her work. The Nazis were looking for her, so she dyed her red hair black and wore clear glasses so she wouldn't be recognized.

She was arrested on March 21, 1945, at a routine military checkpoint in Haarlem, while distributing the illegal communist newspaper *de Waarheid*. Hannie was shot dead three weeks before the end of the war in the dunes of Bloemendaal.

Artist Marijke van Welzen chose Hannie Schaft because she admires her bravery and her willingness to participate as a resistance fighter in the Netherlands during World War II. She is remembered every November during a national event held in Haarlem. Marijke made this textile collage using commercial fabrics which she appliquéd. It is free-motion stitched and quilted.

Marijke depicted Hannie Schaft, known by everyone in the Netherlands, walking through a forest, Het Amsterdamse Bos, with her bag full of flyers, stolen identity cards, food coupons and illegal newspapers.

Marijke wanted to depict her quite small in the immense forest to show how lonely her missions must have been. They must have been scary because behind every tree a German soldier or an enemy might be hiding. Marijke allowed her red hair to show, even though she had dyed it. Marijke has quite a considerable stash of fabrics. She knew she had the perfect forest fabric for this quilt. Marijke made the large tree from a "wood" print fabric. For the soldier and the girl she looked at many pictures and drew the figures first on paper. The gun was the hardest to depict, as Marijke has little knowledge about guns. She appliquéd the pieces to the quilt. The shadows on the ground happened kind of by chance. She likes to use improvisation for these things and find the right solution by trial and error, looking again and again and changing pieces a little at a time. Marijke used free-motion stitching to stitch all the pieces down and free-motion quilting throughout the piece.

Hannah Senesh (1921–1944)

. . . paratrooper trained to rescue Jews during the Holocaust.

The Meaning of Hope
Phyllis Cullen
Ninole, Hawaii

Blessed Is the Match

by Hannah Senesh

Blessed is the match consumed in the kindling flame.
Blessed is the flame that burns in the heart's secret
*   places.*
Blessed is the heart with strength to stop its beating
*   for honor's sake.*
Blessed is the match consumed in the kindling flame.

Hannah Senesh (originally Szenes) was a woman of rare courage, dignity, honor, and pride. Born in Budapest, Hungary, Hannah was acutely aware of the anti-Semitic sentiments all around her. She moved to Israel in 1939, lived on a kibbutz, and wrote poetry and a play about kibbutz life. In 1943, safe in Palestine, away from the Holocaust, she decided to parachute back to the maelstrom to help other Jews. No group of persons, other than the Jews of Palestine, attempted such a rescue. Only thirty Jews did so, including three women, and one of the three was Hannah Senesh.

Hannah joined the British Army, volunteering to parachute behind enemy lines to try to rescue Jewish people. She parachuted into Yugoslavia in March of 1944 where she spent three months with Tito's Partisans, becoming more committed to her mission every day. In June, at the height of the deportation of Hungarian Jews, Hannah crossed the border into her homeland. She was caught almost immediately. She faced the worst the Nazis threw at her, including beatings, maiming, the imprisoning of her mother and threatening her with death, and months of torture and interrogation. She never gave up her comrades, never gave up the Special Operations Executive (SOE) codes, and never betrayed herself, her people, or her country. She was executed by firing squad unblindfolded, looking them squarely in the eye, as the Russian Red Army entered the suburbs of Budapest, and as the Nazis and the Hungarian Fascists grabbed their files and fled.

Hannah Senesh was a hero not only for her people and her country, the Jews and Israel, but for all free men and women, and all who are not free but would be. Even though she did not succeed in her defined military mission, she continued it even while in prison. There, through her friendship and courage, she offered other imprisoned Jews hope that others might come after her to rescue them from Fascist death. What is the meaning of hope? Hannah Senesh provided an answer—her indomitable spirit was the answer.

Artist Phyllis Cullen created this moving collage portrait to tell Hannah's story, an inspiring tale of bravery and self-sacrifice. Hannah is shown in uniform. Parachutists drop behind a line of Jewish Holocaust victims alongside a death train. Phyllis hand dyed the cotton fabric. Her piece was constructed using machine appliqué. It is thread-sketched and quilted. Paint was used to highlight the piece.

Muriel "Mickie" Siebert (1928–2013)

. . . first woman to purchase her own seat on the New York Stock Exchange.

Mickie's Bull
Peggy Fetterhoff
Spring, Texas

"When a door is hard to open, and if nothing else works, sometimes you just have to rear back and kick it open." —Muriel Siebert

Muriel "Mickie" Siebert left Cleveland, Ohio with $500 and a Studebaker bound for New York City. She lied on her resume about having a college degree and secured a job on Wall Street. Siebert was excellent with numbers, detail oriented, and researched investments thoroughly. She took advantage of working for knowledgeable bosses to gain an understanding of the financial industry. Initially, she did mainly research; making sure it was thorough, accurate, and timely. Working on the trading floor, Mickie learned, "crossing the block," which meant providing income from the buy and sell side of a transaction.

She was always paid less than the men around her doing the same work, so she changed positions whenever it helped her career.

Mickie applied for a seat on the New York Stock Exchange (NYSE), inviting member sponsors to avoid borrowing part of the $450,000. Everyone turned her down, but she persisted. On December 27, 1967, she became the first female to purchase her own seat on the NYSE.

In 1969 she formed her own company, Muriel Siebert & Co., Inc. Mickie stood up to sexual discrimination. In 1970 when she worked with Salomon Brothers to underwrite a new bond offer, her company name was at the bottom of the list of companies instead of alphabetically, as was the custom, so Mickie withdrew from the offering.

When the SEC removed restrictions on prices that financial institutions could charge for a trade, she became the first discount brokerage for institutional investors. Many companies went belly up, but she made the necessary changes in order to survive.

In 1977, she entered public service by becoming the Superintendent of Banking for New York State, earning about a tenth of her previous income. She put her company in a blind trust during her tenure there, regulating about $500 billion. No New York banks failed while she was Superintendent.

Mickie, a conservative Republican, discovered that Emily's (Early Money Is Like Yeast) List assisted Democratic women who wanted to run for Congress. So she cofounded the Republican counterpart, WISH (Women in the Senate & House) and the New York Women's Forum.

Eventually, she started her own charity, SEPP, Siebert Entrepreneurial Philanthropic Plan, which contributes fifty percent of the selling commissions on new offerings after cost. This program created opportunities for the buyers of the financial instruments to contribute to charities through their purchases. Through the Muriel F. Siebert Foundation, Mickie developed the "Siebert Personal Finance Program: Taking Control of Your Financial Future," a financial literacy program for middle and high school students and adults, teaching them essential financial skills. Mickie worked unflaggingly to promote financial literacy.

Mickie Siebert was inducted into the Women's Hall of Fame in 1994. She wrote her life story with Aimee Lee Ball in 2002, *Changing the Rules: Adventures of a Wall Street Maverick*. Mickie died at the age of eighty-four on August 24, 2013, in Manhattan.

Artist Peggy Fetterhoff spent a few years of her career as a stock broker, experiencing a small taste of the financial industry male domination. Peggy said that women who succeed in this industry must be twice as smart and every bit as aggressive as their male counterparts. The red bull in this creation is a bit of an oxymoron suggesting a slightly feminine version of the famous Wall Street Bull. She symbolizes the talented, successful women that work in the financial industry. Peggy created this piece honoring Mickie Siebert using cotton fabric. It is machine pieced, machine appliquéd, and machine quilted.

Nina Simone (1933–2003)

. . . songwriter of "Mississippi Goddam" and "To Be Young, Gifted and Black," anthems of the Civil Rights Movement.

Nina: A Theme with Variations
Sherri Culver
Portland, Oregon

"I had spent many years pursuing excellence, because that is what classical music is all about . . . Now it was dedicated to freedom, and that was far more important." —Nina Simone

Nina Simone, a self-described "freedom singer," was a child prodigy. In 1933, Eunice Kathleen Waymon was born in the segregated south. At age two, Eunice began teaching herself piano and surprised her mother one day by playing hymns straight through without a mistake.

Her mother's employer, Mrs. Miller, became her benefactor, supporting her training as a classical concert pianist. After studying with Muriel Massinovitch, Eunice received a one-year scholarship to the Juilliard School of Music in New York. She hoped to earn a scholarship to the Curtis Institute of Music (CIM) in Philadelphia. Unfortunately, CIM rejected her application and Eunice was devastated, later learning that the denial was based on the color of her skin. Eunice began playing piano at the Midtown Bar & Grill in Atlantic City during the summer. At the end of the night, the owner told her that she should sing or not return! This ultimatum sent Eunice on an entirely new trajectory. Concerned about the opinion of her preacher mother and other family members, Eunice changed her name to Nina Simone and became a singer.

Nina signed her first recording contract without reading it or getting advice, something that would haunt her for the rest of her life. Her career took off, and she was overwhelmed with bookings, recording gigs, and travel. Andy Stroud came into her life and quickly became her husband and manager. Becoming entirely dependent upon Andy, Nina suffered physical and emotional abuse as she succumbed to his demands to keep a performance schedule that taxed her physically and led her to depend on alcohol to cope. During this time, Nina became a representative of the American Society of African Culture. Extended visits to Africa became her respite. She became friends with many civil rights leaders including Lorraine Hansberry, the first black writer to have a Broadway hit, *A Raisin in the Sun*. Lorraine convinced Nina to think about herself as a black person in a country run by white people and a woman in a world run by men. Inspired by the title of an unfinished Lorraine Hansberry play, Nina wrote "To Be Young, Gifted and Black." As the Civil Rights Movement progressed, her "Mississippi Goddam" became its anthem. Her love for Africa and her commitment to the Civil Rights Movement led to tension with her singing career.

Her career led her from nightclubs to concert stages and finally onto the world stage. Her style, a combination of classical piano, jazz, gospel, folk, pop, and blues, drew fans from everywhere. Nina's mastery of morphing styles and keys, while interspersing bits of entirely different pieces was magical. Her dream of performing with a full orchestra at Carnegie Hall was ultimately fulfilled, but as a singer, not as a pianist.

Artist Sherri Culver's piece shows Nina squatting on sheet music, symbolizing her classical piano training and her ongoing love of Bach. The microphone and the red and gold shiny fabrics on the rectangular design elements reflect her concert singing career and costumes. The mini-sketch portraits of Martin Luther King, Jr., Malcolm X, and Muhammad Ali represent her Civil Rights activism. The African fabric shows her African heritage and devotion to it throughout her life. Sherri manipulated a photo of Nina in Photoshop to create the contours of the face. The details such as her hairline, her off-center nose, unequal eyes, were added later. Quilting was used to make the contours of the face recede or come forward. A light hand in quilting the face is balanced by a more densely quilted background, frequently using simple geometric designs.

Gloria Steinem (1934–)

. . . founded *Ms.* magazine, Women's Media Center, and National Women's Political Caucus.

Gloria
Bonnie Askowitz
Miami, Florida

"A gender-equal society would be one where the word 'gender' does not exist: where everyone can be themselves." —Gloria Steinem

In 1972 Gloria Steinem became the first woman to address the National Press Club since its founding in 1908, but that accomplishment, unique as it was, pales in the light of her lifetime accomplishments as a journalist, author, lecturer, activist, and feminist leader.

Gloria began her journalism career with an article for *Esquire* about contraception and how women were forced to choose between marriage and a career, a subject later addressed by Betty Friedan. Gloria went undercover as a *Playboy* bunny and wrote an article about the way women were being treated at Playboy Clubs. Artist Bonnie Askowitz believes that Gloria sees herself primarily as a writer. A recent photo shoot with Annie Leibovitz shows her at her writing desk in deep thought. As an author of books and essays, she has covered subjects as diverse as India, Marilyn Monroe, rebellion, ageism, gaining power, and self-esteem.

From the early 1960s, Gloria, the political activist, campaigned for women's equality. She said, "To have democracy outside the home you must have democracy inside." She founded *Ms.* magazine, the Women's Media Center, and the National Women's Political Caucus. She speaks about issues related to women including prostitution, pornography, human trafficking, abuse, and female genital mutilation. She has also spoken against male circumcision as a form of mutilation.

Reproductive rights have been a cornerstone of Gloria's activism since 1969 when she attended a speak-out for *New York* magazine about abortion rights. She credits this event with starting her "life as an active feminist," and Gloria hopes to be remembered as having coined the phrase "reproductive freedom."

Gloria believes that to be heard you must speak out. She fought against the Vietnam War, in support of the Free South Africa Movement, and for LGBTQ rights. In fact, she has spoken out on many subjects, and she is the author of many pithy quotes. Some are found on the art piece.

Currently in her eighties, Gloria is still writing. She is also producing and hosting a documentary series on Viceland Cable TV called *Woman*. This show is about violence of all types against women and plumbs the depths of her interests. Gloria received the Medal of Freedom from President Barack Obama in 2013.

Bonnie created *Gloria*, dressed as Wonder Woman, who was featured on the cover image of the first issue of *Ms.*, in red and blue, in front of a picture collage poster of her life. Bonnie printed pictures from Gloria's website onto fabric with an Epson printer and quilted it. There is a picture of Gloria with Bonnie near the upper left-hand corner. She painted superhero Gloria using Bonnie's daughter's body, giving the image superhero muscles. Wonder Gloria poses in a "ready for anything" stance, wearing a belt with a female symbol buckle. Instead of the Wonder Woman tiara, Gloria sports her iconic glasses atop her head. Gloria could be Wonder Woman's alter-ego, only she fights in street clothes. She truly is a superhero to Bonnie and many others, a symbol of women's rights, children's rights, and equal rights for all as she has spent her entire life seeking truth and justice.

After feminism I suddenly realized: not everyone has to live the same way. Imagine that.

Girls actually need superheroes more than boys.

Any woman who chooses to beha like a full human being should be warned that the armies of the status quo will treat her as some thing of a dirty joke. That's thei natural and first weapon. She wi need her sisterhood.

Without leaps of imagination, or dreaming, we lose the excitement of possibilities. Dreaming, after all, is a form of planning.

Anne Sullivan (1866–1936)

Helen Keller (1880–1968)

. . . opened the world of knowledge to Helen Keller who was blind, deaf, and mute.

. . . first deaf/blind person to earn a Bachelor's degree.

She Knows!
Susanne Miller Jones
Potomac Falls, Virginia

"I have thought about it a great deal, and the more I think, the more certain I am that obedience is the gateway through which knowledge, yes, and love, too, enter the mind of the child." —Anne Sullivan

"The best and most beautiful things in the world cannot be seen or even touched—they must be felt with the heart." —Helen Keller

Anne Sullivan was born with an eye disease that escalated when she and her brother, Jimmy, were sent to the Tewksbury Almshouse in Massachusetts. After Jimmy died, Anne caught the attention of the staff and asked them to send her to a special school. She was sent to Perkins Institute for the Blind and given several surgeries to try to improve her sight. Since Annie had impressed the school's director, Michael Anagnos, she came to mind when Colonel Keller wrote to the school asking for someone to work with their daughter, Helen, who was deaf and blind due to a high fever at nineteen months.

Anne traveled to Ivy Green in Tuscumbia, Alabama. There she found an unkempt, unruly child who did as she wished and was in desperate need of teaching. Annie insisted that she and Helen be allowed to live in the pump house without any interference from Helen's parents. Helen was forced to depend totally on Anne, her teacher. It was at the water pump at Ivy Green that the world opened for Helen through Annie's finger spelling "water" into Helen's hand, using the manual alphabet. All of a sudden Helen knew that things had names and she needed to know the names of everything. Following this awakening, Anne taught Helen to write, read Braille, and to speak. They were Teacher and Helen, friends and companions.

Helen went to college at Radcliffe becoming the first blind and deaf person to graduate from college. It was no small feat, as Anne had to spell the lectures into her hand and spent hours explaining the contents of her textbooks.

Together they traveled wherever folks wanted Helen to speak. Helen wrote books with Anne's help, trying to make ends meet. Anne even played herself in a movie, *Deliverance*, based on their story, which was a colossal flop. Still trying to make ends meet, they went on the vaudeville circuit, and they were a hit!

When Anne's sight grew worse, and her health started to fail, they left the Orpheum circuit. Helen began advocating for the rights of those with disabilities. She became a spokesperson for the American Foundation for the Blind and a founding member of the ACLU. She traveled the world and met with every president from Grover Cleveland to Lyndon Johnson, who gave her the Presidential Medal of Freedom in 1964.

Annie died in 1936, leaving Polly Thompson to accompany Helen until Polly's death in 1960. Helen died in 1968. Anne and Helen rest side by side in the National Cathedral in Washington, DC. Anne Sullivan was the first woman so honored.

Artist Susanne Jones has been an admirer of these two women since she saw *The Miracle Worker* when she was nine years old. The centerpiece water pump was appliquéd with the blanket stitch. The organza water flows freely over Helen's outstretched hand with acrylic beads of water splashing over the edge. In the upper corner, an appliquéd hand puts fingers on jawline, nose, and lips in the Tadoma pose used to teach deafblind people to speak. Sign language hands spell out TEACHER (above the pump) in honor of Anne and WATER (below the pump), the word which opened a world of knowledge for Helen. HELEN is written in Braille made out of micro buttons. The background is stamped with a wood block and fabric paint. Helen Keller's signature is recreated using machine embroidery as are two quotes by Helen Keller.

Everything I touched seemed to quiver with life.

Helen Keller

Pat Head Summitt (1952–2016)

. . . most winning coach, male or female, in NCAA basketball history.

Pat Head Summitt
Ellen Icochea
Alexandria, Virginia

"I won 1,098 games, and eight national championships, and coached in four different decades. But what I see are not the numbers. I see their faces."
—Pat Head Summitt

Pat Head Summitt grew up playing basketball on a farm in Tennessee with her brothers. She went to the University of Tennessee at Martin and played on the intramural basketball club, serving as player, coach, laundress, and fundraiser. Following a near career-ending knee injury, Pat worked hard in therapy to become the co-captain of the 1976 US Women's Olympic Basketball team, leading her team to place Silver. In 1984 as Head Coach of the US Women's Olympic Basketball team, she led the team to a Gold Medal finish. Pat became the first athlete from any country to win a medal as both an athlete and a coach.

Under Pat's leadership, women's collegiate basketball became a fully supported, revenue generating, scholarship giving, sport that has evolved into the Women's National Basketball Association. Pat went on to become the most winning coach, male or female, in NCAA basketball history. Coach Summitt and her Lady Vols won eight NCAA Championships and made 18 Final Four appearances. She was most proud of the fact that her players, who completed their eligibility at the University of Tennessee, experienced a one hundred percent graduation rate.

On August 22, 2011, Pat announced that she had Alzheimer's disease and vowed to fight it. She and her son, Tyler, established the Pat Summitt Foundation. Her career came to an end as Head Coach Emeritus with 1,098 wins out of 1,306 games coached. She was selected SEC Coach of the Year eight times and NCAA Coach of the Year seven times.

Pat was inducted into the International Women's Sports Hall of Fame in 1990 and the Women's Basketball Hall of Fame in 1999. In 2012, President Barack Obama presented her the Presidential Medal of Freedom. She is the only person to have two NCAA Division 1 basketball courts named after her. The Pat Head Summitt Court is at the University of Tennessee at Martin, and The Summitt is at the University of Tennessee, Knoxville. Pat said her most important statistic was 161, the number of Lady Vols that played on her teams. To them, she was more than a coach. She was a friend, a mentor, and a loving mom. Pat brought out the best in them. "I remember every player—every single one—who wore the Tennessee orange, a shade that our rivals hate, a bold, aggravating color that you can usually find on a roadside crew, 'or in a correctional institution,' as my friend Wendy Larry jokes. But to us the color is a flag of pride, because it identifies us as Lady Vols and therefore as women of an unmistakable type. Fighters. I remember how many of them fought for a better life for themselves. I just met them halfway."

Artist Ellen Icochea created this thread painted portrait after getting permission from her son and the Pat Summitt Foundation. After scanning the photograph onto cotton and identifying the perfect thread colors for each section, she layered the quilt sandwich and began thread painting. She proceeded from darkest to lightest. It often meant using seven or eight colors of thread per area. This process took a long time as Ellen sewed and blended each subsequent layer of thread into each area. The colors of the University of Tennessee and the Pat Summitt Foundation are orange and white. Alzheimer's disease is represented by purple. So Pat is pictured in an orange jacket with a purple Alzheimer's ribbon on her coat held in place by the lapel pin of the Pat Summitt Foundation.

Margaret Thatcher (1925–2013)

. . . first woman and the longest-serving Prime Minister of the United Kingdom in the twentieth century.

Margaret Thatcher
Jennifer O'Brien
New Fairfield, Connecticut

"If you want something said, ask a man; if you want something done, ask a woman." —Margaret Thatcher

Daughter of a grocer with Conservative political leanings, Margaret Thatcher studied chemistry at Oxford's Somerville College. Dorothy Hodgkin, a Nobel Prize-winning scientist, was one of her instructors. Margaret was employed as a research chemist before she went into politics. Margaret ran for a seat in the British Parliament, predictably losing. Two months after that loss, she married David Thatcher. She and David became the parents of twins. She studied law, becoming a barrister at the end of her studies. In 1959 Maggie threw her hat in the ring again. This time she won a seat in the House of Commons. She continued to win elections, rising in power with each win. She was appointed Secretary of State for Education and Science in 1970.

During Prime Minister Heath's term in office, Maggie felt like she went unheard and doubted whether there would be a female Prime Minister of the United Kingdom in her lifetime. She proved herself wrong, becoming the leader of the Conservative Party in the United Kingdom in 1975, the first woman leader to hold this powerful position in a major party in the UK. Maggie became Prime Minister of the United Kingdom in 1979 and held the position until 1990. She was the longest-serving British prime minister in the twentieth century and the first woman to hold that office. In the USSR they called her the "Iron Lady," a nickname that stuck because of her uncompromising politics and leadership style.

During her three terms, she cut social welfare programs, reduced trade union power, and privatized certain industries. She was best known for her destruction of Britain's traditional industries through her attacks on labor organizations such as the miners' union, and for the massive privatization of social housing and public transport. Margaret Thatcher, through her three terms in office, molded the future direction of the United Kingdom and set them up to prosper in the new millennium.

Artist Jennifer O'Brien created these images reflecting important aspects of Margaret Thatcher's life. The Union Jack flag of the United Kingdom represents the country and those she served. Big Ben represents Parliament where she spent a significant portion of her working life. The black door with the iron work is an image of 10 Downing Street, the Prime Minister's official residence. Margaret Thatcher always carried a purse instead of a briefcase, so it is featured on the piece. The background is a map of the London Underground. Jennifer thought this was appropriate as London is the seat of the government and the home of the royal family. The crowns in the border symbolize the royal family and Maggie's long association with them. This work uses raw-edge appliqué, free-motion thread-painting, and embellishments. Jen first planned the location of all the appliqué images. Next, she layered the backing, batting, and top. Finally, she created all the thread-painting, appliquéd the separate images, and quilted to add texture and dimension.

Wilma Vaught (1930–)

. . . responsible for the establishment of
the Women in Military Service for America
Memorial at Arlington Cemetery.

*The Women in Military Service for America
and General Wilma L. Vaught, Retired*

Starla Phelps
Alexandria, Virginia

"What I wanted to be when I grew up was—in charge."
—Wilma Vaught

Wilma Vaught joined the Air Force to lead, not just to serve. Although never a combat fighter, she served a full tour in Vietnam and was just a block away from bombs. She was outspoken and paved the way for the many successful women in uniform who followed her. In every position she held throughout her career, she was the first female to hold the position. She continued to lead and support women after she retired. Her vision was to honor all of the American military women from the Revolutionary War to the present. She spent almost twelve years crusading to establish a memorial to honor women in military services; her efforts led to the raising of over twenty million dollars.

Graduating from the University of Illinois in 1952, Wilma Vaught received a Master's degree from the University of Alabama. When she joined the military in the 1950s, there were limits on how many women could be in the military and how they could serve. In 1957 Vaught was commissioned a Second Lieutenant in the US Air Force. From 1957 to 1968 she was promoted to increasingly important positions. She was the first woman to deploy with a Strategic Air Command squadron to Guam. The following year she deployed to Vietnam. She served a full tour in Vietnam; in recognition of her contributions, she was awarded the Distinguished Service Medal and the Bronze Star Medal. In 1972 she became the first female officer to attend the Industrial College of the Armed Forces. In addition to her many challenging assignments she also served as Chairperson of the Committee on Women in the NATO Forces and was the senior military woman representative to the Defense Advisory Committee on Women in the Services. In September 1980 she was the first woman selected for promotion to Brigadier General in the comptroller field. General Vaught was the only woman to hold the position of President of the Board of Directors of the Pentagon Federal Credit Union (1976–1982).

Artist Starla Phelps' goal was to display General Vaught's vision on this quilt. The quilt is in four parts. Across the top are summary tabs of the roles and significant accomplishments of servicewomen. Next, is a drawing of General Vaught's achievement, the Women in Military Service for America Memorial, which Starla drew and then quilted. At the bottom of the quilt is Starla's copy of *Athena's Watch* by Michael Solovey, depicting today's military fighting women. Overlaid onto the memorial is Starla's version of Annette Polan's portrait of General Vaught. Starla selected sheer for the overlay to depict General Vaught's vision drawing forth the Memorial. You can see the Memorial through her portrait; it is her vision. Trapunto was used to add dimension.

Barbara Walters (1929–)

. . . first female cohost of a nightly major
network news show.

And the Glass Ceiling Came Tumbling Down . . .
Sherri Culver
Portland, Oregon

*"I have affected the way women are regarded, and
that's important to me." —Barbara Walters*

Daughter of Lou Walters, a successful booking agent, Barbara
Walters met many performers and developed an enviable list of
contacts. She was valuable behind the scenes but was not
considered for screen opportunities. In 1961, she went on-screen
for the first time on *Today* to fill a temporary need. In 1974 she
became cohost of *Today*, the first woman to cohost on any
network news or public affairs program. There was a clause in
her contract that gave Barbara the right to the position which
she took advantage of, leading to a surge in ratings for the show.

During the early years of TV, she was considered an
"upstart" when she became the only woman on Richard Nixon's
trip to China in 1972. On that trip and beyond, she was excluded
from conversations and the companionship of other journalists
who were jealous of her. Barbara Walters plowed forward,
gaining the respect of viewers and trust of celebrities and
newsmakers. When cohosting *Today*, she was not allowed to
ask the first two questions in on-air interviews. Barbara simply
went out of the studio and recorded interesting interviews
where she asked *all* of the questions.

While her assignment as coanchor of the *ABC Evening
News* was a historical breakthrough for women, it was a bitter
experience for Barbara. Her $5,000,000 contract caused an
outcry. There was a backlash from NBC when she left for ABC.
Her cohost, Harry Reasoner, was publicly outspoken in his wish
not to work with her and was disrespectful to her during telecasts.
Barbara went on to coanchor *20/20* for twenty-five years and to
create and cohost *The View*, both highly acclaimed ABC programs.

Part of her anchor contract with ABC was the agreement
to do four one-hour specials each year. She became known for
those in-depth interviews. It would be easier to create a list of
the notable people Barbara Walters did not interview than a
list of those she did. Diligently working her list of contacts,
she planned "chance" encounters, researched those she wanted
to interview, and persisted until she landed them. She prepared
for each interview, often surprising the subject with little-known
facts that unleashed memorable moments. She tried to uncover
the real person behind the personality and give them the
opportunity, in some cases, for redemption. Many highly
sought-after interviewees agreed to speak only to Barbara.
Barbara Walters crashed through the glass ceiling and opened
it up for women journalists.

This portrait shows Barbara Walters backed by newsprint,
in her early days on air, appearing on a black and white TV
with rabbit ears. Set against a 1970s-era wallpaper background,
the glass shards tumbling down from above represent her
achievement of cracking the glass ceiling in TV broadcasting
when she became the first in many areas.

Artist Sherri Culver manipulated the photographs in
Photoshop to create the value based background of the contours
of the face. Details such as her hairline and lines around the
eyes were added to the face. Small print commercial fabrics
add texture and give the viewer a different experience when
viewing the art from a distance and then up close. Hair lends
itself to unusual use of large prints. Leaves, flowers, animal
prints, grass, and other designs, when fussy cut into smaller
pieces, are amazing in a head of hair.

Betty White (1922–)

. . . first female producer in Hollywood.

Betty White: A Television Legend
Birgit Ruotsala
Green Bay, Wisconsin

"Friendship takes time and energy if it's going to work. You can luck into something great, but it doesn't last if you don't give it proper appreciation. Friendship can be so comfortable, but nurture it—don't take it for granted." —Betty White

According to *Guinness World Records 2014*, Betty White has had the longest TV career for a (female) entertainer, seventy-five years at that point. Born in 1922, Betty started entertaining audiences in 1939 singing on an experimental television station in Los Angeles. In 1950 she hosted a show called *Hollywood on Television*, a five-and-a-half hour ad lib show six days a week, which earned her an Emmy nomination. From 1953 to 1955 she starred in her first series called *Life with Elizabeth* which she produced—becoming the first woman producer in Hollywood. Consequently, she was given the honorary title of Mayor of Hollywood.

Betty was a favorite on game shows in the early days of television and in 1961, while appearing on *Password*, she met her third husband and the love of her life, Allen Ludden. Following Allen's death, Betty has remained single indicating that she had already had the best with Allen. She appeared so frequently on game shows that she was christened "The First Lady of Game Shows." She later became the first woman to win an Emmy for Outstanding Game Show Host for her show, *Just Men*.

For ten years, Betty White was the host of NBC's Macy's Thanksgiving Day Parade, and for twenty-one years, she hosted NBC's Tournament of Roses Parade. As Betty's star rose at CBS on *The Mary Tyler Moore Show*, NBC felt that they had to move in another direction.

Betty played diverse roles on popular sitcoms, from Sue Ann Nivens on *The Mary Tyler Moore Show* in the 1970s to Rose Nylund on *The Golden Girls* in the 1980s. Her role on *The Mary Tyler Moore Show* won her two Emmy Awards. Her work as Rose Nylund won her another Emmy. Both shows are listed by the Writers Guild of America as two of the 101 Best Written TV Series of All Time.

When *The Golden Girls* ended in 1992, Betty did many guest appearances. During the Super Bowl in 2010, her career received a shot in the arm as she was the star of a Snickers ad, one of the audience's favorite commercials. That led to a grass roots campaign to get Betty White to host *Saturday Night Live*, which she did in May of that year, becoming the oldest person ever to host the show. Her career revival led to a five-year run as Elka Ostrovsky on *Hot in Cleveland*.

Betty published seven books about her life and work and became an activist for animal rights, especially with the Los Angeles Zoo. Her work with the zoo was documented in a book that she wrote, *Betty and Her Friends: My Life at the Zoo*. She once said that if she hadn't been an actress, she would have been a zookeeper.

Betty White's Rose Nylund was a favorite character in artist Birgit Ruotsala's Midwestern Scandinavian home. In creating the quilt of Betty, Birgit chose a black and white palette to represent Betty's early years in television. Betty looks a lot like Birgit's mother. So Birgit blew up a photo that she had taken of her mother and then changed the details to match the photos of Betty's features. A pen and ink sketch was done to portray Betty in her later years. Betty actually has Birgit's mother's lips, earrings, and hairdo. The black background was created with a very faint listing of the shows in which she appeared. Overall quilting was done in a fine white thread to give the piece texture and bring the sketch to life.

Jody Williams (1950–)

. . . Nobel Peace Prize winner for her work to ban anti-personnel mines; founder of the Nobel Women's Initiative.

Jody
Gabriele DiTota
Melbourne, Florida

"We must teach ourselves to believe that peace is not a 'utopian vision,' but a responsibility that must be worked for each and every day." —Jody Williams

In 1997 Jody Williams received the Nobel Peace Prize along with the International Campaign to Ban Landmines (ICBL), of which she was the founding coordinator. Jody's work to ban and clear landmines started in 1992 with the development of the ICBL which has grown into an international organization of 1300 non-governmental organizations in ninety countries. The result of Williams' efforts was the adoption, at the Oslo Diplomatic Conference in 1997, of a treaty prohibiting the use, production, transference, and stockpiling of anti-personnel mines.

At the time of her award, Jody Williams was only the tenth woman, and the third American woman, to win the Nobel Peace Prize. *Forbes* magazine named Jody Williams one of the most powerful women in 2004. In 2006, after discussion with the other female Nobel Peace Laureates, Williams took the lead in establishing the Nobel Women's Initiative. Their mission is to use their influence to support women's groups around the world in campaigning for justice, peace, and equality.

In an interview with *Real Leaders* magazine, in 2015, Williams made the following statement: "The image of peace with a dove flying over a rainbow and people holding hands singing Kumbaya ends up infantilizing people who believe that sustainable peace is possible. If you think that singing and looking at a rainbow will suddenly make peace appear then you're not capable of meaningful thought or understanding the difficulties of the world."

Artist Gabriele DiTota's work is an extension of her life and art quilts are her canvas. She employs raw-edge appliqué in her pieces. Gabriele's father, who was still in his teens, was drafted post–World War II to clear fields of land mines in southern Denmark. Growing up, Gabriele heard the stories of the difficulty disarming mines in crumbling wooden casings and of the accidental detonations that routinely occurred. Her father still carries the shrapnel in his back from a mine explosion. After clearing a field, the young recruits would have to link arms and walk across the field to assure the farmer that it was safe to begin cultivation again.

When Gabriele started researching Jody William's work into banning and clearing landmines, it touched a chord. The images she found online of survivors of landmines, many of whom were children with badly mutilated limbs, were profoundly disturbing. The universal non-language specific danger symbol of skull and crossbones seemed to be a universal warning to stay away from an area which may still have hidden mines. It was this symbol that she chose to illustrate the work of Nobel Peace Prize Winner Jody Williams. While Gabriele was working on the piece, she found a used CD in the garbage, and it became the inspiration to use mini CDs as the eyes. The CDs give an eerie effect, which to Gabriele makes the piece all the more unsettling. Behind the bleach discharged image of the skull and crossbones, there is a graffiti-like scattering of crosses symbolic of lives lost to the horror of mines. The mines under the central image are hidden in the grass just as real mines are. The work includes discharged fabric, painted fabric, and raw-edge appliqué.

Oprah Winfrey (1954–)

. . . American television host, actress, producer, philanthropist, and entrepreneur; recipient of the Presidential Medal of Freedom.

Oprah Winfrey: Overcoming and Conquering
Leo Ransom
Sherman, Texas

"I've come to believe that each of us has a personal calling that's as unique as a fingerprint—and that the best way to succeed is to discover what you love and then find a way to offer it to others in the form of service, working hard, and also allowing the energy of the universe to lead you." —Oprah Winfrey

Oprah Winfrey has been a talk show host, actress, producer, philanthropist, and author. She was born in poverty to an unwed mother and lived on a farm with her maternal grandparents. Her father learned of her birth when he received a printed baby announcement in the mail with a note that said: "Send clothes!" At six, she went to live with her mother, a housekeeper. Her mother was rarely at home. Winfrey was sexually abused by a cousin beginning when she was about nine years old. Following the birth of Oprah's sibling, her mother sent Oprah, fourteen, to live with her father in Nashville. He was very strict and adamant about her getting a good education. So she went to Tennessee State University in 1971. Oprah won the Miss Black Tennessee pageant when she was seventeen, attracting the attention of a local radio station where she was hired as a newsreader.

In 1976 Oprah moved to Baltimore, Maryland, and hosted a TV chat show, *People Are Talking*. A Chicago station recruited her to host *A.M. Chicago*, opposite *Phil Donahue*, and she was beating him in the ratings within a few months. Steven Spielberg cast her in *The Color Purple*, for which she received an Oscar nomination.

In 1986, Oprah launched *The Oprah Winfrey Show*, an instant hit. She took over control of the show from ABC and put it under her own production company, HARPO. In 1994, Oprah vowed to keep tabloid stories off of her show and took the high road, filling the airwaves with uplifting discussions.

In 1999, Oprah entered the cable and internet market with the Oxygen Network, dedicated to women's programming. She began publishing *O: The Oprah Magazine* in 2004. In 2005, she coproduced *The Color Purple* on Broadway which ran for three years. Her 2015 revival of *The Color Purple* won the Tony Award.

Oprah, the richest African American of the twentieth century, uses her money to help others through Oprah's Angel Network. She has raised millions to help others, including educating girls in South Africa. Children everywhere can count Oprah as one of their advocates. During the Clinton administration, the president signed into law a bill creating a nationwide database of convicted child abusers. Oprah was responsible for suggesting the bill to Congress. She is the founder of the Family for Better Lives Foundation. In recognition of her good works, she received the Academy of Television Arts & Sciences' Bob Hope Humanitarian Award in 2002.

She supported Barack Obama during his campaigns for the White House, telling the crowd, "Dr. King dreamed the dream. But we don't have to just dream the dream anymore. We get to vote that dream into reality by supporting a man who knows not just who we are, but who we can be." Oprah is known for her concern for the rights of all and has worked to ensure those rights. In 2013, Barack Obama awarded her the Presidential Medal of Freedom in recognition of her contribution to our country.

Artist Leo Ransom created this portrait of Oprah by drawing the pattern onto fabric and filling in areas with different shades of small thumbnail sized pieces of fabric, a technique that he calls fused confetti. It is an effective technique for creating shadings and highlights. Her hair alone took Leo close to ten hours to complete while the body took over twenty-four hours and the clothing about six hours. The "HARPO Studio" silhouette in the background is a symbol of Oprah's accomplishments. The background fragments represent how unstable her life was when she was a child.

197

Beatrice Wood (1893–1998)

. . . first female accepted into the avant-garde art movement: The Mama of Dada.

Beatrice Wood: A Life Colored by Art
Mary McLaughlin
Portland, Oregon

"Hardships and handicaps can . . . stimulate our energy to survive them. You'll find if you study the lives of people who've accomplished things, it's often been done with the help of great willpower in overcoming this and that." —Beatrice Wood

Beatrice Wood was born into a wealthy family in San Francisco, California in 1893. She was expected to grow up to be a genteel society woman. Willful and independent by nature, she wanted to become an actress. Her mother sent her to Europe hoping she'd abandon the idea. In Europe, away from her conventional family, Beatrice blossomed. She learned French, developed an appreciation for art, and was the object of admiration by several men.

Returning to America, she settled in New York City and joined the art community. She fell in love with Henri-Pierre Roche, a writer and collector of avant-garde art. Through Henri-Pierre she met Marcel Duchamp, and the three of them formed a complicated love triangle. Although the war didn't reach the US shores, it was a turbulent time, and the Dada art movement gave voice to sadness and dystopia. Beatrice was the first woman accepted into the avant-garde art movement. She was nicknamed "The Mama of Dada." At the first New York exhibit, in 1917, Beatrice's *Un peut (peu) d'eau dans du savon* (*A Little Water in Some Soap*), a painting of a nude woman with a bar of soap strategically placed, received the most outcry.

On a trip to the Netherlands, Beatrice purchased a pair of plates with a beautiful, iridescent finish. She wanted a matching teapot, but couldn't find one. So she enrolled in a ceramics course at Hollywood High and began her adventure in pottery making. She built a home and studio in Ojai, California. She opened her studio to students and shared the secrets of her all-over luster glazes. She described glazes as alchemy, saying that opening the kiln was like Christmas morning. She often included primitive figures in her pottery showing her feminist side and her humor. Although she had many lovers, she never married nor had children. One of her most famous quotes is "I owe everything to art books, chocolate, and young men."

Although she abandoned her acting career, Beatrice Wood has a legacy in film. Roche's 1956 novel *Jules et Jim* was said to have been based on the relationship of Wood, Duchamp, and Roche. Years later, James Cameron partially based the 101-year-old character Rose in the 1997 film *Titanic* on Beatrice, having read her biography while developing the film.

In an interview when she was ninety-seven, she said "I'm blessed to have freedom to do what I wish, which is pottery and chasing men. But they don't know it." Then she laughed. She lived to be 105, joyfully.

Artist Mary McLaughlin admires Beatrice Wood as a woman determined to make and share her art! Returning to college at thirty-one, Mary was well aware of the age difference between her classmates and herself. She delighted in finding Beatrice's autobiography, *I Shock Myself*, written in 1983 when Beatrice was eighty. Here was a woman of a certain age who joyfully celebrated creative living and embraced her age and her clothes! She dressed exclusively in Indian saris and Native American jewelry for the last several decades of her life. Even sitting at her potter's wheel, her sari was protected from the clay by an apron, and her jewelry was on display. Mary says she was charming and she wishes she had known her. This portrait based on the photo by Tony Cunha was created using fabric manipulations, and machine appliquéd using an Indian sari, fabric from a recycled patio umbrella, and sequined fabric. The jewelry was created by using thread play. Her eyes are painted with textile paint. It is machine quilted.

Malala Yousafzai (1997–)

. . . youngest recipient of the Nobel Peace Prize, recognizing her advocacy for girls' education.

Malala Yousafzai was born on July 12, 1997, in the beautiful Swat Valley in Pakistan where the local Taliban banned girls from attending school. She entered the world with a thirst for knowledge and a father, Ziauddin Yousafzai, who is a poet, an educational activist, and the owner of a chain of private schools. Ziauddin felt that Malala's education was as important as a boy's formal schooling. This idea was unheard of in the Pashtun culture, the ethnic group of Malala's family. In fact, the birth of a Pashtun girl is thought of as a solemn experience, while sons are celebrated with great joy.

Malala grew up in the schools where her father taught, thereby feeding her desire to learn. The Taliban began to take control of the Swat Valley in 2007 and not long after, girls were banned from attending school. With the support of her father, Malala refused to let the Taliban dictate what she saw as her fundamental right.

Malala had garnered a reputation as an outspoken advocate against the Taliban at an early age. In 2008 at the age of eleven, Malala, who was fluent in Pashto, Urdu, and English started to blog anonymously for BBC Urdu, using a fake name, about living under Taliban rule. She recorded her fears of war and the destruction of her country. Malala also wrote about her anger at being forced to stay at home rather than go to school. Her diary entries often denounced and questioned the tactics of the Taliban, which drew their attention and anger.

Rather than quieting Malala, her voice seemed to grow. Despite death threats from the Taliban, she and her father continued to be fierce advocates for the right for girls to be educated. In 2011, she was nominated for the International Children's Peace Prize, and she won Pakistan's National Youth's Peace Prize.

As she became more recognized, threats against her increased until 2012 when the Taliban decided to kill her. On October 9, 2012, Malala was on her way home from school when a member of the Taliban stopped her school bus. He boarded the bus and asked, "Who is Malala?" He fired three shots directly at her, and one of those entered the left side of her forehead. Miraculously, Malala survived, but only after she was transported to a hospital in Birmingham, England. The Pakistani government paid for her transport to the UK for treatment. She has not been back to her homeland since the day she was shot.

The assassination attempt led to worldwide outrage, media coverage, and an outpouring of sympathy. It also resulted in the first Right to Education Bill in Pakistan and Malala Day at the UN on her sixteenth birthday calling for worldwide access to education. In 2014 Malala went on to become the youngest recipient of the Nobel Peace Prize. Prior to winning this prize, she and her father cofounded the Malala Fund. As a Nobel Laureate, she donated all of her prize money to finance a secondary school for girls in Pakistan. Through the Malala Fund, she continues to fight for the rights of children all around the world to have twelve years of safe, quality education.

Malala
Gabriele DiTota
Melbourne, Florida

"Let us remember: One book, one pen, one child, and one teacher can change the world."
—*Malala Yousafzai*

Artist Gabriele DiTota's work is an extension of her life, and this piece really hit home. When Gabriele hears the news of refugees fleeing war-torn areas, particularly in the Middle East and on the African continent, her thoughts always turn to the children. There is a whole generation of children whose sense of security is threatened by outside influences and who have no access to schools because of the very problems that they are fleeing. Gabriele's mother's education in Bedlin, Germany, was cut short due to World War II. Schools were turned into infirmaries, and the young preteens and teenagers were pressed into service as nursing help. Gabriele has heard her mother's stories of her refugee trek fleeing these atrocities, and the lost opportunities due to a lack of education. Her mother's stories made Malala's story resonate with Gabriele.

Gabriele was impressed with Malala's desire for education for all, but particularly for girls. Malala's story takes place during a time of oppression from the Taliban in Pakistan. The tyrannical similarities remain even though Malala is from a different time and place than Gabriele's mom.

Gabriele tweaked the coloration of the image of Malala. She used a shibori dyeing technique to create the fabric for the hair and acrylic inks to paint fabrics for the head covering. The quote was the inspiration for the seriousness of the expression because unfortunately, women's lack of access to education is all too common. The fabric on the right is stamped with a repeating motif reminiscent of Pakistani ornamentation.

I tell my story not because it is unique, because it is not. It is the story of many girls.

Malala Yousafzai
Nobel Peace Prize 2014

Malala Yousafzai

Nicki Allen

Springfield, Virginia

"I speak not for myself but for those without voice . . . those who have fought for their rights . . . their right to live in peace, their right to be treated with dignity, their right to equality of opportunity, their right to be educated." —Malala Yousafzai

When artist Nicki Allen was designing this quilt, she spent a good deal of time researching. She read *I Am Malala* by Malala Yousafzai and Christina Lamb. Nicki went on the Internet to find images and quotes to inspire her creativity. She developed quite a list to work from, but had difficulty tracking down the necessary permissions. Nicki ultimately got permission for the image she used, but not for the quotes she wanted. So Nicki wrote her own text based on the events of the day Malala was shot. As a quilt artist, Nicki often struggles with keeping her work "uncluttered." Sometimes it's difficult for her to know when to stop creating. It is machine pieced, raw-edge appliquéd using batiks, and it is machine quilted.

On October 9th 2012, 15 yr old Malala Yousafzai was on her way home from school when a member of the Taliban stopped her school bus. The gunman boarded the bus and fired three shots directly at Malala. One of those bullets hit the left side of her head. She was not silenced.

203

The Bletchley Girls

. . . helped change the course of history by cracking secret Nazi codes, thereby shortening World War II by at least two years.

The Bletchley Girls
Alison Laurence
Auckland, New Zealand

"The geese that laid the golden egg and never cackled."
—Winston Churchill, British Prime Minister

"We knew how vital it was not to give away what we were doing. That could have caused a real disaster. And so I blocked most of it out!" —Jean Tocher, Bletchley Girl

Under the strictest code of secrecy, the women of Bletchley Park assisted in breaking the German codes during World War II. Bletchley Park, a mansion seventy kilometers from London, was Britain's most secret establishment and home of the Government Code and Cypher School. It housed a secret team whose mission was to crack the Nazi codes and ciphers, the most well-known being Enigma.

Women from all areas of life joined the war effort. Bletchley enlisted members of the Women's Royal Naval Service (WRNS) nicknamed Wrens, members of the Woman's Auxiliary Air Force (WAAF), and civilians. The 1,600 personnel in 1942 grew to more than 8,000 by the end of 1944. Three-fourths of these were women known as "the Bletchley Girls."

They were sworn to secrecy about their work, told that if they talked, they could be shot. Secrets were to be kept for the rest of their lives, even from their families. Posters stressed the need for secrecy with slogans such as "Loose Lips Might Sink Ships," and "Careless Talk Costs Lives."

The Bletchley Girls undertook a variety of jobs, often repetitive, boring, and carried out in cold wooden huts. Some were tasked with tracking the enemy radio, carefully logging every letter or figure. Messages were sent to Bletchley Park (Station X) to be deciphered, translated, and fit together like a puzzle to produce a complete picture of what the enemy was doing. Some worked on the BOMBE, an electromechanical machine designed by Alan Turing, to decipher the Enigma encrypted messages.

Deciphering the coded communications between Hitler, his High Command, and their front line, revealing the strategies of the German regime, was essential to victory. A machine was built to help analyze their contents—the Colossus. It consisted of valves and transistors, was the size of a large room, and was very noisy.

Some Bletchley Girls became operators of this machine, the first electronic computer in the world. It was precision work, with long, tiring hours. On May 8, 1945, the wireless said that the fighting would stop at one minute past midnight. The European war was over, and the Bletchley Girls were the first to know! It was VE Day. The work for the Bletchley Girls ceased. There was great rejoicing, and they all left Bletchley Park.

Stories about the Bletchley Girls and Bletchley Park remained secret until 1974 when permission was given for a book, *The Ultra Secret*. William Stevenson wrote another titled *A Man Called Intrepid*.

Artist Alison Laurence was inspired to tell this story as the mother of her friend worked at Bletchley Park on the Colossus and Alison feels it is a story that must be kept alive. Her friend's mother still refuses to discuss her work as a Bletchley Girl, maintaining the vow of silence that she took at the time. Alison chose to fly the Union Jack at the top of the quilt to express the patriotism felt by all who worked tirelessly at Bletchley Park. Alongside the flag, she has shown the letters as they appeared on the Enigma machine. They represent the codes and ciphers from Enigma, the Morse codes intercepted, the Colossus, and earlier BOMBE machines.

The image of Bletchley Park sits as a backdrop, fittingly pale, as more than seventy years have passed since the end of the War. Finally, three Wrens represent the Bletchley Girls. The faces are featureless—symbolic of the Oath of Secrecy the Bletchley Girls signed. The cotton linen quilt was made using fusible appliqué, fabric printing, and hand embroidery. It was machine quilted and enhanced using fabric pencils.

ENIAC Programmers

. . . six women who programmed ENIAC, the world's first electronic general-purpose programmable computer.

The ENIAC Programmers

Jayne Gaskins

Reston, Virginia

"I was told I'd never make it to VP rank because I was too outspoken. Maybe so, but I think men will always find an excuse for keeping women in their 'place.' So, let's make that place the executive suite and start more of our own companies." —Jean Bartik

In 1946, the US military introduced Electronic Numerical Integrator and Computer (ENIAC), the world's first electronic general-purpose programmable computer. The war ended a few months before ENIAC could be completed but, recognizing that the potential went far beyond missile trajectories, the military pushed on to completion. The original objective was to find a way to project the trajectories of missiles quickly. Most men were fighting in World War II, so they recruited female mathematicians to do the programming and, having only schematics to work with, six women did just that. Most women had to relinquish their jobs to returning soldiers, but these programmers were requested to remain longer so they could teach men how to do the jobs. Most went on to make even more significant contributions to the development of the computers that are an integral part of our lives today.

ENIAC was presented in a front-page public relations extravaganza including a prestigious dinner celebration. The programmers were not mentioned or invited. Fifty years later another celebration paid tribute to the creators of ENIAC. Only two of the women were invited, and then only because of other significant contributions they had since made in the field of computer science. Again, their original accomplishments went unrecognized.

Deep within the heart and soul of every computer we touch today are the spirits of these ENIAC programmers: Francis "Betty" Snyder Holberton, Betty "Jean" Jennings Bartik, Kathleen McNulty Mauchly Antonelli, Marlyn Wescoff Meltzer, Ruth Lichterman Teitelbaum, and Frances Bilas Spence.

HERstory recognizes their accomplishments and contributions:

Francis "Betty" Snyder Holberton (1917–2001) was the coleader ENIAC programmer who went on to help create COBOL and FORTRAN computer languages. She came up with mnemonic character commands that made sense like A for add and B for bring. She suggested replacing UNIVAC's black exterior with gray-beige that has become the standard for computers.

Betty "Jean" Jennings Bartik (1924–2011) was the coleader ENIAC programmer who went on to work on BINAC, the first computer to use magnetic tape instead of punch cards, and was responsible for designing UNIVAC's logic circuits, then became one of the early editors of computer information publishing at Auerbach Publishers, Data Decisions, and McGraw-Hill.

Kathleen McNulty Mauchly Antonelli (1921–2006) married ENIAC co-inventor John Mauchly and raised five children. She later worked on BINAC and UNIVAC I, whose hardware was designed by John. After John's death, she gave lectures on ENIAC, often with Jean Bartik.

Marlyn Wescoff Meltzer (1922–2008) married and volunteered at Shir Ami Library. She delivered Meals on Wheels and knit more than 500 chemotherapy hats for the Susan B. Komen Foundation.

Ruth Lichterman Teitelbaum (1924–1986) taught the programming tools that she had developed to the next generation of ENIAC programmers.

Frances Bilas Spence (1922–2012) continued working with ENIAC after the war.

In 1997, all six of these women were inducted into the Women in Technology Hall of Fame.

Artist Jayne Gaskins' work is an abstracted assembly of six sheets of very basic binary code. Each is a different color to honor the unique contributions of the six women. All they had to work with on this first computer was logical diagrams and the most simple, basic $1 + 0$ binary numbers present on each colored sheet. The silver binding represents the enormous pieces of machinery consisting of approximately 18,000 vacuum tubes and forty-eight-foot panels that filled an entire room. Jayne designed each sheet of code separately in Photoshop and had them printed on silk fabric. The units were assembled over varying thicknesses of batting and then quilted. It was appliquéd and machine quilted.

CAPT Kristen Griest, 1LT Shaye Haver, and MAJ Lisa Jaster

(1989–) • (1990–) • (1978–)

. . . became the United States Army's first three female Rangers.

Triumph
Laura Mosher
West Point, New York

"I was thinking of future generations of women. I would like them to have that opportunity, so I had that pressure on myself." —Captain Kristen Griest

Captain Kristen Griest, 1st Lieutenant Shaye Haver, and Major Lisa Jaster became the United States Army's first three female Rangers in 2015. Graduates of the United States Military Academy at West Point (2011, 2012, and 2000, respectively), they began the Ranger Course at Fort Benning, Georgia in April of 2015. Capt. Griest, a military policewoman, and 1st Lt. Haver, an AH-64 Apache helicopter pilot, graduated on August 21, 2015. Maj. Jaster, a thirty-seven-year-old Army Reserve Engineer officer with deployment experience in Iraq and Afghanistan (and married mother of two), followed on Oct. 16, 2015. They were members of the first class of Rangers to include women (twenty started but did not complete the course), in a class that included 380 men, ninety-four of whom graduated with Griest and Haver in August.

The US Army's grueling sixty-one-day Ranger Course, based in Fort Benning, Georgia, includes phases in the mountains of northern Georgia and the swamps and streams in the Florida Panhandle. It is sixty-one days long if a student completes each phase on the first try, although these women, like many soldiers, had to repeat several sections of the course. Ranger school focuses on challenging soldiers with lack of sleep and little food as they take on battlefield tasks including long marches and mock ambushes. In 2015, just over 1,600 of a total of over 4,000 men who began the course graduated—a rate of 40%. Approximately 3% of Army men are eligible to wear the Ranger tab. They include some service members who serve in the Ranger Regiment, but also many others who serve in jobs ranging from military police to helicopter pilot.

Major Jaster, the oldest of the female officers to complete the course, endured the long months she spent in training by focusing on her goals. She had a quick comeback for younger, male soldiers who whined about the adversity. "I'm old enough to be your mother; I've been here nine weeks. Shut up," she told them.

First Lieutenant Haver said whenever she became discouraged while clambering through woods, swamps, and mountains; she'd look to her male comrades and gain strength. "The ability to look around at my peers and see that they were sucking just as bad as I was kept me going," she said.

Since graduating Ranger school, Capt. Griest has again made history by becoming the Army's first female infantry officer. She recently graduated from the Maneuver Captain's Career Course and earned the right to wear the distinctive blue infantry cord.

Both Haver and Griest admitted that they felt the weight of their historical assignment. "I was thinking of future generations of women," Griest said. "I would like them to have that opportunity, so I had that pressure on myself."

These strong, determined women have broken through the Army's "camouflage ceiling" and now proudly wear the Ranger tab and serve as role models to the women following in their footsteps.

Artist Laura Mosher, a librarian at West Point, created this tribute to the West Point graduates using cotton, felt, and fabric from a female Army officer's Army Combat Uniform. It was machine appliquéd, machine quilted, and embroidered. The three Rangers are represented by female symbols crossed with Ranger patches. At the center of the patches are insignia: the wings represent the Aviation branch, the castle represents Corps of Engineers, and the crossed pistols represent the Military Police. These are the three branches represented by these women when they graduated from Ranger School. Since graduation, Griest has transferred to the Infantry branch, but Laura chose to use the insignia that she wore when she graduated.

Las Sinsombrero (1927–1939)

. . . Spanish women who fought for rights for women.

Las Sinsombrero
Marisa Márquez
Madrid, Spain

"Las Sinsombrero were many, each of them with a feat that belonged to them . . . Their greatest achievement was to be able to be themselves in the midst of a society that took the time to accept that they had to look at them . . ." —Tània Balló, translated from Las sinsombrero: Sin ellas, la historia no está completa (Las Sinsombrero: Without Them, the Story Is Not Complete)

In 1927 a group of students, males and females walked the streets of Madrid without wearing their hats, an insult to the status quo of the time. They wanted to fight the conservative minds and bring new ideas into a very traditional society.

A liberal government was elected in 1931 in which women were given responsibilities. With the new constitution, the equality of men and women became a real possibility. There was no right to vote for women yet, but they could be elected to be representatives, and two women were elected, Clara Campoamor and Victoria Kent. Clara Campoamor fought for equal rights for women, focusing on making it illegal to discriminate against women because of their sex in being hired to work for the government.

During this time women fought for their rights and some laws were approved in the parliament; divorce and abortion became legalized due in 1936 to the influence of Federica Montseny, health minister (the first woman in Europe to be minister in a government).

In 1927 there was a generation of artists and writers that were very influential in their time: Salvador Dalí, Rafael Alberti, Federico Garcia Lorca, and Luis Cernuda. There was also a group of women who are virtually forgotten because they were erased from the textbooks: Concha Méndez-Cuesta, María Teresa León, Ernestina de Champourcín, Rosa Chacel, Josefina de la Torre, María Zambrano, Margarita Gil Roësset, Margarita Manso, Maruja Mallo, Angeles Santos, and Remedios Varo.

Las Sinsombrero represented a group of women that fought against the status quo to become a whole people, independent of their spouses and family. They became writers, artists, or politicians but their careers were cut short when in 1939 Spain became a fascist dictatorship under Francisco Franco, and the majority of them were exiled, silenced, or killed. The new government deleted all the achievements of these women. Spanish women did not have the same rights again until 1975.

Artist Marisa Márquez says that they are still fighting for equality. In this tribute to women who tried to make a difference in Spain, Marisa painted the pieces, machine appliquéd them to the background, and machine quilted her piece. Her quilt represents the women in the generation from 1927 to 1939 that fought for their rights and the right to choose the way to live their life equal to men. They don't have faces because Spaniards don't study their achievements, they don't remember their names, and they have disappeared from the textbooks and from Spanish culture. Books written by female authors of that period aren't mandatory reading in school. Books by male authors of the same period are required reading. Paintings that were produced by female artists from that time aren't in museums. Their political achievements are not in the history books. Their names are just forgotten. That's why there are only silhouettes, no faces. Their names are in the falling hat, left behind.

Betty Heinrich Berkstresser (May 12, 1919–)
Barbara Willis Heinrich (May 30, 1916–)

. . . serving as WASPs, flew during World War II, relieving men for duty overseas.

Taking Flight: My Great Aunts
Debra Goley
Goodyear, Arizona

"Men were off to war. It was the first time women flew in our service and we were being useful. Women were considered second class and not useful. You had to fight for your place." —Barbara Heinrich

From artist Debra Goley, great-niece of the two honorees:

My aunts were Women Airforce Service Pilots (WASP) of World War II. Under the leadership of Jacqueline Cochran, their mission was to ferry aircraft from factories to air bases across the country, relieving men for combat. More than 12,000 aircraft were utilized. A WASP candidate must have had 150 hours of flying time and have the boldness of spirit to leave home for Sweetwater, Texas, for basic training. In 1942, First Lady Eleanor Roosevelt declared, "This is not a time when women should be patient. We are in a war, and we need to fight it with all our ability and every weapon possible. Women pilots, in this particular case, are a weapon waiting to be used."

Two such women are my great-aunts, Betty Heinrich Berkstresser and Barbara Willis Heinrich. I am proud of their achievement and want to honor their service. World War II was raging, and there was a manpower shortage. More than 25,000 women applied to be WASPs, 1,074 were chosen, and two of them were my aunts. After going through basic training, my two great aunts raised their right hand and received their wings directly from Jackie Cochran, evidenced by a photo I found of Betty, showing Jackie Cochran pinning flight wings

on her. Both of my aunts, still living, are "forces to be reckoned with." They are bold in spirit and good at flying.

My Aunt Betty's math professor at the University of Houston in 1943 noted an ad in the Houston newspaper asking for pilots to serve. My aunt dropped everything to join the Sweetwater gals. I had the pleasure of interviewing her in November 2016, and she gleefully noted: "the best memory of being a WASP is flying." She flew missions daily from Hondo Army Airfield base in Texas to destinations as far away as New York. She was featured on the front cover of the base paper *Beam*, Vol. II, No. 26, 28 July 1944, suited up to fly a C-60. It was the photo that I used to portray her looking over her shoulder in what seems pure joy.

My great-aunt Barbara Willis Heinrich was recently featured on *CBS San Francisco*. It was her 100th birthday on May 30, 2016, which happens to be the date of the original Memorial Day. The taped interview called "100 Years" was to celebrate her centenarian day and honor her service. In the interview, she talked about being fearless when doing spins. In the pictures shown to me by the Heinrich family, I stared at a confident young female pilot leaning on her plane while standing on the wing of a C-47 with the ease of a fly girl. She is Aunt Bobbie to me, and her stance had to be incorporated into my analysis of what the base, the uniforms, the aerial view might have been like if I could see through time.

In 2010, my aunts received the Congressional Gold Medal, the highest possible civilian award given by Congress, in Washington, DC, at the Capitol. My Aunt Betty seemed quiet when I asked her about this important honor and the ceremony. I could tell in her eyes; it was just part of the mission.

Artist Debra Goley designed a composite of portrait, aerial, and elevation photos provided by her aunts. In her piece, you can see the aerial of the runway, the elevation of her aunts and the detail of Betty's jacket. When Debra makes a composite drawing, she highlights areas that are important to the subject. She circled Aunt Bobbie's head with the body of the plane.

Jean Little (1932–)

. . . internationally acclaimed Canadian children's author whose books tackle challenging issues.

Reading a Little
Maggie Vanderweit
Fergus, Ontario, Canada

"You pay a price for the 'gift' of an active imagination. While mine played a major part in making me a writer, it also made me adept at transforming run-of-the-mill molehills into towering mountain ranges."
—Jean Little

Jean Little was born legally blind in Taiwan in 1932. Her parents, Canadian doctors, were medical missionaries. The family moved back to Ontario in 1939, and Jean started school. She graduated from the University of Toronto in English Literature.

Her first novel, *Mine for Keeps*, about a girl with cerebral palsy, was written to offer a spunky, realistic role model for children with special needs. It won a major award, the first of many. Jean has written forty-five children's works on a talking computer. She travels with a seeing-eye dog.

Jean takes on timeless, universal, and challenging themes—disease, loss, death, abandonment, addiction, war, disabilities, and bigotry. Her resilient children learn to cope, to build or rebuild relationships, to change, to trust, to be very brave, to examine their own flaws, and to help each other. They accept and move through their problems, to become hopeful and strong. Adversity does not get in the way of living a full and happy life.

Jean Little's books have been translated into over twelve languages and made into movies. Jean is a member of the Order of Canada and a recipient of six honorary degrees. She has worked as an adjunct literature professor and has a school named after her. She travels extensively, talking to audiences about the joys of reading and writing. She remains one of Canada's most important and best-loved children's authors.

Maggie shares the story of her admiration for Jean Little:

"One of the conditions for immigrants to be allowed into Canada from Holland after World War II was that some family members had to go into 'service' for a while to take the place of all the men lost in the war. My mother worked for the Little family as a maid for a number of years. She cooked, cleaned, and did laundry for the family and the two medical practices operating from the house. (Both of Jean's parents were doctors.)

Jean has been legally blind from birth. My mother, Rose Vanderweit, was fifteen when she started working for the Littles, and so was Jean, so they became friends. Mom went to school with Jean part-time to learn English. After that, they worked at a camp for disabled children and taught together at a special needs school. My mother became a nurse; surely influenced by the Doctors Little. They remain lifelong friends, and I grew up reading all of Jean's books. Always, for gifts, we got extra special hand-printed volumes of her poetry and stories. The earliest books included stories about Dutch immigrants finding their way in Canada. My childhood best friend is Jewish, and Jean wrote a few stories about two girls who were a lot like us.

During my teen years, I attended a summer camp which Jean sometimes directed. I learned all the songs and participated in the activities she often writes about.

When I went to university in Toronto, I attended the same college Jean graduated from and sometimes helped her when she was doing book lectures. The children Jean and her sister Pat adopted and my sons are all part First Nations, so we have that in common too.

Jean herself is an amazing example of what you can do in spite of adversity. Jean's characters and stories and the way people interacted and solved life's dilemmas have profoundly influenced me. I feel I am so much stronger and better for having her moral compass to guide me."

Maggie used photo transfer on cotton to create this machine-pieced and machine-quilted work. The notes on the quilt are from Jean to Maggie through the years.

Margit Louisa Olson (1956–2014)

. . . pursued excellence in everything,
touching lives and blazing the trail for others
with Down syndrome.

Margit Olson, Lady of Love
Birgit Ruotsala
Green Bay, Wisconsin

"Excuse me, may I have a hug?" —Margit Olson

Margit Olson, born with Trisomy 21 Down syndrome was a trailblazer her whole life and gives a face to those born with mental and physical disabilities. When Margit was born on August 9, 1956, the trend for people born with Down syndrome was to institutionalize or at best, keep them at home hidden and sheltered. Margit was kept at home, and she began the mission of her life to engage with everyone around her touching the hearts of each person who interacted with her.

From a very early age, Margit was tenacious and persistent. To perfect her handwriting, she spent one summer vacation copying the whole family edition of Webster's Dictionary. She reveled in her gymnastic prowess demonstrating her capability to do the splits every chance she got. She was the most popular baseball player in the neighborhood as children rallied to her side to play and as they grew older and had their own children, she taught generations how to slug the ball out of the yard.

Being a very loyal person, Margit championed children in school and stood up to bullying before it became a topic of discussion. Her primary modus operandi was to show and practice love and respect for all life—both human and animal. Margit lived her life in love with those who surrounded her. When Alzheimer's stripped her of the ability to do anything for herself, she still had the power to interact with her hospice nurses to impart gratitude and love.

Her artwork which borders this quilt was sought after by friends, neighbors, and family. She showed her work in several exhibitions and won awards for her sense of color.

Artist Birgit Ruotsala is Margit's sister. She wanted to honor her because she is part of what is good in our lives in this world. Her face reflects all that the human condition can achieve that is positive: love, generosity, tenderness, boldness, creativity, perseverance, compassion, kindness, humor, a sense of adventure, integrity, and a spirit of innocence. Margit exemplifies the good in everyone and gives a face to people that each of us knows. According to the National Down Syndrome Society, one in every 691 people is born with Down syndrome. Birgit lifts this woman up as a person who achieved all that she set out to do. She lived her life to the fullest, and through striving to achieve excellence in all she did with all the capabilities she possessed, she was a role model for children growing up in her midst. Her accomplishments may seem small in our world, and yet, she blazed trails for many Down syndrome people following her in the education system, in Special Olympics, in her social setting, and in her faith community.

Margit died on May 25, 2014. At her memorial service, attendees shared "Margit" stories that showed how she impacted their lives. There are many special education teachers working in the field because of her influence, many pastors who have stories to share about her Christ-like love, and there are many people in the Down syndrome community that have an example of what is possible in their own lives because of Margit.

Birgit scanned a photo of her sister which she lightened and then printed on cotton fabric. Details were first put in with thread painting. Color was added with textile paint, markers, and Inktense colored pencils. The word cloud was designed on the computer and printed and added behind the portrait to describe her. The border was a scan of the original artwork of Margit. It was printed, pieced, and quilted.

Anna Marie Peterson (1916–)

. . . became a professional artist at age ninety-three.

My Mom Anna Marie Peterson: Artist, Age 100

Betty Hahn

Sun City, Arizona

"I sat down with it and made the awfulest looking thing you can imagine, but it was fun. But then I tried again, and it came out looking pretty good."
—Anna Marie Peterson

From artist Betty Hahn, who just happens to call Anna Marie "Mom":

Anna Marie Peterson was born the only child to a Norwegian immigrant father and a second generation Norwegian mother in Ames, Iowa. She loved school, eventually graduating from Iowa State College, majoring in applied art. Having become an accomplished pianist, she began playing for her church first as a pianist, and then as organist. She was a church organist from her late teens to her late 80s.

Her artistic abilities were used as a homemaker and didn't blossom until her ninety-eight-year-old father moved in with her and her husband. He had worked until then as a shoe repairman/shoemaker and was bored just watching television; she decided to see if he could hook a rug with some yarn and canvas she had intended to use herself. Over the course of the next seven years, they made and sold over 275 wall hangings that she designed and he hooked. He did his last one at age 105 and he lived to be 106.

She then put her talents to work making quilts for three children, eight grandchildren, twenty-two great-grandchildren, and a recent great-great-grandchild. In 2007 they moved from Iowa to Sun City, Arizona, near us. She began taking art quilting classes with me, and during one where we were using bleach, she begged off because of the smell. I set her up instead to demonstrate needle-felting, which she hadn't known how to do. Hand needle-felting involves using a barbed needle to punch wool or other fibers into a felt background. The process is not typical in the modern art world, but the results are breathtaking and incredibly realistic. Initially, she made a self-declared awful piece but said it was fun. What would she do with this new talent? She was ninety-three years old at the time. I suggested she make portraits of birds because of her love for them. Her animal and nature portraits leave gallery owners, judges, and art connoisseurs speechless. She has now completed over one hundred pieces, had forty of them accepted into art shows, and at age ninety-seven began writing a blog, http://grammaannsfelting.blogspot.com, to share her new art career with the world. Now, at age 100, she has had over 12,200 views of her blog, which she maintains herself.

She recently accompanied me to the Houston International Quilt Festival. She happily shared her business cards, which she makes herself. She hopes to reach the age of 106 as her dad did. She will need that much time to use her stash of fabric and felting supplies!

Anna Marie is my mother. How do you show one hundred years of a remarkable woman who is "Mom"? I gathered photos from stored boxes, scanned and printed them, and laid them under my silk. I put myself on autopilot and started drawing with a fine tip pen, then filled in the images with paint. Somehow she appeared there on the silk, as a baby, a toddler, a young woman, an organist, a mother of three, a fan of "cool" cars, a grandma making quilts for the babies, and an artist getting accepted into galleries. I was so afraid, something I almost never am, making this quilt. When I finished, we were all amazed to see her there, vibrant and beautiful. This is a silk crepe de chine whole cloth quilt painted with acrylic paint and Tsukineko inks.

Marna Williams (1926–)

. . . worked in the Civil Rights movement, helping African Americans obtain rights previously denied them.

Planting the Mustard Seed
Susanne Miller Jones
Potomac Falls, Virginia

"We were not protesting against injustice but rather cooperating with the political and religious leaders in seeing that the justice of the Civil Rights Act of 1964 be provided to all of Birmingham citizens."
—Marna Williams

In the words of artist Susanne Jones, Marna's daughter-in-law:

When the four little girls Denise McNair, Carole Robertson, Cynthia Wesley, and Addie Mae Collins were killed in the Sixteenth Street Baptist Church bombing of 1963 in Birmingham, Alabama, Marna Williams was raising four children of her own. It haunted her that it could have been her children killed in that church. Marna had to do something. She joined with some other women from her Presbyterian Church family. They sought out resources and found cooperation from the local Catholic Church and the Greater Birmingham Ministry. Together they formed the Mustard Seed.

They began a preschool and an after-school program in the black segregated neighborhood near their church. The women met with the children's parents and listened carefully to their needs. They went with them to community agencies to get those needs met. The Mustard Seed's Men's Brotherhood sponsored a baseball team and built a baseball field in the cow pasture formerly used by a dairy. (They rented the cow pasture for $1 a year.) The boys competed in integrated tournaments sponsored by the Police Athletic League, which began as a means for law enforcement to interact with the city youth.

The community grew to become the Social Service Program at the Southtown Housing project, and a model for the United States housing project. The women were not protesting against injustice but rather cooperating with the political and religious leaders in seeing that the justice of the Civil Rights Act of 1964 was provided to all Birmingham citizens. It was evident to all that the Mustard Seed community was united in love for one another. At the same time, their actions created conflict with family and friends who believed that the Mustard Seed's actions were a threat to life as their family and friends knew it. At the time, Marna wondered about who she was and what her choice had to do with the meaning of her life. The Mustard Seed transformed not only the Southtown community but Marna herself.

I made this quilt to honor my mother-in-law and friend, Marna Williams. I covered the state of Alabama with pictures of Denise, Carole, Cynthia, and Addie Mae printed on organza to give the photos a haunting quality. In the center is a thread-sketched Marna talking to a small boy. Vignettes from the Mustard Seed Project show a boy sliding into base on the softball team, a child being read to, and food being picked up at the cooperative food pantry. In the lower left-hand corner is a fabric recreation of a watercolor, originally painted by Marna, of children of all races playing peacefully together. That was the dream of Martin Luther King, Jr. and the Civil Rights movement. It is Marna's dream too.

Susan "Lucky" Shie (1950–)

. . . teacher and producer of award-winning art quilts; founder of the Green Quilts Project.

Lyrical Lucky Shie
Karol Kusmaul
Inverness, Florida

"I hope that my way of working has turned art quilting into a way to communicate social justice issues, and help people be inspired." —Susan Shie

From artist Karol Kusmaul, Susan's friend and student:

Susan "Lucky" Shie was born with albinism. She is legally blind. Her eyes are very sensitive to light. She must be very close to her work to see what she is doing. She has never let her vision challenges stop her from following her passions—to create art, to document current world and personal events, to raise awareness about social, political, and environmental issues worldwide.

I interviewed Susan, who spoke about developing and managing the Green Quilts Project, encouraging artists to communicate ideas about the environment through art quilts. Susan described the art quilts as "storage batteries of caring, to cover the earth with healing energy." Quilt National presented a Green Quilt Award to one of Susan's art pieces. The work was photographed and registered. Susan asked the International Quilt Study Group (IQSG) to archive the entire fifteen years of the project. IQSG accepted the proposal, accepting six large file boxes. Michelle Merges Martens, Robin Schwalb, and Susan Faeder assisted Susan.

Susan Shie runs the Lucky School of Quilting in which she encourages her adult students to draw without fear, and express themselves with childlike courage and abandon, not worrying about perfection. Susan says, "Every artist in the history book was an iconoclast and broke from tradition. The ones who hatched the ideas were not followers. They had strong passion. No matter what your style, you throw it together in an instinctive and natural way, with your heart. If you want to be recognized, be pigheaded! Have a look that's just yours. Stay thirsty, curious. Stay in 'what if?' mode."

Susan has earned two college degrees in painting, researched and produced thousands of award-winning art quilts, and maintained a rigorous worldwide teaching schedule. She also fights for peace and for social, environmental, political, and women's rights. She enjoys spending time with friends, family, her garden, her dog Libby, and in her kitchen. Susan's work has earned acceptance into Quilt National thirteen times. In 1990, she was awarded a $50,000 grant from the National Endowment for the Arts, and she has received several grants from the Ohio Arts Council. Susan says, "I hope my way of working has turned art quilting into a way to communicate social justice issues and help people be inspired. My work has always been too loud, feminist, and kooky for corporate purchases. I might as well say what I really think."

This quilt is not made in my usual style. I made it in Susan's style, having taken an extended class with her, learning her art quilt processes. Susan is a painter, talker, thinker, activist, and writer. She constantly records world and personal events, drawing and journaling in her sketchbooks and on fabric. I've spent two separate weeks with her at retreat events, getting to know her well. I find her brilliant, prolific, and delightful. I am impressed with her artistic accomplishments despite the fact that Susan lives with albinism and is legally blind. Because of my admiration for Susan and her accomplishments, I interviewed her to learn more about her passions and her life's work. I've highlighted that information in the quilt. Drawn and painted symbols are covered with text—including quotes and descriptors, Susan's accomplishments and opinions. It is a whole cloth quilt drawn and painted on white fabric. Text and details were added with a permanent Rub-a-Dub marker. It was embroidered, machine quilted, and bound using Susan's methods. I feel like the lucky one to have had the chance to get to know and learn from her! There is a purchased embroidered bird appliquéd to the quilt.

Yvonne Porcella (1936– 2016)

. . . founder of Studio Art Quilt Associates and godmother of art quilting.

May I Take Off My Hat?
Susanne Miller Jones
Potomac Falls, Virginia

"I have enjoyed a life of travel to exotic destinations, meeting extraordinary people, experiencing more joys than sorrows . . . I am forever grateful to those who made it possible for me to live life to the fullest."
—Yvonne Porcella

Yvonne Porcella was raised in California on an almond farm. One of two girls, she was given an opportunity for a nursing education that was too good to pass up.

In 1962, she began making unique garments, quilts, and wall hangings. Her work was featured in major exhibits, museums, and galleries. Yvonne worked in a series, exploring new techniques before moving on to the next new thing. Her work was vibrant and bold. She adored black and white checkerboards, half square triangles, and log cabins. She often hand painted her fabrics to create subtle pastel watercolor effects. She machine pieced, hand appliquéd, and hand quilted her pieces. She wrote nine books along the way tracing her artistic journey and inspiring others to join her in creating art quilts.

In 1989, Yvonne founded Studio Art Quilt Associates and served as the President of the Board of Directors for twelve years. She was traveling extensively, teaching and lecturing both nationally and internationally. The Renwick Gallery of Art of the Smithsonian Institution bought her quilt *Takoage* in 1994. Along with 300 objects from all of the Smithsonian museums, it traveled in a celebration exhibit of the 150th anniversary of the Smithsonian Institution. She served on the Board of Directors for the Alliance for American Quilts (now The Quilt Alliance) from 1997 to 2004. Yvonne was inducted into the Quilters Hall of Fame in 1998 and was the fifth quilter to be given the Silver Star Award at the International Quilt Festival in Houston, Texas.

Yvonne inspired us all with her enthusiasm, energy, and talent. She was kind to everyone and loved being surrounded by her art quilting community, the one she nurtured and encouraged.

This piece was created by artist Susanne Jones after she spent time with Yvonne at Sacred Threads 2015 during the last year of her life. Yvonne was going through another round of cancer treatments, fighting the good fight for her last six years. She was not about to let that keep her at home in California when Sacred Threads and the Quilt Alliance's Not Fade Away conference were happening on the east coast. So she traveled all day to be there. When she got in Susanne's car at Dulles Airport, she asked, "May I take off my hat?" Susanne was impressed by her concern for everyone else's comfort. Susanne's first thought was, "Dear lady, you can do whatever you want." Susanne used that event as the inspiration for this portrait of Yvonne in a gold wool beret surrounded by her favorite colors: red, white, and black; and her favorite traditional piecing techniques.

225

Karey P. Bresenhan

. . . founder of International Quilt Market and Quilt Festival and cofounder of the International Quilt Association.

Karey
Gabriele DiTota
Melbourne, Florida

"We know dedicated quilters don't regard quilting as an optional hobby, but as part of their lives. They, like quilters throughout history, quilt during good times and bad. Their quilting is both a means of expressing themselves creatively and also of expressing what is going on in their lives and how they are dealing with it." —Karey P. Bresenhan

Karoline "Karey" Bresenhan, who is descended from a long line of quilters, has made quilts her life's work. In 1974 she opened Great Expectations, a retail antique shop in Houston, and grew it into one of the largest quilt shops in the country. Her first Quilt Fair that same year was the forerunner of the International Quilt Festivals to come. In 1976 Karey, with her mother, founded the Quilt Guild of Greater Houston.

Karey Bresenhan is recognized as a visionary and a driving force in promoting and cultivating the quilting industry. Karey's foresight led to the International Quilt Festival and International Quilt Market. In 1979, Karey held the first International Quilt Market where quilt shop owners could come to buy wholesale fabrics, supplies, and books. The same year she also established Quilts, Inc., the parent company for her shows and ventures. It was also this year that she cofounded the South/Southwest Quilt Association, which later became the International Quilt Association (IQA).

Concern over low-priced copies of quilts being made overseas prompted Karey, along with several others, to begin the Alliance for American Quilts (currently The Quilt Alliance) to safeguard American quilt history. Their projects include Quilters S.O.S. (Save Our Stories), Boxes Under the Bed, Quilt Treasures, and the International Quilt Index.

Karey has written multiple books inspired by her love of antique quilts and Texas Lone Star Quilts, and for documentation of special exhibits such as America: From the Heart. She is also a collector of more than 250 quilts. One of her most recent projects is the opening of the Texas Quilt Museum in LaGrange.

Karey's enthusiasm for quilting and her business insights have helped her establish and cultivate the quilting industry in the US and Europe.

Artist Gabriele DiTota started as a traditional quilter, learning the skills and the challenges of this unique craft form. In this way, she learned to appreciate the skill that is required to create very exact seams and angles that when joined created the exquisite and detailed quilts that Gabriele has seen on display in quilt shops and shows and sometimes in homes. She was bitten by the art quilt bug and now considers her quilts more of a canvas. She enjoys experimenting with hand-painted, dyed, and printed fabrics. Gabriele used raw-edge appliqué to create this piece honoring Karey, whom Gabriele considers a force in the quilt world. Next to Karey are some of the books that she has authored or coauthored. In her hand are brochures about Quilt Market and Quilt Festival and the Texas Quilt Museum, which Karey was instrumental in establishing. A Texas Star quilt was a logical choice for the background. The Texas Star is painted with acrylic inks as are Karey's face and hands. The scarf is hand-dyed silk.

Acknowledgments

Thanks, first of all, go to my supportive and loving family, I couldn't have done this without you. I am so very grateful to:

My grandmother, Anna Bruce Miller: She taught me how to sew when I was five or six. I'm grateful that she taught me a skill that has become my passion and given me great joy.

My parents, Sue and Bruce Miller: They always supported, encouraged, and believed in me. I am so very thankful that they taught me to follow my dreams.

My grandmother, Annie Gragg Mullins: Her perseverance inspires me even now, and her belief in me still undergirds me every day.

My husband, Todd Jones: Behind every strong woman should be a man like you. I couldn't have planned the exhibit, written the book, or gotten the quilts mailed to venues without your support and assistance. Thanks so much for taking all of the photos for the book and for the fact checking and technical editing that you did. You are the best!

My children, Sarah Jones and Doug Jones: Thanks for looking at every quilt I make and cheering me on. I enjoyed all of your special talents and events and was always your biggest cheerleader. Thanks for returning the favor and for your enthusiasm.

To my daughter Sarah and her friend Bree Cox: Thanks for coming up with a super title for this collection. Your help was invaluable!

My pals from the quilting community were instrumental in helping me, and I am grateful:

To my Sacred Threads Committee friends: Thanks for getting me involved in art quilting. Your support and challenges, no matter how large or small made a huge difference. A big shout-out to Lisa Ellis, Diane Dresdner, Sarah Entsminger, Elaine Evans, Sandi Goldman, Barbara Hollinger, Bunnie Jordan, Lauren Kingsland, Susan Lapham, Audrey Lipps, Vivian Milholen, Carole Nicholas, Starla Phelps, Shana Spiegel, and Anne Winchell for encouraging me.

To Donna Marcinkowski DeSoto: Thank you for including me in *Inspired by the Beatles* and *Inspired by the National Parks* and for encouraging me along the way with advice and

enthusiasm. You showed me how to create a community of artists, and I'm grateful.

To Lisa Ellis: Thank you for mentoring me and introducing me to the wonderful quilting community. You taught me all of the quilting basics, advised me on guilds and organizations to join, introduced me to wonderful people, and encouraged me always. Thank you for all of that and for jurying this collection.

To Cyndi Souder: Thank you for teaching me so much about art quilting during our Art Quilt Journey group. Your encouragement has been instrumental in my development. I value every "Holy crap" and "I love my job" that I get. Thanks for encouraging me and for jurying this collection.

To my Art Quilt Journey sisters, Wren Grumbles, Nancy Hershberger, Helen Hollingsworth, Sue Redden, and Jenny Winchell: Thank you for your support and encouragement. You are great cheerleaders.

To Schiffer Publishing, Pete Schiffer, and my editors Cheryl Weber and Sandra Korinchak: Thanks for all of your help and encouragement. You were always an email or a phone call away. I'm thrilled to be working with you and the whole team at Schiffer again.

To Janet Marney: Thank you for editing the final draft. I learned a lot from your edits. It was great to have fresh eyes on it.

Last but not least I send kudos and boatloads of thanks to the talented artists who created these wonderful tributes to strong women. You made this collection possible. You also provided the research hours on these wonderful women. Thank you for making my job easier by writing about these amazing ladies' groundbreaking accomplishments. I value the connections that we have made, virtually and in person. The world is a little smaller now, and I cherish the friendships that we have made through needles and thread. Thank you from the bottom of my heart.

Appendix

Ain't I A Woman?
Attributed to Sojourner Truth

Delivered in 1851 at the Women's Convention in Akron, Ohio

Well, children, where there is so much racket there must be something out of kilter. I think that 'twixt the negroes of the South and the women at the North, all talking about rights, the white men will be in a fix pretty soon. But what's all this here talking about?

That man over there says that women need to be helped into carriages, and lifted over ditches, and to have the best place everywhere. Nobody ever helps me into carriages, or over mud-puddles, or gives me any best place! And ain't I a woman? Look at me! Look at my arm! I have ploughed and planted, and gathered into barns, and no man could head me! And ain't I a woman? I could work as much and eat as much as a man—when I could get it—and bear the lash as well! And ain't I a woman? I have borne thirteen children, and seen most all sold off to slavery, and when I cried out with my mother's grief, none but Jesus heard me! And ain't I a woman?

Then they talk about this thing in the head; what's this they call it? [member of audience whispers, "intellect"] That's it, honey. What's that got to do with women's rights or negroes' rights? If my cup won't hold but a pint, and yours holds a quart, wouldn't you be mean not to let me have my little half measure full?

Then that little man in black there, he says women can't have as much rights as men, 'cause Christ wasn't a woman! Where did your Christ come from? Where did your Christ come from? From God and a woman! Man had nothing to do with Him.

If the first woman God ever made was strong enough to turn the world upside down all alone, these women together ought to be able to turn it back, and get it right side up again! And now they is asking to do it, the men better let them.

Obliged to you for hearing me, and now old Sojourner ain't got nothing more to say.

Letter to Theodore Roosevelt from Elizabeth Cady Stanton
(presented as dictated to her secretary)

New York, October 25, 1902.

Dear Sir,

As you are the first President of the United States who has ever given a public opinion in favor of woman suffrage, and when Governor of New York State, recommended the measure in a message to the Legislature, the members of the different suffrage associations in the United States urge you to advocate in your coming message to Congress, an amendment to the National Constitution for the enfranchisemoit [sic] of American women, now denied their most sacred right as citizens of a Republic.

In the beginning of our nation, the fathers declared that "no just government can be founded without the consent of the governed," and that "taxation without representation is tyranny." Both of these grand declarations are denied in the present position of woman, who constitutes one-half of the people. If Apolitical [sic] power inheres [sic] in the people—and women are surely people—then there is crjring [sic] need for an amendment to the National Constitution, making these fundamental principles verities.

In a speech made by you at Fitchburg, on Labor Day, you say that you are "in favor of an amendment to the Constitution of the United States, conferring additional power upon the Federal Government to deal with corporations." To control and restrain giant monopolies for the best interests of all the people is of vast import, but of far vaster importance is the establishment and protection of the rights and liberties of one-half the citizens of the United States. Surely there is no greater monopoly than that of all men in denying to all women a voice in the laws they are compelled to obey.

Abraham Lincoln immortalized himself by the emancipation of four million Southern slaves. Speaking for my suffrage coadjutors, we now desire that you, Mr. President, who are already celebrated for so many honorable deeds and worthy utterances, immortalize yourself by bringing about the complete emancipation of thirty-six million women.

With best wishes for your continued honorable career and re-election as President of the United States.

Elizabeth Cady Stanton.

WASP Requirements

Required qualifications for acceptance into WASP program

ARMY AIR FORCES
Headquarters Flying Training Command
Fort Worth, Texas

Present requirements:
a. Age: 21 to 35 years
b. Education: High school or equivalent
c. Experience: 150 hours previous flying, logged and certified
d. Personal interview with Miss Cochran or person designated
    by her
e. Medical examination by Army Flight Surgeon

Course:
    If applicant is accepted after personal interview and having
passed medical examination, the course will include:
- Approximately 100 hours flying, 25 of which will be
    under the hood
- Fifteen hours in Link Trainer
- 180 hours ground school course

Progress will be based on proficiency of student

Pay:
    While in training—$150 per month
    When assigned to duties—$250 per month

Applicant will have to be qualified at the end of above training
to pass commercial, written and flight test, and instrument
rating. Applicant can be eliminated at any time during the
process of the course at the discretion of the instructors.

Jacqueline Cochran
Director, Women's Flying Training

Glossary

Angelina® Fiber: very fine, unique fiber that is light reflective and light refractive. Adds sparkle and shine to art quilts.

Apliquick™: applique shapes traced onto lightweight fusible interfacing, cut out, and ironed on the wrong side of the fabric. Apliquick™ rods and glue stick are used to turn under the seam allowance prior to hand or machine stitching.

appliqué: a process, which can be done by hand, machine, or with fusible web; using small amounts of fabric which are then sewn onto a background

art quilt: an art quilt is defined by Studio Art Quilt Associates as "a creative visual work that is layered and stitched or that references this form of stitched layered structure"

batik: fabric designs made by covering an area with wax to prevent dye from penetrating the fabric in that area

batting: the middle layer of a quilt sandwich, usually cotton, wool, or polyester

beading: decorating or embellishing with beads, usually stitched on by hand

binding: a strip of fabric sewn over the raw edges of the quilt

broderie perse: French for "Persian embroidery," popular in the early 1800s; a type of appliqué where motifs are cut from printed fabric and appliquéd to the background

Colorhue® Silk Dye: instant-set concentrated silk dyes

couched: yarn or other threads are placed on the background fabric and fastened in place with small stitches.

Craftsy: an online site that offers classes in quilting, sewing, knitting, and art as well as other crafts

Derwent Inktense®Pencils: watercolor pencils, can be used dry for intense color or with water added to create a translucent effect. The color is permanent when dry.

diptych: a piece of art created over two panels. They are meant to hang side by side.

dupioni: a rough slubbed silk fabric woven from the threads of double cocoons. Also spelled doupion, doupioni, dupion, and douppioni.

Dye-Na-Flow: concentrated liquid color for use on untreated fabric, flows freely like dye. It is especially good for use on silk.

embellish: add interest to the piece with the addition of buttons, crystals, paint, ink, decorative threads, etc.

encaustic wax: hot wax to which color is added and used to paint cloth which is then heat set

free-motion quilting: machine quilting, using a darning foot, with the feed dogs lowered or covered while the quilter moves the quilt sandwich under the needle

fused: adhered to fabric via iron-on webs or interfacing

fussy cutting: cutting a detail or targeted piece of a pattern from the fabric, instead of cutting a piece at random

Galaxy® Fabric Markers: markers that have acid-free ink in them. They are permanent, non-toxic and non-bleeding.

hand-dyed fabric: fabric that is dyed by hand, often by the artist using it. Each piece of hand-dyed fabric is one of a kind with unique markings and textures.

hand-pieced: the method of assembling the quilt top without using a machine. The stitching is done by hand.

hotfix: trims that have a heat-sensitive glue that, when heated, forms a tight bond with fabric and other surfaces.

Jacquard™: manufacturer of supplies, artists' quality textile, mixed media, and craft products

juried: selected by a panel of experts in the field

Kraft-Tex™: paper that looks, feels, and wears like leather, but sews, cuts, and washes like fabric

lamé: silk, cotton, or wool fabric that has been interwoven with thin threads of metallic fiber

Lutradur®: a multimedia material made by Pellon® that is a cross between fabric and paper

machine-pieced: the method of assembling the quilt top using a sewing machine

metal leafing: thin foil used for decoration

monofilament: a thread that has a single filament and is translucent

monoprint: unique print created by spreading paint on a surface such as a gelli plate, making the design, and placing the fabric on top to accept the design

needle-turn appliqué: appliqué motif to the background by hand using the needle to turn the edge of the piece as you go

noil: short fiber removed during the combing of a textile fiber and often separately spun into yarn

ombré fabric: comes from the French word *ombrer* which means "to shade." Ombré fabric shades from light to dark across the width of the fabric.

paint appliqué: objects painted on cloth and then appliquéd on a background

Pearl or Perle Cotton: a two-ply mercerized cotton thread used in hand needlework. It is sold in weights 3, 5, 8, and 12.

posterize: print or display an image in a posterlike fashion using only a small number of different tones

potato resist: resist is a substance applied to a cloth surface that blocks the penetration of dye or paint. Potato resists produce lace-like patterns and crackle lines similar to batik once the resist is washed out.

Prismacolor®: professional artists' supplies manufactured by Newell Brands. Items in the Prismacolor® line that are popular with fiber artists are colored pencils, Art Stix, pastels, watercolors, and alcohol-based permanent art markers.

quilted: two layers of fabric with batting in between stitched to hold it all together

rattail binding: binding the edge of the quilt by laying a cord along the edge and satin stitching it to the quilt

raw-edged appliqué: shapes are cut to the finished size and sewn with a straight stitch to the background. Edges are left raw. Fraying is intentional as it adds texture.

reverse-appliqué: a technique in which a line is cut in the top layer of fabric and the raw edges are turned under and stitched to expose the layer of fabric underneath

roving: a soft strand of fiber that has been twisted readying it to be made into yarn

Sharpie®: a brand of permanent marker

shibori: a set of traditional Japanese resist-dyeing techniques created by manipulating, folding, stitching, and binding the cloth before dyeing

Shiva Oil Paintstiks: solid oil paints in stick form

Spoonflower®: a fabric print-on-demand site that prints original designs on various fabrics and paper

stash: a supply of fabrics, thread, and embellishments used for making quilts

Sulky® Thread: thread manufactured for embroidery, quilting and embellishing

Superior Threads®: manufacturers of thread for quilting, piecing, appliqué, embroidery, and garment construction

Swarovski® crystals: high-quality Austrian crystals which add bling to fiber art

Templar® plastic: heat resistant template material

Terial Magic: spray on liquid that can replace stabilizers and fusibles

Texture Magic®: steam-activated shrinking fabric made of polyester. The fabric shrinks thirty percent in all directions when steam is applied.

thread-painting: "painting" something using a machine and thread as the paint and the fabric as the canvas

thread-sketching: using the machine to "sketch" in the essential elements without all of the details; a highlighting

thread-work: work made with threads or the process of doing so

trapunto: a part of a quilt that is stuffed by adding another layer of batting to cause that portion to puff out

Tsukineko®: a quick-drying craft ink that must be heat set when used on fabric

Tulip Fabric Markers: markers that have non-toxic premium quality inks that resist fading

turned-edge appliqué: appliqué motif to the background by hand, after pre-turning the edges using glue, a fusible, or freezer paper

Tyvek®: a spun polyethylene film manufactured by DuPont

Ultrasuede®: a highly tactile and versatile material with the feel of suede and a very soft texture

Uni-ball markers: will mark on a variety of surfaces with permanent, water-resistant color

Valdani®: a thread company that produces thread, floss, and yarn in cotton, silk, polyester, rayon, and wool

whole cloth quilt: a quilt in which the top is one single piece of fabric that is quilted with a complex design

Organizations

Quilt Alliance

http://quiltalliance.org

Quilt Alliance is a nonprofit 501c3 organization established in 1993 with a mission to document, preserve, and share our American quilt heritage by collecting the rich stories that historic and contemporary quilts, and their makers, tell about our nation's diverse peoples and their communities.

Sacred Threads

http://sacredthreadsquilts.com

Sacred Threads, a biennial exhibition of quilts, explores themes of joy, inspiration, spirituality, healing, grief, and peace and brotherhood made by artists from across the United States and Canada.

Studio Art Quilt Associates (SAQA)

http://www.saqa.com

SAQA is an international non-profit organization dedicated to promoting art quilts and the artists who create them. It is an information resource for all things art quilt related for our members as well as the public. Founded in 1989 by an initial group of fifty artists, SAQA members now number more than 3,400 artists, teachers, collectors, gallery owners, museum curators, and corporate sponsors.

Sponsor

eQuilter

http://www.equilter.com/

References

Marian Anderson
Anderson, Marian. *My Lord What a Morning: An Autobiography of Marian Anderson*. Champaign: University of Illinois Press, 1984.
www.marian-anderson.com

Lucille Ball
Ball, Lucille. *Love, Lucy*. New York: Penguin Books, 1996.
Monush, Barry, and James Sheridan. *Lucille Ball FAQ: Everything Left to Know About America's Favorite Redhead (FAQ (Applause))*. New York: Applause Theatre & Cinema Books, 2011.
Sanders, Coyne Steven, and Tom Gilbert. *Desilu: The Story of Lucille Ball and Desi Arnez*. New York: William Morrow & Co., 1993.

Mary Blair
Canemaker, John. *Magic Color Flair: The World of Mary Blair*. New York: Walt Disney Family Foundation Press, 2014.
Canemaker, John. *A Mary Blair Treasury of Golden Books*. New York: Golden Books, 2012.
www.d23.com/walt-disney-legend/mary-blair/

Karey P. Bresenhan
Waldvogel, Merikay, Rosalind Perry, and Marian Ann Montgomery. *Quilters Hall of Fame: 42 Masters Who Have Shaped Our Art*. Charleston: Voyageur Press, 2014.

Marie Curie
www.aps.org/publications/apsnews/201312/physicshistory.cfm

Simone de Beauvoir
www.karenkarbo.com/simone-de-beauvoir-iconoclast
www.nytimes.com/1986/04/15/obituaries/simone-de-beauvoir-author-and-intellectual-dies-in-paris-at-78.html

Geraldine Ferraro
www.scholastic.com/teachers/articles/teaching-content/geraldine-ferraro

Aretha Franklin
www.paper-research.com/biographies/Aretha-Franklin-27413.html

Rosalind Franklin
Rossiter, Margaret. *Women Scientists in America: Before Affirmative Action, 1940-1972*. Baltimore: Johns Hopkins University Press, 1998.
www.profiles.nlm.nih.gov/KR

Betty Friedan
www.observer.com/2013/02/into-the-mystique-betty-friedans-feminist-classic-at-50

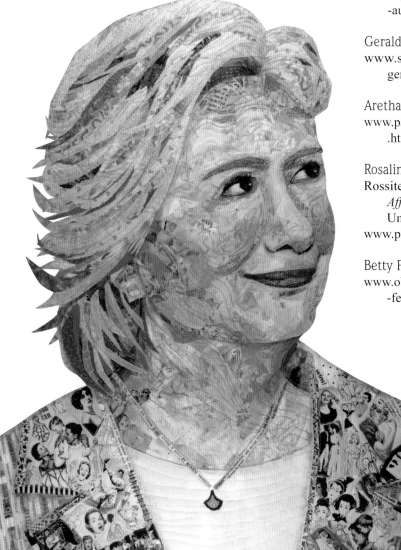

Wally Funk
www.wallyfly.com/

Maria Goeppert-Mayer
Dash, Joan. *A Life of One's Own: Three Gifted Women and the Men They Married*. New York: Harper & Row, 1973.
Mayer, Peter. *Son of (Entropy) 2: Personal Memories of a Son of a Chemist, Joseph E. Mayer, and a Nobel Prize Winning Physicist, Maria Goeppert Mayer*. Bloomington: Author House Publishing, 2011.
Rossiter, Margaret. *Women Scientists in America: Before Affirmative Action, 1940-1972*. Baltimore: Johns Hopkins University Press, 1998.
www.aps.org/publications/apsnews/201312/physicshistory .cfm
www.nasonline.org/publications/biographical-memoirs/memoir -pdfs/mayer-maria.pdf
www.nobelprize.org/nobel_prizes/physics/laureates/1963/ mayer-bio.html

Jane Goodall
www.janegoodall.org

Viginia Hall
www.cia.gov/news-information/featured-story-archive/2015 -featured-story-archive/virginia-hall-the-courage-and -daring-of-the-limping-lady.html
www.smithsonianmag.com/history/wanted-the-limping -lady-146541513

Fanny Lou Hamer
Mills, Kay. *This Little Light of Mine: The Life of Fanny Lou Hamer*. New York: Penguin Books, 1993.
Weatherford, Carol Boston. *Voice of Freedom: Fannie Lou Hamer, Spirit of the Civil Rights Movement*. Somerville: Candlewick Press, 2015.

Dorothy Hodgkin
Rossiter, Margaret. *Women Scientists in America: Before Affirmative Action, 1940-1972*. Baltimore: Johns Hopkins University Press, 1998.

Golda Meir
http://www.jewishvirtuallibrary.org/golda-meir

Lee Miller
Byrski, Liz. *Gang of Four*. Tuggerah, Australia: Pan Macmillan, 2004.

Louise Nevelson
www.theartstory.org/artist-nevelson-louise.htm

Yvonne Porcella
Porcella, Yvonne, and Rebecca Phillips Abbott. *Yvonne Porcella, A Memoir: Defining Why*. New York: Iris Karp, 2014.
Waldvogel, Merikay, Rosalind Perry, and Marian Ann Mont-gomery. *Quilters Hall of Fame: 42 Masters Who Have Shaped Our Art*. Charleston: Voyageur Press, 2014.

Rangers
www.insideedition.com/headlines/11538-meet-the-first-ever -female-soldiers-to-graduate-from-ranger-school-i-was -thinking-of
www.time.com/4005578/female-army-rangers/

Hannah Senesh
http://www.jewishvirtuallibrary.org/hannah-senesh

Nina Simone
Simone, Nina. *I Put a Spell on You: The Autobiography of Nina Simone*. Boston: Da Capo Press, 2003.

Sojourner Truth
www.sojournertruth.org

WASPs
www.twu.edu/library/wasp.asp

Jody Williams
www.real-leaders.com/nobel-peace-laureate-jody-williams -admits-im-no-mother-theresa/

Index

Susanne Miller Jones has been creating all of her life. Fiber art opened many doors and introduced her to fiber artists around the world who have become friends through the magic of social media. A retired elementary school teacher and mother of two, Susanne and her husband Todd live in Potomac Falls, Virginia, enjoy traveling, and hope to accompany this exhibit as it travels the world. Susanne's work is in private collections, has been exhibited in many national shows, and has been in several books. She is the author of *Fly Me to the Moon: An Art Quilt Journey* (Schiffer). She enjoys curating fiber art collections and getting to know other artists. Susanne is a member of Studio Art Quilt Associates and the Quilt Alliance and serves on the Sacred Threads committee.